# A Guide to Psychological Understanding of People with Learning Disabilities

Who are the people we describe as having learning or intellectual disability?

Many clinical psychologists working in a mental health setting are now encountering people with learning disabilities, in some cases for the first time. This book provides the background information and understanding required to provide a basis for an inclusive and effective service for people with learning disability.

In *A Guide to Psychological Understanding of People with Learning Disabilities*, Jenny Webb argues that we need a new, clinically-based definition of learning disability and an approach that integrates scientific rigour with humanistic concern for this group of people, who are so often vulnerable to misunderstanding and marginalisation. Psychological approaches need to be grounded in an understanding of historical, theoretical and ethical influences as well as a body of knowledge from other disciplines. The Eight Domains is a simple but holistic method for information gathering, while the Three Stories is an integrative model of formulation to use with those people whose needs do not fit neatly into any one theory. Divided into three sections, the book explores:

- Understanding the context
- Understanding the person: Eight Domains
- Making sense: Three Stories.

This book provides an invaluable guide for trainee clinical psychologists and their supervisors and tutors working with adults with learning disability. It will also be helpful for clinical psychologists working in mainstream settings who may now be receiving referrals for people with learning disability and want to update their skills.

**Jenny Webb** has worked with learning disabled people for more than 20 years. She is a Consultant Clinical Psychologist and is on the British Psychological Society Specialist Register of Clinical Neuropsychologists. She can be contacted through the consultancy *Agency and Access*, which is for the support of people whose intellectual impairments may render them vulnerable.
www.agencyandaccess.co.uk
jenny.webb@agencyandaccess.co.uk

# A Guide to Psychological Understanding of People with Learning Disabilities

Eight Domains and Three Stories

**Jenny Webb**

Routledge
Taylor & Francis Group

LONDON AND NEW YORK

First published 2014
by Routledge
27 Church Road, Hove, East Sussex BN3 2FA

Simultaneously published in the USA and Canada
by Routledge
711 Third Avenue, New York, NY 10017

*Routledge is an imprint of the Taylor & Francis Group, an informa business*

*British Library Cataloguing in Publication Data*
A catalogue record for this book is available from the British Library

*Library of Congress Cataloging in Publication Data*
Webb, Jenny, 1948–.
  A guide to psychological understanding of people with learning
  disabilities: eight domains and three stories/Jenny Webb.
    pages cm.
  Includes bibliographical references.
  1. Learning disabled – Psychology.  2. Learning disabled –
  Mental health.  3. Learning disabled – Intelligence levels.
  4. Learning disabilities – Psychological aspects.  I. Title.
  RC394.L37W44 2013
  616.85'889 – dc23
  2013003476

ISBN: 978-0-415-60114-6 (hbk)
ISBN: 978-0-415-60115-3 (pbk)
ISBN: 978-0-203-79877-5 (ebk)

Typeset in Times
by Florence Production Ltd, Stoodleigh, Devon

MIX
Paper from
responsible sources

FSC
www.fsc.org    FSC® C013056

Printed and bound in Great Britain by
TJ International Ltd, Padstow, Cornwall

To Bill
for your thoughtfulness
and for all the little shared jokes

# Contents

# List of figures and tables

## Figures

## Tables

# Acknowledgements

I owe a great debt to all the people who have supported and inspired me during the long gestation of this book. First and foremost I must thank all those people with learning disability, their families and carers, who have given me their trust and worked with me over the past 25 years. This book is their story. Particular thanks to Josephine Goddard, who contributed the artwork for the cover, and Toby Edwards, who wrote the opening poem. Adele Armistead from moonloft produced Figure 6.3. I would also like to thank the staff at Dunhill Library in Chichester for the patience, efficiency and good humour with which they met all my requests for publications.

Early in my career my erstwhile supervisor and friend Jenny West taught me to accept people as they are rather than trying to push them into the mould in which we want them to be. More recently, she read every word of this book and made many helpful suggestions. My daughter Leonie Nimmo read the final draft, and her perceptive comments helped improve the structure. Gillian Roose carried out the therapeutic work that resulted in the opening poem. Several people gave me the benefit of their expertise on particular chapters, including Sarah Boyd, Mary Boyle, Hilary Brown, Shona Daynes, Sophie Doswell, Mark Haydon-Laurelut, Margaret Henning, Pauline Oldroyd, Martin Stent, Simon Whitaker and the late Les Carr. Margaret Henning introduced me to the world of narrative therapy and guided me in its use. Janeen Prinsloo supervised me in neuropsychology. My many clinical conversations with Martin Stent have helped me to critically consider and develop my ideas.

My thanks to my editors, particularly Kristin Susser, who initially encouraged me to submit a book proposal, and to Joanne Forshaw, who was understanding about missed deadlines. Thanks also to all the friends and family who have supported me over the past three years, above all my husband Bill McMellon. His influence is to be felt throughout the book, particularly in its emphasis on historical understanding, and in its conclusions. I could not have written it without him.

The errors and omissions are all my own.

# Abbreviations

| | |
|---|---|
| AAIDD | American Association on Intellectual and Developmental Disability |
| AAMR | American Association on Mental Retardation |
| APA | American Psychiatric Association |
| BILD | British Institute for Learning Disabilities |
| BMA | British Medical Association |
| BPS | British Psychological Society |
| CBT | Cognitive-Behavioural Therapy |
| CPS | Crown Prosecution Service |
| CQC | Care Quality Commission |
| DCP | Division of Clinical Psychology |
| DCR-10 | The Classification of Mental and Behavioural Disorders: Diagnostic Criteria for Research |
| DH | Department of Health |
| DSM-IV | Diagnostic and Statistical Manual of Mental Disorders, 4th edition |
| HO | Home Office |
| ICD-10 | International Classification of Mental and Behavioural Disorders – 10th edition |
| IMCA | Independent Mental Capacity Advocate |
| MCA | Mental Capacity Act |
| NCCL | National Council for Civil Liberties |
| PMLD | Profound and Multiple Learning Disabilities |
| RCP | Royal College of Psychiatrists |
| SALT | Speech and Language Therapy |
| UN | United Nations |
| WAIS-IV | Wechsler Adult Intelligence Scale, 4th edition |
| WHO | World Health Organisation |

# Introduction

I am just me
I am not unusual
I couldn't be anyone else
I am comfortable being me
Other people are different to me
We are all different
And that's OK
                    Toby Edwards


Toby is a young man with a diagnosis of learning disability and autism, who was referred to the psychology service for help with his challenging behaviour. He wrote this poem after a clinical psychology trainee worked with him on his life story and helped him understand the nature of his condition and his feelings. But how did this come about? What was the process by which he was assessed and a decision made as to the type of intervention that might be helpful to him?

Toby was not able to explain his problems to us. Nor could he tell us about the way he liked to be treated by his support workers, or the relationships in his family, or his need for routine or his sensory sensitivity. We had to discover these things, and feed them back to him and his carers in a way that aided their understanding and helped Toby learn how to cope with the difficulties he faced in everyday life.

Getting to know Toby, and others like him, is a journey of discovery. In this we have to consider the whole possible range of factors that could be contributing to the person's presenting problems. We bring to the task both a scientific curiosity and a humanistic interest in whole people, in all their wonderful complexity, their resources as well as their deficits. In this process, our relationship with the person is central. They entrust us with insight into their lives, and we give back to them, consciously or otherwise, our thoughts, hunches and feelings. It is a constantly evolving and reciprocal process. Though I no longer see most of the people I have written about, I feel they are still part of me.

My experience in working with people with learning disability began in 1976, when I took a job as a healthcare assistant. *'Are you interested in children?'* said the roughly scrawled note on the imposing Victorian door. Of course, I then had no idea that 'children' referred to any 'boy' between the age of five and 50. What a hell-hole it turned out to be. Sometimes I think that the whole of the rest of my career has been a quest to lay to rest the spectre of those early experiences.

Within 20 years this mental handicap hospital would be closed down. Its passing signalled the welcome end of the 19th-century asylums, an alternative universe in which the staff had absolute power over the 'patients'.

> I moved to St Lawrence's when I was seven. . . . That was 1952. . . . When you first went there you could hear people screaming and shouting outside . . . There were bars on the windows when I first when to St Lawrence's, it was just like a prison. . . . You couldn't open the windows. . . . You didn't have toys, no toys whatsoever. . . . There was no school there, . . . As you got older you could stay doing baskets or you could go down the laundry or the workshops in the grounds. . . . The worst thing was, I couldn't wear my own clothes, you had to wear other people's . . . the beds were too close together, so you didn't have a locker or anything, you just went to this big cupboard and helped yourself . . . you couldn't wear your own shoes in them days, you had to wear their shoes and they were horrible. They made them there, in the hospital. You never went out for anything because they did everything in the hospital.
>
> (Mabel Cooper, quoted in Atkinson et al, 1997)

We are told that Mabel Cooper was keen to tell her life story, to let people know what it was like to spend most of her life in an institution, without family and with little recognition of her individuality. Mabel eventually freed herself from institutional care, and found someone who was willing to listen to her story. Others have lacked the words to tell stories, or lacked the people willing to listen. Many of the elderly people we see today spent a good part of their lives in such institutions. Some suffered decades of abuse.

Sadly, reports of horrific physical, emotional and sexual abuse still surface in the media from time to time. When they do, they are met with universal shock and opprobrium. It would seem that the humanity of people with learning disability is beyond question. However, there is also a worrying resurgence of stigmatising attitudes and oppressive behaviour towards people with disabilities. The problems we face in attempting to meet their needs remain, as does the vulnerability of a group of people who are less able than others to represent their own interests.

This book reflects my belief that, while continuing to respect our scientific heritage, we also need to carry out our work within the broad humanistic tradition. Part of our responsibility is to work to ensure that the voices of the learning disabled are heard, that their rights are respected and their humanity recognised in meaningful ways. This may mean seeing ourselves as advocates as well as professionals. It also means being aware of our own position within a broader cultural and social context. But being well-meaning and self-aware is not enough. We hope that our training as clinical psychologists provides us with a foundation in the tools we need to help people meet their needs.

In this enterprise we need to be theoretically eclectic. One theory is rarely adequate to provide an understanding of the person, and how we may help them. For example, we may suspect that a person with behavioural problems is suffering from insecure attachment; we also know they have difficulty in communicating their feelings. At the same time, we may suspect that those people currently supporting them are reinforcing problem behaviours. And we are also aware that the support workers are themselves suffering from a high level of stress and are poorly managed. All these factors, and the theories that help to explain them, need to be brought into our formulation and fashioned into a coherent narrative.

This holistic, theoretically eclectic and integrative approach is expressed in the structure and content of the book. Part I covers issues relating to definition, ethics, history, theory and law. It provides a context within which we can better understand the nature of the work we are doing, and its contingent character. Part II presents a framework for our understanding of the person, which I call the *Eight Domains*. These are: the Inner World, Neurological, Cognitive, Physical, Behavioural, Attachment, Social and Ecological Domains. Part III presents a fresh approach to the integrative process of formulation, which I call *Three Stories*. These are: the Core Story, the Supporting Story and the Sparkling Story.

This book is about *understanding*, and its methodological counterpart, assessment. Intervention is only covered insofar as there is a particular assessment technique associated with the intervention, or the intervention can itself function as a form of assessment. Even with regard to understanding, limited space or limitations in my own clinical experience have meant that I have had to deal with many important topics only briefly, and some topics have been omitted altogether. For example, I do not address issues of forensic psychology or ethnic diversity. Some recommended reading is given at the end of each chapter. This usually comprises two or three books that give an overview of the subject.

The book is grounded in my own clinical experience, and I write as a practitioner rather than an academic, attempting to tread the precarious path between reflective practice and scientific objectivity. Examples given from the literature are illustrative rather than definitive. I have included anonymised case vignettes, and fragments from other sources that hopefully serve to ground the book in a broader cultural context, and to model an aspect of reflective practice.

Toby chose to use his own name. He continues to pursue his own path, but in an environment that offers him both safety and respect for his distinctive needs and unique talents. That is a big achievement, both for Toby and for the many people who support him.

You may be reading this book as a trainee clinical psychologist embarking on your Learning Disability placement, or as a trained clinical psychologist working in a mainstream setting and starting to see learning disabled clients. Like me at the start of my career, you may be assailed by a combination of heroic good intentions and feelings of ignorance and impotence. I hope that this book will provide a framework within which you can begin to make sense of the problems faced by people like Toby and see a way forward to help resolve them. I hope you find it interesting, stimulating and useful. I hope it will help to further our shared enterprise of making life better for people with learning disability.

# Part I

# Understanding the context

# 1 Defining the construct of learning disability

As I begin this book, I face a quandary. How am I to write about this subject without using some of the terminology that is the subject of study? After long consideration, I have decided to adopt the term 'learning disability' when referring to contemporary usage. This chapter explains this decision, and what I mean by the term 'learning disability'.

The history of learning disability is partly the history of changes in terminology. In the United Kingdom the term 'idiocy' was replaced by the terms 'mental deficiency', 'mental handicap' and latterly 'learning disability'. 'Mental impairment' is used in some legislation, and 'special needs' is the term in common usage to describe children with developmental disabilities and others. Members of the self-advocacy group People First have expressed a preference for the term 'learning difficulties'. In America the term 'feeble-minded' was replaced by that of 'mentally retarded', and 'intellectual disability' is the term now generally adopted by the international scientific community.

Such changes in terminology and classificatory systems have to some extent been driven by the ongoing attempt to escape the stigma attached to earlier terminology, but they also reflect changes in the concept of learning disability itself. In the positivist tradition such changes would be viewed as attempts to get ever closer to the 'true' definition of learning disability as a medical diagnosis. Alternatively, the change in language may be seen as representing changes in social structure, power relationships, values and in the abilities needed for survival in specific cultures.

Current definitions are given by the diagnostic manuals of the WHO and the APA, as well as national bodies such as the AAIDD. The ICD-I0 and DSM-IV are currently being revised. Most current definitions refer to three criteria, involving (i) early age of onset, (ii) cognitive impairment (represented by IQ score) and (iii) functional disability. For example, the ICD-10 identifies four degrees of severity of mental retardation, which it defines as an:

> arrested or incomplete development of the mind, which is especially characterized by impairment of skills manifested during the developmental period, skills which contribute to the overall level of intelligence, ie cognitive, language, motor, and social abilities.
>
> (WHO, 1994: F70–79)

A radical challenge to the general diagnostic manuals came from the AAMR that, in 1992, influenced by the social model of disability, published a revised diagnostic manual. While it broadly accepted the usual three criteria given for classification of mental retardation and the IQ < 70 cut-off, it also stated, in a memorable phrase, that mental retardation 'is not something you "have" like blue eyes or a bad heart' (AAMR, 1992: 9). The importance of social environment was acknowledged in the Levels of Support model, referring to the frequency and intensity of support people need in particular social contexts. The four levels of support were described as: Limited, Intermittent, Extensive and Pervasive, and were not associated with IQ scores.

The White Paper *Valuing People* also referred to a four-part classification, though without defining the categories (DH, 2001a). Also in 2001, the BPS produced its own guide to definitions. This acknowledged the fact that learning disability is a social construct but nevertheless went on to provide a definition of the concept close to that of the diagnostic manuals. This was on the grounds that it is enshrined in our social and legal systems and so affects people's legal and civil rights. However it stressed the importance of flexibility and clinical judgement in diagnosis. It stated that IQ score should only be interpreted in the context of a holistic assessment, covering 'biological, psychological and interactional factors, within the broader social/cultural and environmental context' (BPS, 2001: 2). These guidelines are also currently being revised.

The BPS suggested collapsing the four-level classification into a two-level classification, since it found no reliable or valid psychometric instruments to make the distinction between the Moderate, Severe and Profound categories. The BPS also introduced its own nomenclature. Thus, 'mild mental retardation' became 'Significant Impairment of Intellectual Functioning', and the other three categories (less than IQ 55) (confusingly) became 'Severe Impairment of Intellectual Functioning'. This means that 'Severe' is defined at IQ 35 internationally, whilst being set at IQ 50–55 in the UK, though only if this is associated with a need for an Extensive Level of Support.

In the UK, the psychiatric and psychological systems co-exist, with implications for individual entitlement to support, governmental planning and legal judgements. The construct of learning disability is thus mired in confusion. This is partly because its scientific foundations are shaky.

## Theoretical issues in the definition of learning disability

The vignette on p. 9 illustrates the gulf that exists between lay and scientific concepts. In contrast to lay concepts, the criteria for acceptance of hypothetical constructs in science are rigorous. In everyday life, we may all vary in the way we define a construct such as 'intelligence', and yet we will probably be able to engage in a dialogue without too much misunderstanding, since in such a conversation meanings are constantly checked and refined. Scientific investigation, on the other hand, requires a foundation of shared meaning. This foundation

## The trainee and the tutor

The tutor's small stature and delicate appearance belie the sharpness of her intellect and the force of her personality. Week after week the clinical psychology trainees are forced to question all the assumptions with which they entered training. In particular they are taught the limitations of the medical model and the need for psychologists to think through their ideas from first principles.

The tutor packs up her files and leaves the room after a particularly taxing seminar. The trainees turn to look at each other. Finally, one breaks the silence:

'Well!' she proclaims. 'Mental illness might not exist in this college, but it bloody well exists in the day hospital where **I'm** working!'

is comprised of two key pillars: the theoretical status of the hypothetical construct and its relationship to the theoretical network of which it forms a part.

### *Hypothetical constructs*

Scientific theories contain observables (directly involving sense data) and unobservables. An unobservable is an 'abstract concept inferred from overt behaviour or from verbal reports of behaviour and experience' (Boyle, 2002: 2). MacCorquodale and Meehl (1948) suggest that unobservables may be one of two types: 'intervening variables' and 'hypothetical constructs'. 'Intellectual disability' falls into the latter category. It is an abstraction, not reducible to a statement about behavioural correlations.

### *Ontological status*

Do hypothetical constructs 'really' exist? And, if so, in what sense? The positivist view is that they do, and that scientific endeavour is directed towards helping us uncover and understand them:

> Since hypothetical constructs assert the existence of entities and the occurrence of events not reducible to the observable, it would seem to some of us that it is the business of a hypothetical construct to be 'true'. . . . The ultimate 'reality' of the world in general is not the issue here; the point is merely that the reality of hypothetical constructs like the atom . . . is not essentially different from that attributed to stones, chairs, other people and the like.
>
> (MacCorquodale and Meehl, 1948: 104–105)

According to Boyle, this statement ignores the distinction between those hypothetical constructs that are assumed to 'really exist', and for which scientists may search (e.g. an atom), and those that will always be abstractions, as is the case with both learning disability and intelligence. Nevertheless, both in service delivery systems and in academic research, the view that these constructs do have a 'real' existence prevails.

## Validity

The theoretical status of a hypothetical construct is often described in terms of its validity, i.e. the extent to which it measures what it is claimed to measure. Various types of validity have been identified, including content, concurrent, predictive, construct, ecological, social, convergent and discriminant (Chaytor and Schmitter-Edgecombe, 2003; Cronbach and Meehl, 1955; Wechsler et al, 2008).

## Correspondence rules

A hypothetical construct forms part of a *theoretical network* that relates observables to each other and to unobservables. This network is described in terms of correspondence rules that link observable events and unobservable constructs. They specify 'what must be observed before the concept can be inferred and may specify quantitatively the relationship between variation in what is observed and variation in the inferred construct' (Boyle, 2002: 4). The correspondence rules also provide the means for examining the predictions from a construct and may evolve as more observations are made over time.

## Medicine

Medicine is a branch of science, within which the construct of 'disease' is usually seen as an entity with a discrete and unchanging identity. The correspondence rules for inference of the disease or syndrome in question constitute its diagnostic criteria, and have predictive power.

Correspondence rules/diagnostic criteria involve an observed cluster of symptoms and signs. A *symptom* is a phenomenon that is subjectively experienced by the person, whereas a *sign* is an independently measurable event that is reliably associated with a cluster of symptoms, and theoretically linked with it as an antecedent (e.g. a blood test result) as well as being linked theoretically to the construct. Observations made over time may result in the evolution of diagnostic criteria. From the positivist point of view, this is the means by which diagnosticians may come closer to the 'true' definition of the disease. On the other hand, Boyle (2002) suggests that disease names are simply concepts that are inferred from clusters of signs and symptoms. When correspondence rules/signs and symptoms change over time, this does not change the nature of the disease, but the theoretical network in which the construct is embedded.

Pilgrim (2011) criticises the scientific integrity of psychiatric diagnoses on four grounds: their lack of predictive validity (e.g. regarding prognosis); their lack of concept validity (e.g. overlapping categories); their lack of treatment specificity; and their definition in terms of symptoms rather than 'hard biological signs'.

## Learning disability as a medical diagnosis and hypothetical construct

The inclusion of learning disability in the diagnostic manuals implies that it is not merely a summary description but a scientifically respectable medical hypothetical construct. Whether it merits this status depends on whether it meets the necessary and sufficient conditions for such a construct.

The diagnostic criteria for learning disability have been, and continue to be, subject to regular revisions, made on the basis of discussion among respected academics and practitioners. We would expect that such revisions would be made on the basis of empirical evidence or theoretical developments but instead the process can seem arbitrary.

The current proposal for revision of the DSM is that a change be made from a descriptive to a more aetiological focus (Andrews et al, 2009a). But suggested changes have been criticised on the grounds both of their lack of validity and of their overly rigid reliance on test results (AAIDD, 2009; Wittchen et al, 2009). The category of learning disability will be subsumed under a broad category termed Neurodevelopmental Disorders. The evidence for the existence of this category seems to have been taken mainly from studies of people with autistic spectrum disorder, which constitute nearly half of the references given. Many of the other references relate to ADHD (attention deficit hyperactivity disorder), dyslexia and stuttering! Notwithstanding the fact that 'genomic screens have not identified "neurodevelopmental" genes common to *all* these disorders . . . it is presumed that disorders within clusters will co-aggregate, do support some common neurodevelopmental genetic risk' (Andrews et al, 2009b: 2015).This analysis leads Andrews et al to come to the astounding conclusion that 'Autism and Asperger's disorders fall at the "severe" end of the genetic spectrum whereas disorders such as mild mental retardation occur at the "mild" end of the spectrum' (Andrews et al, 2009b: 2016).

### *Learning disability and intelligence*

The construct of learning disability piggy-backs on the further construct of intelligence, since it is intelligence testing that is used to assess learning disability. This brings us to the issue of the validity and reliability of intelligence tests and of the cut-off point used to define learning disability. This complex issue is one that I can only skate over here.

### Validity

The cut-off for diagnosis of learning disability is usually given as two standard deviations below the mean, which equates to IQ 70, covering 2.28 per cent of the population. This is an arbitrary figure, made more problematic by the 'Flynn effect' that has resulted in the periodic re-norming of IQ tests. As a result of such changes, the proportion of people classified as learning disabled has fluctuated between 1 in 23 (in 1949) and 1 in 213 (in 1989). The 'the hidden history of IQ testing shows huge fluctuations in the IQ criterion of mental retardation and paucity of evidence for any particular criterion' (Flynn, 2000: 197).

There is also a circularity about the use of the 2.28 per cent cut-off. It is based on the assumption that intelligence is normally distributed in the population, and this is demonstrated by administering a test that is statistically designed to ensure that this is in fact the case. But even this does not really work. The confidence interval for IQ 70 on the WAIS-III is 67–75. If people with IQ up to 75 are included in the category of mild learning disability, then the number of people jumps from 2.23 to 4.74 per cent of the population (Whitaker, 2003).

If IQ score were ecologically valid, then this would mean that if we knew a person's IQ score, we would be able to predict their adaptive behaviour, as well as a range of other possible features. However, the relationship between IQ and measures of adaptive behaviour is only moderate (Whitaker, 2003). One study of self-determination or autonomous functioning found that intellectual capacity was much less of a significant contributor to these abilities than the opportunity to make choices (Wehmeyer and Garner, 2003).

It is often stated that IQ scores are correlated with academic performance and occupational achievement (e.g. Sternberg et al, 2001). However, even this relationship is problematic, thrown into question by the fact that, at the same time that IQ scores were rising in America, academic performance was falling (Flynn, 1987). Flynn concludes that this can only be explained by the hypothesis that intelligence tests do not in fact measure intelligence, but are instead a measure of Abstract Problem Solving Ability, a term that 'accurately conveys our ignorance'. It involves problems that are so abstracted from reality that ability to solve them 'can diverge over time from the real-world problem-solving ability called intelligence'.

### Validity of the WAIS-IV

The Manual for the WAIS-IV states that there is evidence for a general factor of intelligence (g), as well as a hierarchical structure, and 8–10 'broad cognitive domains' that are 'interrelated, functionally and neurologically'. It refers to content validity, response processes, internal structure, correlational studies and external relationships. Confirmatory factor analysis is used to justify the use of a model based on one second-order and four first-order cognitive domains (Wechsler et al, 2008).

But elsewhere the validity of the test is described in terms of:

> the degree to which the evidence supports the interpretation of test scores for their intended purpose . . . as a result, examination of a test validity requires an evaluative judgement by the test user . . . evolving conceptualizations of validity no longer speak of different types of validity but speak instead of different lines of validity evidence, all in the service of providing information relevant to a specific intended interpretation of test scores.
>
> (Wechsler et al, 2008: 57)

It claims evidence for ecological validity, but no evidence is provided for this. It seems to me that by this analysis the authors of the test are giving *carte blanche* to test users to interpret the test in whatever way suits them.

### *Reliability*

The issue of the validity of the WAIS is compounded by its doubtful reliability (Webb and Whitaker, 2012). This has been calculated to mean that the confidence interval for the test at lower levels of ability is +/– 15 points, a finding that makes nonsense of attempts to define the diagnosis of learning disability partly in terms of IQ score (Whitaker, 2008a).

Various factors contribute to the poor reliability of the WAIS in the context of learning disability. These include the unrepresentative nature of the standardisation samples; the extremely low number of learning disabled people likely to be in each of these samples; the assumption of a normal curve, which probably does not apply in the low IQ range; irregularities in test administration by clinicians; arbitrary changes in test content; the use of split-half rather than test–retest reliability for some subtests; and the fact that performance may well be more variable in learning disabled people.

## The social constructionist critique

> The terms in which the world is understood are social artefacts, products of historically situated interchanges among people.
>
> (Gergen, 2003: 15)

Both 'intelligence' and 'intellectual disability' are the product of a particular social and historical context and in turn 'actively constitute the "truths" which we assume' (Rapley, 2004: 10).

Current diagnostic criteria suggest that learning disability, like physical illness, is something inside the people concerned, independent of social context. For example, in the DSM-IV it is stated that a person with Moderate Mental Retardation 'may learn to travel independently in familiar places', and that they 'adapt well to life in the community' (APA, 2000: 41). But these abilities are entirely context-dependent. There is a world of difference, for example, between catching a rural bus that finishes its route at the local town, and navigating a complex underground train system. Similarly, whether a person is able to adapt to life in the community depends on what that life involves, who the neighbours are, what practical and social support is given, what activities are available and so on; in other words to the 'fit' between the capabilities of the individual and the demands of a particular environment. This means that using IQ score to judge people's real life abilities is misleading. For example, IQ score is often used as an indicator of parenting ability, but Booth and Booth stress that parental competence is not a quality inherent in individuals, but is 'a distributed feature of the parents' social network' (Booth and Booth, 1998: 98).

Furthermore, a person's IQ score reflects their social context. Sternberg et al (2001) suggest that each additional month spent in school is likely to increase a child's IQ in comparison with what would otherwise have otherwise been expected.

The socially constructed nature of learning disability is illustrated by its cultural and historical relativity.

### Cultural relativity

In Taiwan there is no precise translation of the word intelligence, and related words refer to qualities such as intellectual self-effacement. In Kenya parents define intelligence in their children as 'the ability to do without being told what needed to be done around the homestead'. Some Africans describe people as being intelligent if they are 'slow in thought and action' (Sternberg et al, 2001: 27). Sternberg et al also suggest there is a distinction between academic and practical intelligence. Among other examples, they cite Brazilian street children, who often fail maths at school, but have the mathematical skill to run a successful street business.

Jenkins (1998) puts forward the idea of 'competence' as a way of considering intellectual ability that is not culturally specific. In Eastern Uganda, rather than valuing independence, people value the qualities involved in social competence. These are: advisability (being socially aware); intentionality (being organised); civility; conversation; and cleverness (that includes liveliness and curiosity) (Reynolds Whyte, 1998). These qualities are worlds away from Western definitions of learning disability.

Nuttall (1998) describes concepts of personhood in Greenland, where life is characterised not by Western categorical concepts but by a general sense of continuity, between the natural and supernatural, the individual and the community, and the sick and the healthy. People are described not as 'having' a learning disability, but as being 'slow at learning/understanding', a state that may be temporary. Moreover, judgements about a person's competence are based on them having the means, knowledge and skills to survive in a community based on hunting.

Edwardraj et al (2010) used focus group methodology to explore attitudes towards learning disability in South India, and discovered the co-existence of many varying and contradictory models of disability.

The cultural relativity of learning disability is recognised in the *ICD-10 Diagnostic Criteria for Research*, which states that detailed diagnostic criteria cannot be specified for mental retardation, since 'low cognitive ability and diminished social competence, are profoundly affected by social and cultural influences' (WHO, 1993: F70–77). This rarely seems to be acknowledged. There is a danger that, through the international scientific community, Western notions will be imposed on cultures that have their own, valuable, concepts of competence.

### Historical relativity

The term 'intellectual disability' and its precursors emerged from lay and legal concepts of incompetence, overlaid by hundreds of years of professional and popular influences that reflect socio-economic conditions. This will be discussed further in Chapters 3, 4 and 13.

### Diagnosis as the exercise of professional power

Through the 'ideology of privatisation', psychiatry and psychology take centre stage in the resolution of human distress. Diagnosis plays a crucial role in this:

> Diagnosis purports to an expert form of knowledge only to be wielded by a skilled few – giving those with access to this knowledge the power to label and define distress and unusual experiences.
>
> (Coles, 2010: 23)

It involves the 'construction of a huge edifice of spurious certainty, backed up by institutional and political power' (Midlands Psychology Group, 2010: 50). Professional judgements are generally in terms of pathology. This can be disempowering for clients and disrespectful of their experiences and the meanings they attach to those experiences. The process also has wider implications, with social categorisation based on testing contributing to 'the legitimization of modern forms of social stratification – with their awards and punishments, their inclusions and exclusions, and their benefits and losses' (Trent, 2011: 1).

### Limitations of the social constructionist approach

There is a danger that the social constructionist approach can involve a denial of impairment, ignoring the real problems that people face in their everyday lives, and their need for support in order to lead normal lives (Goodey, 2011). For example, minority cultures in the UK may conceptualise disability in distinctive ways, and to accept their views unquestioningly could result in people being denied access to the help they need (Dobson and Upadhyaya, 2002).

> Intellectual disability is also an ontological reality that makes a real difference to one's experience of being in the world. . . . Rarely do [social constructionist accounts] seek in any way to enter into the lived realities of people with intellectual disabilities.
>
> (Klotz, 2004: 98)

Klotz advocates an approach that focuses on the social experiences and perceptions of people with learning disability. This, he says, requires 'long-term and intimate engagement with the people in question' (Klotz, 2004: 100).

In the context of UK society at present, acceptance of culturally relative concepts of disability could result in people being denied access to the help they need.

The social constructionist approach necessarily generates hypotheses that are particular to specific societies, cultures or even individuals. This may not be a disadvantage. However, if cross-cultural research and practice is to proceed, there will also be a need for a language of competence and disability that transcends local definitions.

## A solution?

So, what term shall I use in this book to describe the people to whom it refers? Jenkins (1998) suggests replacing the idea of intelligence with that of competence. Flynn (2000) suggests the use of direct tests of impaired adaptive behaviour to assess learning disability. Greenspan (1994) suggests defining learning disability in terms of deficits of conceptual, practical and social intelligence that result in a need for supports in order to succeed in culturally relevant roles. In his later work, influenced by his work in the American criminal justice system, he suggests that impairments are demonstrated by the person's history of academic, practical and social risk (Greenspan et al, 2011). Whitaker (2008b) has produced a definition that links competence, environmental demands, intellect, risk and distress.

My solution to this dilemma is to extricate myself from the psychiatric definition, and the search for a 'true' definition of learning disability. Instead, for clinical purposes and in this book I will use the term *learning disabled* to describe:

> *those people who, due to cognitive deficits beginning at birth or during childhood, are unable to fulfil social roles in a way that is expected in a particular society at a particular time, and hence are considered to be at risk, practically, physically, socially or emotionally.*

This is consistent with recent moves within Clinical Psychology to begin to 'develop coherent, credible alternative forms of categorisation which are based on psychological theory and which have direct implications for both aetiology and intervention' (BPS, 2011).

With regard to the description of people at different levels of ability, I shall sometimes refer to the levels of support the people are judged to need. Where appropriate, I shall use the term PMLD (Profound and Multiple Learning Disabilities). These are people

> whose degree of learning difficulty is so severe that they are functioning at a developmental level of two years or less . . . and also they have one or more other severe impairments, for example they may be unable to walk, be severely visually impaired, or both.
>
> (Ware, 2003: v)

In discussing the history of services, I will generally use the terminology of the time. And sometimes I will simply refer to 'people'.

## Conclusion

The medical framework used to define the construct of learning disability has been given a spurious scientific respectability through the practice of intelligence testing. But we need to recognise the historical and cultural relativity of the terms we use, the theoretical and statistical weaknesses of the intelligence tests we use, and the distributed nature of social competence. This is a debate that needs to beyond the cloisters of the American Psychiatric Association. In the meantime, I propose leaving 'intellectual disability' to the international research community, and using, for clinical purposes, a definition of 'learning disability' based on the linked criteria of early onset, cognitive deficits, social competence and risk.

## Recommended reading

The current diagnostic manuals and guidance from the BPS
Boyle M (2002) *Schizophrenia: A Scientific Delusion?* (2nd edition) London: Routledge
Goodey C F (2011) *A History of Intelligence and Intellectual Disability: The Shaping of Psychology in Early Modern Europe* Farnham, Surrey: Ashgate

# 2　The scientific and ethical context

Most clinical psychologists see themselves as being part of a scientific intellectual tradition. This has its roots in the 17th century, with Galileo and other scientists who dedicated themselves to establishing the truth through observation. In the following century, David Hume suggested the centrality, not just of observation, but of the ideas of cause and effect, in helping us understand phenomena:

> Here is a billiard ball lying on the table, and another ball moving toward it with rapidity. They strike; and the ball which was formerly at rest now acquires a motion. This is as perfect an instance of the relation of cause and effect as any which we know either by sensation or reflection.
>
> (Hume, 1740, quoted in Fromm and Xirau, 1968: 169)

And another hundred years later, Comte described the Positive or Scientific state, in which the mind 'endeavours now to discover, by a well-combined use of reasoning and observation, the actual *laws* of phenomena' (Comte, 1842, quoted in Fromm and Xirau, 1968: 207).

The scientific paradigm still defines almost every publication appearing in the academic psychology journals, and we as a profession describe ourselves as 'scientist-practitioners'. The linear, causal model of understanding is represented in a therapeutic encounter in which the therapist carries out an assessment, develops a formulation and then implements an intervention that sorts out the problem.

But the nature of science itself, with its claim of unique access to truth, is open to question. Kuhn (1996) suggests that science is not travelling on a single, inexorable path towards an ever-closer grasp of the truth. Instead, it develops incrementally only within non-scientifically ascribed limits, given by the currently acceptable 'paradigm'. Paradigms serve to delimit the field of activity and the assumptions on which investigation will be based, as well as what counts as legitimate theory and methodology. Ultimately, paradigms rest on untestable, value-based assumptions. Science itself is a form of social knowledge, conditional and defined by a particular community of scholars. The assumptions of science at any one time may therefore legitimately be questioned. Kuhn states that it is not possible for the practitioner to step outside a paradigm. However, the fact that 'scientific revolutions' can take place does imply that, at times of change, practitioners do consider alternative paradigms in order to evaluate their relative merits and find a way forward.

The application of the assumptions and techniques of science to human beings raises particular questions. MacIntyre (2007) suggests that the behaviour of any particular person is inherently unpredictable. The explanations provided by the 'objective' scientific approach can feel uncomfortable when applied to living, feeling human beings. Explanations in terms of behaviour alone can feel partial and unsatisfactory. The manipulation of variables with little reference to the inner life of the person is disempowering and could be ethically questionable. Moreover, the primacy accorded to scientific methodology can serve to stifle debate and development of alternative paradigms (Goodey, 2001). This can have dangerous implications. The history of our profession shows us that what passes for objectivity may disguise the most pernicious of philosophies and policies (see Chapter 4).

In Clinical Psychology in Learning Disability, theory and practice may be seen as having evolved from a strictly positivistic view to one that has become more fluid and permeable to different ideas. There is now greater recognition of a humanistic imperative in our work, and also the possibility of alternative narratives, each of which is valid (in the everyday sense of the term). But this creates a tension both in our theory and our practice, since positivism, humanism and social constructionism all have different implications for ontology, explanation, methodology, values and the very nature of human beings.

## Comparing the three paradigms

### *Ontology: what exists?*

'An ontology is a theory of what exists and how it exists' (Goodley, 2011: 49). According to the scientific view, there is a 'truth' existing as an objective reality, which is waiting to be uncovered by the scientist. From a humanist perspective, as expressed in phenomenology, reality exists in subjective experience. Schutz (1962) suggests that the difference between studying things and studying people is that, unlike the objects studied by natural scientists, people have already interpreted themselves, and it is therefore their individual and collective interpretations that are the appropriate object of study for the human sciences.

The postmodernist view is that there is no objective reality and both positivism and humanism are simply stories we tell ourselves and others. In the field of psychology, postmodernism is expressed in social constructionism. This is influenced by Wittgenstein in its emphasis on language as the medium by which meaning and reality are socially constructed.

> Our idea of what belongs to the realm of reality is given for us in the language that we use. The concepts we have settle for us the form of the experience we have of the world . . . the world is for us what is presented through those concepts. That is not to say that our concepts may not change; but when they do, that means that our concept of the world has changed too.
>
> (Winch, 1958: 15)

This statement gets to the heart of narrative therapy. In the therapeutic process a new, shared narrative emerges, and this retelling has a transformative effect on people's perceptions of reality. Our role is both to facilitate this process and to be a part of it.

### *Explanation: reasons and causes*

According to the positivist view, the true state of things is defined by causal relationships, which are described in universally applicable laws that link observable phenomena. The work of science is therefore to uncover these laws. The phenomenological view is that explanations should be in terms of intentions, reasons and meaning rather than causes. Social constructionists also emphasise meaning, but see this as being constructed through relationships and conversations. They are more likely to include cultural context in their explanations (Gergen, 2003).

There is a longstanding philosophical debate as to the relationship between reasons and causes. This centres partly on the question whether reasons can be causes, and, associated with this, whether an explanation in terms of reason can be scientific. But according to Hill (1982), the two types of explanation are not necessarily mutually exclusive, since the same clinical issues may originate both in causes and in reasons.

Alternatively, we may see science as a developmental process. The early stages of study and theory-building may involve 'a spectrum of activity from tentative, messy, intuitive exploration through to the development of useful principles and rules for understanding the world' (Keegan, 2007: 33). This may involve using our own mental processes in order to frame hypotheses that we can then test by observation (Winch, 1958).

### *Methodology: the nature of knowledge and knowing*

Scientists justify their claim to know what is true is through their use of objective methods of study, typically using the hypothetic-deductive method. This involves the construction of theories that yield falsifiable predictions in the form of hypotheses. The hypotheses are then tested by reference to observable data, and the results used to confirm or falsify the hypotheses and the theory on which they are based. In this way, the theory may develop into a set of laws that yield real-world predictions.

The phenomenological view is that the methods of science are inadequate for understanding subjective states. Weber, the early sociologist, suggested that where action has a meaning (i.e. symbolic character) then the appropriate form of understanding is not causal but 'interpretive understanding' (*verstehen*) that involves the exercise of empathy.

Sacks (1992) argues that, unlike natural phenomena, culture displays 'order at all points'. This means that, however much or little we examine, it will contain information that reflects the whole. This approach provides a rationale for ethnomethodological approaches (e.g. Goffman, 1961), and Conversation Analysis (see Chapter 14).

### *Values*

Clinical psychologists aspire to be scientists, and science as a discipline is often seen as value-free. However, it seems to me that truth is the ultimate value for scientists. Their aim is simply to tell us what are, so far as current knowledge goes, the facts, unpolluted by values. But is this possible? Scientists express their values in their choice of subject for study and the way in which they study it. They may hide behind their expressed commitment to scientific objectivity to pursue their own political or ethical agenda, as was the case in studies of the racial basis of intelligence. Nowadays the choices scientists are able to make are increasingly constrained by institutional factors such as the direction of government policy, the priorities of funding bodies and the demands of the market economy.

What values should guide our work with people? This cannot be established by reference to rational argument: 'on values reason is silent' (MacIntyre, 2007: 26). MacIntyre argues that contemporary society lacks superordinate principles that might guide our ethical choices between alternative values, such as justice, survival, rights or liberty. We are left only with a 'disquieting private arbitrariness'. Kuhn is untroubled by the *a priori* nature of values, since he asserts that ultimately all theories rest on untestable assumptions.

The professional Code of Conduct for British psychologists includes the requirement to 'value the dignity and worth of all persons' (BPS, 2009: 10) . This humanistic tenet is not so private. It is widely accepted in society and has a long history dating back to the Renaissance. Against the established structure and doctrine of the church, the humanists set the intrinsic value of human beings. This lies in their capacity for free will and the boundless potential that this affords: 'with freedom of choice and with honor, as though the maker and molder of thyself, thou mayest fashion thyself in whatever shape thou shalt prefer' (Mirandola, 1486, quoted in Fromm and Xirau, 1968: 104).

Social constructionism, in its emphasis on the relativity of knowledge, may also be seen as value-free. But this is belied by the sensitivity to individual suffering expressed in much of the writing by social constructionists (e.g. Diversi, 2003). Michael White stresses that social constructionism should not be taken as implying a moral relativism, nor does it negate our moral responsibilities towards our clients:

> if in therapy we collaborate with persons in the further negotiation or renegotiation of the stories of persons' lives, then we really are in a position of having to face and to accept, more than ever, a responsibility for the real effects of our interactions on the lives of others.
>
> (Bubenzer et al, 1995: 14)

### Human nature

The scientific emphasis on causal explanations and invariant laws implies a deterministic conception of human behaviour. This is at odds with both the conception of a person who as an agent, free to make their own choices, and the view that identity is socially constructed.

The three traditions of thought are summarised in Table 2.1. This builds on the analysis given in Goodley (2011).

*Table 2.1* Understanding people: three traditions.

|  | *Positivism* | *Humanism* | *Postmodernism* |
|---|---|---|---|
| Ontology | Belief in the existence of truth and facts | Belief in the reality of subjective experience | Belief in the relativity of knowledge, which is expressed and created in language |
| Explanation | Causal | In terms of reason, meaning and motive | In terms of socially constructed narratives, influenced by cultural context |
| Methodology | Objective, observation | Subjective | Ethnomethodology, Conversation Analysis |
| Values | Truth is the main value | Belief in the dignity and worth of each person | ? |
| Concept of human nature | Human fate is determined | People are agents, acting voluntarily | Identity is socially constructed |

### A rapprochement?

There has been a tendency for theoretical rapprochement between different approaches. Much as Kuhn describes, the anomalies and limitations of a theory eventually become evident, and there is a move either to replace the theory with something new, or to adapt and extend the original theory.

So whereas early behaviourists showed astonishing insensitivity to some of their subjects, present-day behaviourism (in the form of Positive Behaviour

Support) has an altogether more human face (see Chapter 7). And whereas some early humanistic therapists showed quite a cavalier disregard for evidence, present-day therapists are generally eager to demonstrate their scientific credentials. Nowadays, I think most psychologists would claim to aim for both objectivity and humanity.

An early example of the integration of the phenomenological and the causal is the study by King and others of patterns of residential care (King et al, 1970). They used Goffman's insights into the nature of institutional care to develop and carry out a scientific study of ways in which institutional structures militated against child-oriented management practices. A more recent example is Stolk and Kars's (2000) study into the meaning that parents attribute to the lives of their profoundly disabled children.

## Implementing a humanistic agenda for people with learning disability

A starting point for implementing a humanistic agenda for people with learning disability is to clarify our concept of what constitutes a fulfilled human being. The construct of 'need' provides one approach to this question. Needs have been defined as 'experiential nutriments that are vitally important for one's well-being and optimal functioning' (Vansteenkiste and Sheldon, 2006: 71). Newman and Beail (1994) suggest that needs have been neglected in the field of learning disability because of the painful experiences that their study may evoke in the practitioner. Another possible explanation is that assertions about need are seen as untestable hypotheses or assumptions, and therefore take us into philosophical areas in which we feel uncomfortable.

Needs may be seen as being universal, or as varying between individuals. In Social Production Function Theory, needs are conceptualised as being variable, so that the task of the psychologist is to ascertain what they are for each person (Nieboer et al, 2005). The problem is that it is difficult to find out a person's needs if they are unable to speak to us, or unable to conceptualise their own inner states. Kreuger et al (2008) used the proxy views of support workers and family members to rank the relative importance of physical wellbeing, social wellbeing, control/influence and time use. However, we have no way of knowing the extent to which the inferences made by others reflect the feelings of the people for whom they care.

Needs are more commonly seen as being universal and invariant. Maslow conceptualised them as a hierarchical pyramid, with physiological factors at its base, and rising through the needs for safety, belongingness, love and esteem to our need for 'self-actualisation' (Maslow, 1971). Newman and Beail (1994) introduced functional and behavioural needs into the pyramid.

*Self-determination theory* provides an alternative conceptualisation of need. This is a theory of motivation, according to which effectiveness in therapy depends on the extent to which the person's psychological needs are satisfied (Deci and Ryan, 2000, 1985). Three needs are identified as being of particular importance: the needs for competence, autonomy and belongingness. *Competence* refers to a person's propensity to 'seek challenge ... which contributes to their growth and skill development'. *Autonomy* refers to the person's 'sense of choice and authorship with respect to their behaviour'. And *relatedness* refers to a person's involvement in 'supportive, caring relationships in which their feelings, thoughts and beliefs are respected' (Vansteenkiste and Sheldon, 2006: 71–72).

Other psychological theories approach the issue of need tangentially or by implication. Within the normalisation literature, the Five Accomplishments seem to suggest the basic conditions that must be met for people to achieve wellbeing (O'Brien and Tyne, 1981). Similarly, the concept of Quality of Life, largely established by factor analysis, seems to imply that if a satisfactory level is reached on the various factors, then people's needs will be met. Within the broader psychology literature, Gilbert's (2010) identification of our emotional regulation systems seems to imply that the needs for us to act on our environment, achieve affiliation and stay safe are intrinsic to human beings. Positive Psychology lays out the preconditions for happiness: a pleasant life; a good life; and a meaningful life (Seligman, 2003).

There is no *a priori* way of deciding between these different views of what constitutes a fulfilled human being. Perhaps we should turn to what people with learning disability say for themselves.

### The views of people with learning disability

It is only recently, as 'user-participation' has become something of a buzz-word, that this has become a subject for study. In the late 1990s, the British Institute for Learning Disabilities carried out a research project to find out what lifestyle outcomes would be valued by people with learning disability and other key stakeholders. They arrived at ten outcomes:

- I make everyday choices
- people treat me with respect
- I take part in everyday activities
- I have friendships and relationships
- I am part of my local community
- I get the chance to work
- I take part in important decisions about my life
- people listen to my family's views
- I am safe from harassment and abuse
- I get help to stay healthy.

(Fox, 2008: 11)

Studies of women with learning disability who self-injure have found that they would appreciate being able to talk about their experience in an atmosphere of understanding and acceptance:

"If you judge people it actually makes them feel worser. If you say, 'oh well you're stupid for doing it' it makes them 20 times worse than what they already are."

"I just spat it out . . . there was a big ton weight coming off my body to make me feel better that somebody knew. . . . Aye, I was glad, I was very happy with myself that I told somebody."

(Heslop, 2011: 8–9)

Waddell and Evers (2000) asked members of a focus group what they wanted from a psychology service:

Apart from practical requests like teaching football and running computer lessons, they wanted psychologists to help them cope with bullying (nearly all felt they had been bullied at some time), to be more independent and to manage relationship problems (with both boyfriends or girlfriends and family).

(Waddell and Evers 2000: 36)

The concern about physical safety (and physical activity) in these sources of information is a salutary reminder of the importance of ensuring that people meet the most basic of needs in Maslow's hierarchy. Beyond this, people's aspirations in both cases can be seen as falling mainly into two basic areas. The first represents the nature of our relationships with others, and includes qualities such as acceptance, respect, belonging and inclusion. The second represents the ways in which we act on the world and encompasses ideas of choice, competence and autonomy.

Where people are unable to meet their needs, for whatever reason, this will be expressed in problematic feelings, relationships or behaviour. When someone is referred to us for help, we embark on a search to understand the nature of their unmet needs and of the factors that have contributed to this situation. Under the guise of 'Independence' and 'Choice', there has been a tendency to favour autonomy at the expense of relatedness or even competence, and we may find ourselves trying to redress this imbalance on behalf of the person.

## Agency and Access

In working to help the person, our aim is both to understand and enhance the capacity of the individual to meet their own needs, and also to understand and enhance the capacity of the social system to facilitate this process. This dual-level approach is summed up in the concepts of Agency and Access.

Agency may be defined as *the extent to which the individual has the capacity to use their internal and external resources to meet their needs and thereby reduce their discomfort or achieve other positive goals*. It is associated with the idea of 'action', which comes from the same Latin root (*'agere'* – to act).

Bandura identifies the core features of agency as being intentionality, fore-thought, self-reactiveness and self-reflectiveness (Bandura, 2001). Such a definition places the bar rather high for most people with learning disability. In contrast, according to the philosopher Shaun Gallagher: 'The kind of conscious knowledge involved in agency does not have to be of a very high order; it could be simply a matter of a very thin phenomenal awareness, and in most cases it is just that' (2007: 1).

As infants, we develop our sense of Agency in our relationships with responsive caregivers. The newborn baby is helpless, without any sense of their ability to act on their environment. But as caregivers respond to their needs, the child gradually develops a sense of competence, autonomy and confidence. Language plays an important part in this process, helping the child to acquire a sense of identity and to locate themselves in relation to their environment (van Nijnatten, 2010).

Where language is limited or absent, as in the case of some people with learning disability, this therefore reduces the possibility of developing Agency. Lack of the ability to use language may be compounded by other reduced cognitive abilities, physical health problems, social circumstances and lack of material resources. This means that, even with support, it is likely that people's ability to develop Agency in the various contexts of their adult lives will be limited. We must therefore equally consider the capacity of the social systems to which they belong to meet their needs.

The disability rights movement has been influential in gaining acceptance of the idea that inclusion and equality are issues of entitlement rather than something delivered out of the discomfort of the able. Seale and Nind (2010) suggest that this sense of entitlement is encapsulated in the concept of *Access*, which refers to the extent to which society is organised so as to promote the fulfilment of a person's needs.

Access, like Agency, is a gateway to the fulfilment of needs and hence to wellbeing. Access is multi-dimensional, involving not just physical access but social organisation, knowledge and power. It is underpinned by relationships, advocacy and communication, and involves every area of life. Failures of access are legion: being invited to attend a conference where none of the presentations is made intelligible; being invited to health screening by letter; being unable to attend an evening disco because there is no late bus home; being unable to take part in a conversation because nobody allows for differences in hearing ability; being expected to cope with unexpected changes; being included in meeting but not supported to participate. The list is endless.

Removing barriers to access is not an end in itself, but a means by which quality of life is improved and people's needs are met. Access goes beyond legal entitlement and formal social structures. It 'happens in the minutiae of interactions in which new words are explained, practices are modelled, social episodes are opened up, small problems are solved and so on' (Seale and Nind, 2010: 12).

The concept of *scaffolding* is helpful to us in conceptualising the ways in which interactions are structured so as to both ensure Access and enhance

Agency. Bruner introduced the term scaffolding on the basis of Vygotsky's work on the *zone of proximal development.* He used it to represent the way in which the child's environment, and particularly their interaction with helpful adults, is structured so as to promote learning (Bruner, 1983). It is more commonly used in the educational field, where it is described as 'a process in which students are given support until they can apply new skills and strategies independently' (Larkin, 2002). Essential elements include: beginning with what the student can do; establishing a shared goal; understanding the student needs; and assisting internalisation and generalisation. While bearing this guidance in mind, here I am using the metaphor of scaffolding more broadly as a useful and accessible image to help carers and ourselves make the crucial shift from *changing the person* to *changing the environment.* We must also allow for the possibility that the individual, through their Agency, affects changes in Access. These ideas are brought together in Figure 2.1.

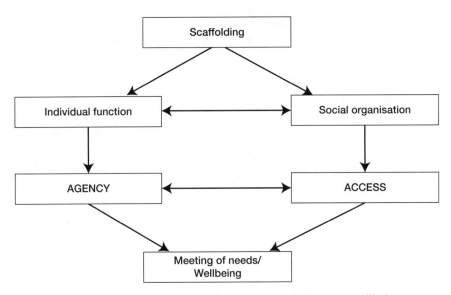

*Figure 2.1* The contribution of scaffolding, Agency and Access to wellbeing.

## Conclusions

People with learning disability, like everyone else, deserve to be able to lead a life in which their needs for physical safety, meaningful social relationships and individual autonomy are met. We can support them in achieving this through working to enhance both their Agency and their Access. But in order to do this, we will first need to develop a clear, thorough and coherent understanding of their problems, drawing on all three of the intellectual traditions described in this chapter.

The rapprochement between science and humanism has been helped by a postmodern climate, in which the certainties of the past now seem more fragile than they did previously. We are perhaps more ready to accept that, if there is such a thing as truth, our grasp of it is only ever likely to be partial. We are more likely to question, and to be flexible in our thinking.

Foucault in 1967 exhorted us to renounce the convenience of terminal truths. Kelly put it rather less poetically:

> When a scientist propounds a theory he has two choices: he can claim that what he says has been dictated to him by the real nature of things, or he can take sole responsibility for what he says and claim only that he has offered one man's hopeful construction of nature. In the first instance he makes a claim to objectivity on behalf of his theory, the scientist's equivalent of the claim to infallibility. In the second instance he offers only hope that he may have hit upon some partial truth that may serve as a clue to inventing something better and he invites others to follow this clue to see what they can make of it.
>
> (Kelly, 1969, quoted in Bannister and Fransella, 1980: 66–67)

## Recommended reading

Goodley D (2011) *Disability Studies: An Interdisciplinary Introduction* London: Sage Publications

Kuhn S (1996) *The Structure of Scientific Revolutions* (3rd edition) London: University of Chicago Press

Seale J and Nind N (eds) (2010) *Understanding and Promoting Access for People with Learning Difficulties* London: Routledge

# 3   The historical context

Through historical understanding we can better understand the present (Marwick, 1970). But there is a 'silence at the centre' of the information we have about the history of people with learning disabilities (Rushton, 1988: 34). Official records do not include their voices. Only with the closure of the asylums were the experiences and feelings of some of the people with learning disability recorded. Academic study is also sparse: 'the social marginality of people with learning disabilities has been mirrored by their academic marginality' (Digby, 1996: 1).

History is not a dispassionate chronicle of events, but a reconstruction, seen through the prism of current concerns and values (Carr, 1961). This means that there are many alternative historical narratives that could be written about people with learning disability and what Goodey (2011) calls their 'historical cousins'. My aim in this account is to provide a context for current issues in learning disability services, particularly focusing on the historical relativity of ideas about people with learning disability and their treatment.

In talking of 'learning disability' I am not necessarily referring to the same group of people that were referred to, say, in the Middle Ages, as 'idiots' and 'fools', or in the 19th century as 'mentally deficient'. Terminology arises in a particular historical and social context and must be understood in that context, not in relation to an invariant medical or social condition. Such labels may have a superficial equivalence, but we need to delve further to understand their meaning as ascribed by the people who used them.

For the purpose of this brief account, I identify four eras, ending in the late 20th century. What has so far passed of the 21st century will be addressed later (see Chapter 13). Each era is characterised by different socio-economic conditions and cultures. And, associated with this, each differently defines and treats those labelled as having cognitive impairments.

## 13th–early-16th century

The medieval literature (much of which is written in Latin) refers, often interchangeably, to 'idiots' and 'fools'. The Latin term idiota means an ignorant or uneducated person and is derived from the Greek idiotes, meaning a private person, one not fit to take part in public life. Due to their lack of understanding of sin, 'fools' could be seen as both holy and depraved (McDonagh, 2008). The 'natural fool' was a person with unique licence to tell the truth, and presumably it is out of this conception that the 'artificial fool', known to us through Shakespeare, came into being.

The Prerogativa Regis, 1255–1290 provided that the king should 'have the custody of the lands of natural fools taking the profits of them . . . and shall find them their necessaries' (Neugebauer, 1996). An idiot was defined as a person who from his birth had lacked understanding. This was decided by a jury of 12 men, who were asked to swear 'whether he be sufficiently witted to dispose of his own land with discretion or not' (McDonagh, 2008). So the legal definition of idiocy was a functional one, linked to property ownership.

We know little about how the various upheavals of medieval society affected the treatment of idiots and fools. Probably many were cared for by their families, found work in agriculture or died young. Some may have been taken to healing shrines or to monastic hospitals. In the late-15th century, people judged to be idiots were taken into the custody of guardians, who were presumed to be upright people, preferably next of kin. In Tudor times, royal appropriation of revenues from the property of idiots gave way to a system that protected their rights and those of their families. So the official discourse at least was one of protection rather than exploitation.

But the Reformation introduced a moral undertone to the conception of idiocy. Protestantism distinguished between sinners and the elect, who could be saved. Since idiots lacked the ability to reason, they were beyond redemption. Their existence in a supposedly God-created world was explained by the changeling myth, according to which the devil had taken away the perfect child and replaced it with its own offspring: 'The devil sits in such changelings where the soul should have been'. They were 'more obnoxious than ten children with their crapping, eating and screaming' (Luther, 1483–1546; quoted in Ryan and Thomas, 1980: 88).

## 16th–18th centuries

The medieval way of life was overturned by the Enclosures, a series of Acts that involved the appropriation of common land into private ownership, or the change in use of land from arable to grazing for sheep. Tenants were evicted or lost their rights to grow crops, graze their animals or to collect firewood. At the same time as swelling the wealth of the landed aristocracy, this agrarian revolution caused widespread destitution and dislocation. The plight of landless labourers was compounded by draconian Vagrancy Acts. Idiots and fools must have suffered from this economic and social upheaval, and the punitive response of the state, at least as much as others. The situation was exacerbated during the reign of Henry VIII by the dissolution of the monasteries (1536–1541), which resulted in the closure of the monastic hospitals.

By the end of the 16th century concern about the maintenance of public order served to usher in what Foucault memorably described as the 'Great Confinement'. From 1575 'Houses of correction' ('bridewells') were set up to deal with criminals. The Poor Law Consolidating Act of 1601 appointed Overseers of the Poor for each parish. They set to work the able poor, but also allowed for some financial provision for poor families. In 1618 those 'naturally disabled . . . in wit . . . as the idiot' were recognised as deserving of Poor Law relief (Allderidge, 1979: 324). The first workhouse was established in Bristol in 1697, and by the end of the 18th century there were 126 of them in England. Exclusion had become systematic.

The 17th century has been described as the Age of Curiosity, the period when science began to develop, with the work of people such as Galileo, Boyle and Newton, and their emphasis on observation and measurement. The 'objective' study of idiocy began, and the scientific view developed alongside, and was often influenced by, the religious and moralistic conception of idiocy. The Protestant demonisation of idiots was continued by Locke (1632–1704). Since 'idiots make few or no propositions and reason scarce at all' (Digby, 1996: 3), they did not qualify as human beings, and infanticide was therefore justifiable (Goodey, 1996).

But at the same time, 17th and 18th-century records show evidence both of loving commitment by families and of a rudimentary system of state support for idiots, delivered through the Courts. This Northumberland widow, speaking in 1711, cared for her two granddaughters:

> the youngest is about thirty years of age and neither of them can tell to twenty . . . I am burthened something with them because they are not capable of service.
>
> (Rushton, 1988: 39)

The 18th century was the age of industrialisation, revolution and the Enlightenment. The traditional communities that previously supported agricultural labourers had broken down. Those seen, for one reason or another, as deviants, continued to be accommodated in bridewells, workhouses and private madhouses. But there was 'no recognition of the mentally handicapped as a category requiring a distinct form of treatment' (Jones, 1972: 3). And within these institutions, cruelty and suffering were endemic, buttressed by a conception of the disabled as subhuman:

> in Bethnal Green, a woman subject to violent seizures was placed in a pigsty, feet and fists bound; when the crisis had passed she was tied to her bed, covered only by a blanket; when she was allowed to take a few steps, an iron bar was placed between her legs, attached by rings to her ankles and by a short chain to handcuffs . . .
>
> (Foucault, 1989: 67–68)

The French Revolution (1789–1799) sent a wave of fear through the middle and upper classes of England. And by the latter half of the 18th century, Britain was transformed by the Industrial Revolution into an urban, industrial society based on wage labour. There was now a new, highly visible industrial working class, as well as an underclass who were unable or unwilling to work. With their rise came perceived potential for the 'rule of the mob', and the need for it to be tamed. But at the same time, science was on the ascendant, in part represented by the medical profession. From 1774 onwards, a medical certificate was required for admission of a person to a madhouse, marking the beginning of medicalisation of services for those seen as idiots.

## 19th–early-20th century

In the 19th century, urbanisation resulted in social problems achieving a new visibility (Jones, 1972). From 1834 onwards Poor Law orders began to refer to people with different categories of disability: idiots, persons of weak intellect, imbeciles, and the mentally infirm (Digby, 1996: 6). Technological change required a more disciplined and educated workforce, and the family was no longer seen as adequate to provide for the socialisation of children. Compulsory elementary education was introduced and as a result 'slow' children, who were unable to progress in regular classrooms, were discovered (Wright, 1996). This resulted in the establishment of the first special schools. By 1903 they had been established in London and 50 other authorities (Gladstone, 1996). In France, Seguin began his physiological education of idiots, combining a belief in their animalistic nature with a conviction that they were capable of improvement (Ryan and Thomas, 1980).

In 1847 the Charity for the Asylum of Idiots (the first institution specifically for idiots) was opened in London, and over the next 20 years, four more institutions were founded (Gladstone, 1996). They were at first seen as educational establishments for children, albeit with medical certification being required. Wilbur, in 1852 identified four groups, based on people's potential for development of functional skills: *simulative idiocy, higher-grade idiocy, lower-grade idiocy* and *incurables* (Trent, 1994).

However, even by the 19th century, doctors had not arrived at a clear definition of idiocy. When children were admitted to the National Asylum for Idiots between 1861 and 1886, certification was based on parental descriptions that emphasised the child's intellectual, practical or social incompetence. For example, the certificate for Tom Alison, granted in 1881, states that Tom is always 'uttering curious noises such as yelling and crying like a cat', whereas that for Thomas Williams, granted in 1871, states 'there is an absence of sympathy with the other children of the Family, either in their grief or joy' (Wright, 1996: 123).

The early asylums were established in a 'burst of therapeutic and social optimism' (Digby, 1996: 5). Children seen as 'educable idiots' were to benefit from fresh air, the association with others, practice, reward and the use of a benign authority. In contrast to their 'inexpressibly filthy' state prior to admission, once in the asylum, the children were 'well clothed, judiciously and regularly fed and exercised . . . [and] from the affection and kindness shewn to them, they are at once much happier' (Gladstone, 1996: 139).

The original intention of the asylums was that children should be admitted at an early age, and remain for a maximum period of five years, eventually improving, being restored to their communities and finding employment. This meant that the more severely disabled were often excluded from the asylums. Even so, early hopes proved to be unrealistic. Financial imperatives resulted in the asylums producing goods for their own consumption or sale, through a programme of industrial training, covering trades such as shoemaking, tailoring and gardening for the boys, and sewing, knitting and laundry work for the girls. A programme of recreational activities and religious observance complemented the education and training. Nevertheless, in 1881 it was estimated that only 3 per cent of the 29,542 idiot inmates of English institutions were in special idiot asylums, the remainder still being accommodated in workhouses, lunatic asylums and prisons (Gladstone, 1996: 140). There continued to be a huge unmet need for places, so asylums became larger, with more adult, long stay inmates. They were built on the outskirts of towns in what became almost self-sufficient communities, with farms, laundries, sewing rooms and 'inmates', who provided a large workforce.

The discourse of improvement and benign authority increasingly turned to one of containment, control and regimentation. The smallest detail of the inmates' life was dictated by the institutional regime and mores. The total institution, later to be so vividly described by Goffman (1961), was born.

In time the asylums were taken over by superintendents, who started to define their charges in medical terms (Trent, 1994: 39). The legitimacy of the medical superintendents was underpinned by their professional status, their monopoly over treatments and their supposed expertise in the conditions of madness and imbecility. These conditions came to be conceptualised as illnesses. The inmates came to be known as 'patients' and at the same time they were turned into objects of scientific curiosity, to be studied, explained, categorised. With the rising power of the medical profession, their conceptualisation of learning disability soon entered the mainstream political discourse, through legislation. Medical diagnosis came to be the lens through which people with cognitive difficulties were seen.

But there was also a more pernicious aspect to the rise of the medical profession. The medical superintendents both reflected and contributed to the vitriolic moral condemnation to which idiots had been intermittently subjected for centuries. In 1859 Darwin's sensational *On the Origin of Species* was published. Although it undermined the religious orthodoxies of the day, this new theory also provided a theoretical rationale for seeing human beings as the highest form of life, and for seeing some people as more human than others. Its social implications were explored by Herbert Spencer (1820–1903), who developed the idea of Social Darwinism and coined the term 'survival of the fittest' (Spencer, 1864). His writing was hugely popular, and it is easy to see how it might have helped to make sense of the incompetences of a particular social group in terms of their innate inferiority within a larger evolutionary scheme.

In the 1860s the term 'feeble-minded' was borrowed from American writings, its meaning being changed to denote those who were both intellectually impaired and a threat to society. This threat was often in terms of their criminality or financial incompetence if they were men, or in terms of their sexual immorality if they were women (McDonagh, 2000).

The experience of different races in the colonies contributed a racist tinge to the mixture of medicalisation and moral condemnation. The most famous exponent of such theories is Langdon-Down, who in 1866 (see McDonagh, 2008: 3) described one group of idiots as Mongolian (later to be renamed Down's Syndrome). Bateman, physician at the Eastern Counties Asylum (where I was later to work as a healthcare assistant), saw idiocy as 'an expression of parental defects and vices . . . a result of the violation of natural laws over several generations' (Ryan and Thomas, 1980: 105).

In the fertile soil of moral opprobrium, Social Darwinism, Mendelian genetics, Degeneracy Theory and medicalisation, 'Eugenics', the science of the improvement of the human race, was to flower. It was brought to life in 1865 by Galton (see Galton, 1883), using the Greek roots meaning 'well' and 'born'. It grew into an international movement, rooted in fear of respectable society being swamped by an alien underclass who bred faster than other people and passed on their disability and degeneracy from one generation to the next. Three policies logically followed from eugenic beliefs: segregation, the regulation of sexual relationships and birth control, including sterilisation.

In 1896 the National Association for the Care and Control of the Feeble Minded was set up. Mary Dendy and others campaigned for the lifetime segregation of 'mental defectives', particularly women, since only the control of reproduction could be 'really efficacious in stemming the great evil of feebleness of the mind' (quoted in Jackson, 1996: 169).

In 1908 the Radnor Report on a Royal Commission reported as follows:

> Investigations compel the conclusion that there are numbers of mentally defective persons whose training is neglected, over whom no sufficient control is exercised, and whose wayward and irresponsible lives are productive of crime and misery . . . and of much continuous expenditure wasteful to the community and to individual families . . . feeble-mindedness is largely inherited; . . . consequently there are strong grounds for placing mental defectives of each sex in institutions where they will be retained and kept under effectual supervision as long as may be necessary . . . to make procreation impossible.
>
> (Ryan and Thomas, 1980: 107)

A parliamentary bill to this effect was drawn up but, despite widespread public support, it was eventually delayed in Standing Committee by some

Ministers who felt uncomfortable about its eugenic assumptions (Abbott and Sapsford, 1988). Eventually it was introduced in a watered down version as the 1913 Mental Deficiency Act. This Act retained clauses establishing a procedure for compulsory certification and detention of mental defectives, though others forbidding marriage and allowing compulsory sterilisation were omitted. Four classes of people were identified: idiots, imbeciles, the feeble-minded and moral defectives. Assessment was based on judgements of competence and morality rather than intelligence. For example, the definition given for idiots is:

> Persons in whose case there exists mental defectiveness of such a degree that they are unable to guard themselves against common physical dangers.

Whereas 'moral defectives' are:

> Persons in whose case there exists mental defectiveness, coupled with strong vicious or criminal propensities and who require care, supervision and control for the protection of others.
>
> (Mental Deficiency Act, 1913)

Local authorities were obliged to identify and make provision for the mentally deficient in their areas. Wide groups of people, including children and people giving birth to illegitimate children, could be detained, with little or no legal safeguard.

> When I was 12 years old the School Board man came round to see my mum to tell her I would have to go away to Essex Hall for playing truancy from school. My mother told him he could not do this without permission from the court, he said 'we can do anything these days, Mrs Lindsey'.
>
> Two days later my mother had forgotten what the man had said, she left me sitting outside on the front doorstep. She asked me to look out for my dad. . . . My mum had given me a bit of bread and jam . . . I had only been out there for about 20 minutes when a car came round the corner. It stopped and four men got out. . . . Although I struggled, they carried me to the car and put me in it and drove off. They didn't even tell my mum.
>
> (Leonard Lindsey, quoted in New Possibilities NHS Trust, 2001: 4)

Women seem to have been disproportionately affected. For example, in Bedfordshire between 1916 and 1918, of 19 adults sent to mental deficiency institutions under the Act, 15 were women. Of these, 11 were described as displaying inappropriate sexual behaviour. Morality seems to have been more important than level of ability (Walmsley, 2000: 68).

> Elizabeth was certified in 1937. In 1993 she told a researcher her story:

> Well me elder sister went down and took her from me when I were in hospital. I didn't know me sister was going to come for it. I thought I was

going to get it all over, meself better and when it were time to go home I was going to take her with me. . . . She brought her up as hers, had her name changed and everything. To think I've never had her . . . that hurt me more than anything. Well I cried and cried – I couldn't help it. And there's been hours I've been in bed at the Park on Villa 4, cried me eyes out.

(Potts and Fido, 1993: 4)

As late as 1952, when Tredgold published the eighth edition of his standard medical textbook, he still felt able to describe idiots and imbeciles as repulsive in appearance, and suggest that their existence should be painlessly terminated. And, of course, 'termination' was the solution that Hitler had decided upon. In Nazi Germany hundreds of thousands of the learning disabled (and physically disabled) were murdered (Burleigh, 2000).

Thankfully, in the post-war years public sentiment was changing and the appetite for eugenic solutions disappeared. However, both adults and children continued to be committed to the new hospitals. The 1944 Education Act, influenced by Cyril Burt, defined and identified by their IQ level a group of children who were 'incapable' of receiving education at school, many of whom continued to live permanently in hospitals. At the height of influence of the Mental Deficiency Act, 65,000 people were placed in institutions, often for many years and without legal redress (Walmsley, 2000).

Leonard Lindsay entered an institution in 1921 and eventually died in it in the 'early 1980s'. Shortly before that he described the harsh life of his childhood in the institution, with children being 'put on bread and water for a week' if they talked in class, and made to wear a notice on their front and back if they tried to escape (New Possibilities NHS Trust, 2001: 4). The hospital magazine reported: 'This zany character, who was full of wit, will be sadly missed by us all' (New Possibilities NHS Trust, 2001).

Other people were restored to their communities too late to remedy the injustices and pain of the past.

In 1937, at the age of 15, Jean Gambell was sectioned as feeble-minded under the Mental Deficiency Act. Her siblings only discovered her existence in the summer of 2007. Weeks after being reunited with her family, she died from pneumonia, holding the hand of her sister Grace, whom she had barely known in her life.

(Midgley, *The Times* 7 November 2007)

## Late-20th century

Influenced by the Great Depression of the inter-war years, the conviction arose that market forces could not be relied upon to ensure a healthy economy or to protect the vulnerable from its failures. In the wake of the Second World War a Labour government was elected, and created the welfare state. This was a universal service, designed to protect everyone from the impact of economic disaster, and people with learning disability were also to benefit. In 1948, with the founding of the National Health Service, asylums for the learning disabled were brought into the hospital network (Race, 2002). And in 1948 the National Assistance Act abolished the Poor Law, and brought the old workhouses under the management of local authorities.

At this time the asylums (now known as hospitals) were still functioning as self-sufficient communities, producing goods on an industrial scale. For example, in 1939 a group of three asylums in Essex produced 220,000 eggs! Shortage of raw materials during the war resulted in production being cut in most areas, but in 1947 the 'patients' still managed to make 25,000 boots (New Possibilities NHS Trust, 2001). However, the days of these institutions were numbered.

Hitler's 'final solution' had finally discredited the eugenics movement. Fear of the 'degenerate' was overtaken by the belief that all human beings had rights and deserved a basic standard of wellbeing in all areas of their life, not only on their own account, but also as 'the foundation of freedom, justice and peace in the world' (Preamble to Universal Declaration of Human Rights, UN, 1948). In 1951 a report from the NCCL described the plight of the learning disabled as one of the greatest social scandals of the 20th century. In 1959, the Mental Health Act recommended setting up comprehensive outpatient services, as well as local authority residential and day centres. The Act allowed for informal (i.e. voluntary) treatment for most people, whilst also providing a new legal framework involving medical certification for compulsory admissions. It stated that no person should be detained for the reason of immoral behaviour alone. Idiots, imbeciles and between half and two-thirds of the feeble-minded were redesignated as 'severely subnormal', which was defined as:

> Arrested or incomplete development of mind which includes subnormality of intelligence and is of such a nature or degree that the patient is incapable of living an independent life or guarding himself against serious exploitation.

'Subnormal' patients, on the other hand, were those with the potential for development:

> Arrested or incomplete development of mind of a nature or degree which requires or is susceptible to medical treatment or other special care or training of the patient.

These definitions anticipate later psychiatric definitions of learning disability in terms of both intelligence and adaptive function.

Enoch Powell's Hospital Plan, published in 1962, envisaged an increase in beds for the subnormal, rising to 63,620 by 1975 (http://studymore.org.uk/

xpowello.htm). But in 1967 there were shocking revelations of patient abuse in hospitals, fuelling the belief that institutional care for the subnormal was wrong. In 1971 a White Paper (DHSS and Welsh Office) introduced the term 'mental handicap' and suggested replacing much of the hospital accommodation with 25-bed hostels and training centres. The UN *Declaration on the Rights of Mentally Retarded Persons*, 1971 affirmed the right of people with learning disability to live in surroundings that were as close as possible to normal life. But it was only in the 1980s that the number of people in mental handicap hospitals began to decline significantly. People then started to live in smaller staffed houses or group homes, often provided by private and voluntary agencies such as Mencap.

A 1980 DHSS report suggested that, at a community level, each agency should contribute to an integrated service for mentally handicapped people and their families. This vision was to develop into the 'single door' concept of Community Mental Handicap Teams. In order to facilitate this shift, the government introduced the provision for joint funding between Health and Social Services. In 1990 the NHS and Community Care Act introduced the term 'learning disability' to replace 'mental handicap'. This Act also introduced the idea of 'supported living' and the purchaser–provider split. This paved the way for later dismantling of public services by ever more market-oriented governments.

During the 1980s and 1990s it became clear that simply decanting people 'into the community' did not necessarily result in either an improved quality of life or a decrease in challenging behaviour. Research focus shifted to the impact of systemic factors such as opportunities for activities and levels of staff support (Mansell, 1993; Lowe and Felce, 1996).

The Disability Discrimination Act was passed in 1995, and this was followed by the passing of the Human Rights Act in 1998. In 2000 the Scottish Executive published *The Same as You: A Review of Services for People with Learning Disabilities* (see also the Scottish Government, 2012) that was explicitly based on the UN *Declaration of the Rights of Disabled Persons*, with its affirmation of people's right to enjoy a decent life, as normal and full as possible (UN, 1975). And in 2001 *Valuing People* (DH, 2001a) was published, and the seal was set on a future that was intended to place beyond question the humanity of people with learning disabilities.

## Conclusions

As socio-economic conditions and ideologies have changed over the centuries, so has the way in which people have been described, understood and treated. At various times, and sometimes concurrently, it seems they were cared for, healed, absorbed, controlled, trained and vilified. In the late-19th and early-20th centuries, the learning disabled became the scapegoats for social evils, and it was believed that, if only they were brought under control, these problems would evaporate. Exclusion became the dominant theme. In the late-20th century, in the aftermath of the Second World War, issues of rights, respect and the need for social adaptation came to the fore. The professions of psychiatry and psychology have played their part in this narrative, as will be described in Chapter 4.

## Recommended reading

McDonagh P (2008) *Idiocy: A Cultural History* Liverpool: Liverpool University Press
Ryan J and Thomas F (1980) *The Politics of Mental Handicap* Harmondsworth: Penguin
Wright D and Digby A (eds) (1996) *From Idiocy to Mental Deficiency* London: Routledge

# 4   The professional and theoretical context

## Intelligence testing

Nowadays, we do not consider testing to be at the centre of our clinical work. But the history of psychology input to the care of learning disabled people begins with the history of testing. In the mid-19th century, Seguin's pioneering work on the 'physiological education' of idiot children laid the groundwork for later development of nonverbal tests (Anastasi and Urbina, 1997). In the 1870s, Galton was working in England on the study of individual differences (see Galton, 1883), and in 1890 James McKeen Cattell coined the term *mental test* for the set of cognitive and physiological tasks that he had devised (Anastasi and Urbina, 1997). Spearman was much influenced by Galton's early work, including his eugenic ideas. He invented the statistical technique of factor analysis to analyse correlations among variables. In experimenting with school children he discovered significant correlations between different intellectual abilities, and developed the idea that in addition to specific abilities there was a 'general intelligence', $g$. This could be assessed by measuring a number of different abilities and pooling the results (Tulsky et al, 2003).

In 1905 Binet and Simon published a set of tests linking and comparing mental and chronological age. Binet grouped the tests into age levels on the basis of the performance of a sample of 'normal' children. The child's score on the whole test could then be expressed as a 'mental age', which corresponded to the age of 80–90 per cent of normal children achieving at that level. Binet stressed that children did not possess a fixed quantity of intelligence: 'Intelligence . . . was a pliant structure that could be developed through good health and educational instruction and in a good environment' (Trent, 1994: 157).

Goddard was much influenced by the evolutionary ideas of his cousin, Charles Darwin. Unlike Binet, Goddard believed in the idea of a fixed, inherited intelligence, which could be assessed using his tests. In 1910 the American Association for the Study of the Feeble-Minded, under Goddard's influence, agreed to adopt Binet's intelligence tests as basis for a tripartite classification system based on mental age. The three groups were *idiots* (with a mental age of two years and less; *imbeciles* (with a mental age of 3–7 years); and *morons* (with a mental age of 8–12 years).

Since mental age was to be established by intelligence testing, Goddard thus succeeded in persuading both the medical profession and other psychologists to use intelligence testing to underpin the medical model of learning disability. In England, in 1924 the Board of Education reported on the use of psychological tests as a way of discriminating between normal and defective children. The idea of a fixed, inherited intelligence had taken root: 'Thousands of people became fascinated by the [Binet-Simon] test, but most employed it while ignoring Binet's insistence on the pliancy of intelligence' (Trent, 1994: 158).

At this time there was increasing public concern about the supposed threat posed by the rising tide of immoral and criminal feeble-minded in the population. This concern was fed by Goddard's (1912) notorious study of supposedly inherited degeneracy in the Kallikak family. Americans also became increasingly concerned about the influx of migrants and a perceived link between these new citizens, feeble-mindedness and degeneracy. Doctors, given the responsibility of weeding out those who posed a possible threat to society, devised Binet-style verbal intelligence tests to weed out the feeble-minded immigrants. They added to these measures non-verbal tests that could be used with people who did not speak English and lacked formal education.

In 1916 Terman published the Stanford-Binet intelligence test. It included the innovative Intelligence Quotient, which involved dividing the subject's mental age by his chronological age and multiplying the resulting figure by 100. Terman had no qualms about the fact that intelligence itself remained undefined:

> to demand ... that one who would measure intelligence should first present a complete definition of it, is quite unreasonable ... electrical currents were measured long before their nature was well understood.
>
> (Terman, 1916, quoted in Murdoch, 2007: 56)

He saw intelligence testing as the tool that would bring both the social deviancy and the reproductive capacity of 'defectives' under control.

Terman produced a group version of his tests for use with recruits during the First World War. For the first time these tests included the use of multiple choice questions. They were divided into 'Alpha' tests that were for use with literate recruits; and 'Beta' tests that were picture-based and could be used with non-literate recruits. By the end of the war psychologists had tested 1.7 million men. They reported that the Beta was a splendid test for Negroes, who had on average a mental age of ten years, as opposed to white recruits, whose average mental age was 13.08 years. Such data were used as evidence for a racist conception of intelligence. After the war, intelligence tests were widely adopted by American schools, and intelligence testing turned into a profitable industry. The tests were also adopted by psychologists in the asylums, providing a supposedly scientific underpinning to the new profession of psychology and its classification of clients.

One of the army's test administrators during the First World War was David Wechsler. In the 1930s, whilst working at a psychiatric hospital, he developed the Wechsler-Bellevue Intelligence Scale (Wechsler, 1939). This 'new' test amounted to a reorganisation and standardisation of existing tests, and had little theoretical underpinning. Seven of the subtests originated in the Binet-Simon Tests, the tests of immigrant screening or the army tests of 1923. Wary of the risk of over-diagnosing feeble-mindedness by using verbal tests, he combined the Alpha and Beta tests into one test with Verbal and Performance Scales (Boake, 2002). He made the test appropriate for adults by basing IQ score on a comparison of the subject's score with those achieved by others in the same age group rather than on the ratio of mental to chronological age.

Wechsler was aware of non-cognitive influences such as planning, persistence and enthusiasm on performance. He was unsuccessful in developing subtests to assess these features, but believed that they were to some extent incorporated into his test through the Performance Scale, which was more sensitive to 'temperamental and personality factors'. Despite producing a test that provided a single score, he wrote that what IQ tests measure was not something that can be expressed by a single factor such as 'g' (Tulsky et al, 2003). But ever since, psychologists have assumed that this is indeed what intelligence tests measure. The centrality of intelligence testing to the understanding of the construct of intelligence is such that the words of Boring in 1923 have now achieved near-mythical status: *'Intelligence is what the tests test'.*

Testing has also driven theoretical developments and this in turn has influenced everyday thinking about the nature of human beings and knowledge:

> The technical and instrumental forms that psychology has adopted . . . have come to delimit and shape the space of psychological thought itself . . . statistical norms and values become incorporated within the very texture of conceptions of what is today's psychological reality. . . . Psychology . . . has altered the way in which it is possible to think about people. . . . What is more, it has endowed some ways of thinking about people with extra credibility on account of their apparent grounding in positive knowledge.
>
> (Rose, 1991: no page numbers given)

## Behaviourism

Behaviourism was to provide clinical psychologists with a second string to their professional bow. Skinner wrote: 'If we are to further our understanding of human behaviour and to improve our practices of control, we must be prepared for the kind of rigorous thinking which science requires' (1953: 42). This meant an exclusive focus on observables, in other words behaviour, which could be explained in terms of learning theory (particularly reinforcement contingencies). The inner world of the subject was irrelevant to this. In the 1960s, for psychologists working in the institutions, behavioural theory and techniques provided a new set of tools to justify and enhance their professional status. Until then, they had mainly to serve the psychiatrists, brought in for the purposes of IQ testing when 'inmates' were proving particularly recalcitrant. Now, psychologists could use their understanding of classical and operant conditioning to reduce some of the most extreme manifestations of behaviour, particularly since total institutions offered the possibility of complete control over reinforcement contingencies.

But by the 1970s the deinstitutionalisation movement was well under way. Eysenck (1972: 609) suggested that the term 'behaviour therapy' should be applied to 'all methods of therapy which are based on modern learning theory'. This included techniques such as desensitisation, shaping, fading, forward and backward chaining, modelling, extinction and prompting, which were seen as helpful in preparing people for their new lives, living independently 'in the community'. These were the days of detailed skills assessments and behavioural programmes.

In the 1980s the description of behaviour in terms of rewards and punishments evolved into its description in terms of function. In the first place this simply specified the form of the relationship between variables, i.e. whether a behaviour was rendered more or less frequent by the presence of a specified reinforcer. Later, it took on board the anthropological or socio-logical meaning of the term, by identifying the function that a behaviour serves (Owens and Ashcroft, 1982). Wahler and Fox (1981) drew attention to the importance of antecedent events, such as the physiological state of the person and the physical condition of the setting, in influencing the frequency and function of behaviours, and the ABC model (Antecedents–Behaviour–Consequences) was born. The model came to be known as Applied Behaviour Analysis, and 'functional analysis' became the procedure for integrating its various elements.

Despite the increased sophistication of their methods, behaviour therapists developed a reputation for being coldly analytical, controlling and a-moral or even immoral. Their theories seemed to deny people's feelings and remove their capacity for self-determination. Carr (1996: 267) made a plea for them to adopt the language of ethics: 'We engineer environments and speak of factors that control human behaviour not because we worship power, but because we are trying to find the means for enhancing personal freedom'.

By the time Carr wrote this, change was already on the horizon, and not only because of the sweeping impact of normalisation. It turned out that behaviour therapy was not the panacea once imagined. In a research study, observations could be carried out systematically and 100 per cent consistency could be achieved in reinforcement contingencies, resulting in very effective interventions. However, in everyday practice, this proved impossible. Consequently, good assessment data were hard to obtain, and interventions often resulted in clients inadvertently being put on a regime of intermittent reinforcement for their challenging behaviours. Clements pointed out that there were many other influences on behaviour, beyond reinforcement contingencies. He proposed a broader concept of Antecedents and Consequences, so that functional analysis became a means of integrating information of different types, as in the STAR model (Zarkowska and Clements, 1994). McGill (2003) suggested that the functions served by behaviour are understandable in terms of both the individual features of some people with learning disability and the typical features of some services for people with learning disability – a conceptualisation that was later to appear in the Challenging Behaviour Guidelines.

The shift in emphasis from the Consequences to the Antecedents of behaviour involved a more preventive approach to challenging behaviour, grounded in understanding rather than control. In the 1990s the concept of Quality of Life was taken up, generating a flurry of research (e.g. Cummins, 2005a). These developments contributed to the Positive Behaviour Support model of behaviour management, with its focus on changes in setting conditions and real life outcomes (e.g. Allen et al, 2005)

## Deinstitutionalisation

The value and morality of keeping people in institutions had been questioned from the late 1950s. In Denmark the Mental Retardation Act defined the aim of services as being 'to create an existence for the mentally retarded as close to normal living conditions as possible' (Emerson, 1992: 1–2). In 1961 Goffman published his seminal study *Asylums*. This threw a cold spotlight on the plight of people incarcerated in asylums, and on the dehumanising techniques used to rob them of their identity. The book provided powerful ammunition to the deinstitutionalisation movement.

Tizard and his colleagues were in the forefront of the attempt to apply scientific method in the field of learning disability, and to espouse the value of community care. They carried out a number of studies demonstrating the potential of those incarcerated in the learning disability hospitals (e.g. Tizard and Loos, 1954). Studies also explored the link between living environments and performance, behaviour and IQ (e.g. Tizard, 1953). When children with learning disability were moved out of an institution into a large house, where staff adopted a developmental approach, a positive impact on their language was reported (Williams, 2005).

## Normalisation

In 1967 Blatt and Kaplan published clandestine photographic recording of the life of adults and children in four institutions, *Christmas in Purgatory*. In a caption to a heart-rending photo of an incarcerated child, Plato was quoted: 'The offspring of the inferior, or of the better when they chance to be deformed, will be put away in some mysterious, unknown place . . .'. It seemed that little had changed in the intervening centuries. Blatt wrote:

> More important than the desperately needed increased per capita expenditure for institutional care . . . is the necessity of infusing a fundamental belief among all who work with the mentally retarded that each of these individuals is equally human.
>
> (Blatt, 1969: 46–47)

In 1972, Wolfensberger published *The Principle of Normalisation in Human Services*, articulating what became the most well-known definition of normalisation. He later described this as the

> utilization of means which are as culturally normative as possible, in order to establish, enable or support behaviours, appearances, experiences and interpretations which are as culturally normative as possible.
>
> (Wolfensberger, 1980: 9)

This definition shifted attention from the experience of the stigmatised person to the perceptions of others. It seemed to involve not only the idea of normality, but also the sociological concept of *norm*, which refers to the expectations attached to social roles. Wolfensberger made this explicit when he renamed the concept *social role valorisation* (SRV). This, he said, incorporated 'The most explicit and highest goal of normalization . . . the creation, support, and defence of *valued social roles* for people who are at risk of devaluation' (1983: 234). Without such valued social roles, Wolfensberger claimed that people suffer from a devalued identity, will be badly treated and will then be more likely to behave in the deviant way expected of him. Interventions may involve enhancement of people's social image, or enhancement of their competencies. Wolfensberger identified seven core themes in service development. These included: the role of the unconscious in human services; the relevance of role expectancy to deviancy-making; the conservatism corollary, with its 'implications of positive compensation for people's devalued or at-risk status', and the importance of social integration (1983: 236).

According to Emerson, Wolfensberger changed normalisation 'from an egalitarian imperative to a *theory* regarding the modification of the social status of deviant groups' (1992: 11). But the theoretical status of normalisation is doubtful. Its force derives less from its scientific credentials than from the overtly ideological assumptions on which it is based. These are delivered in Wolfensberger's distinctive writing style, a potent mix of outrage and acute observation. Also not to be underestimated are PASS and PASSING, the service evaluation tools, which were used as a form of training to convey the philosophy of normalisation.

---

### Alf

It is 1986. The trainee clinical psychologist has arrived for her supervision at the portakabin that houses the psychology department. Her supervisor sits, elegant and composed, behind a large desk. The window behind her looks out on to the extensive grounds of the institution. The trainee is distracted by the appearance outside the window of Alf, standing with a fixed stare, and his penis hanging out. The supervisor swivels round, coming almost face to face with Alf. She rises, opens the window wide and shouts at the top of her voice: **'fuck off!'** Alf covers himself up and scuttles off.

The trainee is shocked and at a loss for words. The supervisor resumes her position behind the desk and straightens her jacket. 'Well!' she says eventually. 'I thought to myself: what's the normalised way to react to Alf?'

---

Participants on PASSING courses were taught to rate service systems on a number of dimensions, including physical and social integration, access, age-appropriateness, culture-appropriateness, model coherency and quality (Wolfensberger and Glenn, 1975). Training was given intensively, with participants reported to work late into the evenings, and subjected to a number of exercises that encouraged them to examine their own prejudices and values. People (like my supervisor) returned from these courses with evangelical zeal and determination to implement normalisation, though the way they did it may have veered somewhat from Wolfensberger's intentions.

Prior to the advent of normalisation, psychologists had been hesitant to introduce the ideas of value-driven practice into their avowedly scientific way of working. Normalisation made values professionally acceptable, and was initially received with enthusiasm by clinical psychologists. But at the same time as it was being taught to trainees, the near-messianic enthusiasm of the advocates of normalisation was generating a sceptical reaction. Psychologists began to question the scientific status of normalisation, and its empirical evidence (Rapley, 1990).

Feminists and others also questioned whether it was right for practitioners to try to change people so that their behaviour and appearance were acceptable within a flawed dominant value system. Should we not be attempting to change the inegalitarian society and the devaluing culture rather than the devalued individuals? Normalisation did not provide an analysis of the roots of devaluation in the distribution of power in society, nor did it challenge the infrastructure that creates devalued roles. It was accused of attempting to 'shake the branch without the tree' (Burns, 1992: 23). Clinicians found a tension between the rigid demands of normalisation and the rights of individuals to make their own choices. What if the individual would be happier staying in an environment seen by others as devaluing? In reply, it was pointed out that happiness is not necessarily the highest value if it is bought at the expense of other valued outcomes such as independence and the respect of others (Pilling and Midgley, 1992).

---

### Ethel

Ethel is well known in the hospital for her cheeky, toothless grin, a legacy of the days when inmates' teeth were routinely removed to stop them biting staff. Ethel is often to be seen walking round the hospital grounds, clutching Annie under her arm. Annie is her battered and much-loved doll.

The psychologist has been asked to follow up some training the nursing staff have received on normalisation. When the psychologist enters the ward, she is surprised to see Ethel sitting on the verandah, vacantly staring into space. There is an untouched jigsaw puzzle on the table in front of her. The psychologist goes and sits down next to her. 'Hello Ethel', she says. 'Where is Annie today?' The nursing assistant who is in attendance answers for Ethel. 'Oh, we decided to get rid of that old doll', she says. 'It's not right for a woman of Ethel's age to be seen carrying a doll around'.

---

In 1981 O'Brien and Tyne produced a version of normalisation/social role valorisation that was both more respectful of individual rights and more accessible to front line services. They called this the *'five accomplishments'*. These were: community presence, choice, respect, competence and community participation. They stressed that these should be pursued in the context of the life experiences, wishes and needs of individuals. This version of normalisation proved popular in England. It partly provided a foundation for the philosophy of Inclusion that later informed the 2001 White Paper *Valuing People* and the development of Person Centred Planning (DH, 2001a; 2002b). Wolfensberger's concept of normalisation proved to be extraordinarily influential and its impact continues to reverberate throughout service systems.

### The disability rights movement

In the heady days of the 1960s the discourse of rights was increasingly entering into the public arena. The sense of their distinct identity, needs and rights by disabled people was expressed in a statement by the Union of the Physically Impaired Against Segregation (UPIAS, 1976). This put forward the revolutionary idea that disability, and the social exclusion associated with it, was not an attribute of the individual, but the outcome of the way society is organised. This analysis was encapsulated in the distinction between *impairment, disability* and *handicap*, a categorisation that was taken up by the

WHO (1980), and that achieved widespread acceptance. Oliver labelled this 'outside–in' approach the 'social model' of disability, contrasting it with the individualistic focus of the 'tragedy' model and the 'medical' model (Oliver, 2004). People with physical disability for the first time started to organise themselves and speak up for themselves, through the advocacy movement.

People with learning disability were largely ignored in the early days of the disability rights movement. But a series of academic studies, together with the momentum of the ideas and campaigns of the 1970s and 1980s eventually resulted in both professionals and relatives accepting that learning disability was also socially constructed, and that the problems people face in attempting to lead fulfilling lives lay in the disabling beliefs and practices of society. In England the foremost self-advocacy group is People First, which was set up in 1984. It describes itself as promoting the social model of disability:

> We should not have to change to fit in with society. . . . At People First . . . we don't look at what doctors say is 'wrong with us'. We look at people's support needs. . . . Self advocacy is important because many people with learning difficulties spend their lives being told what to do. . . . Professionals and carers . . . should ask us what we want because no one knows better than us ourselves.
>
> (www.peoplefirstltd.com)

But the social model has had its controversies. Its proponents are accused of ignoring the reality of impairment in people's lives, and the physical and emotional suffering it can engender, regardless of social organisation (Thomas, 1999). Associated with this is a failure to investigate the nature of the relationships through which people are devalued and excluded in everyday life (Corker and Shakespeare, 2002). Oliver dismisses such criticism on the grounds that 'the social model is not about the personal experience of impairment but the collective experience of disablement . . . the limitations that our impairments impose upon us are an inadequate basis for building a political movement' (2004: 8).

More recently, criticism of 'socio-structural determinism' has come from a postmodernist perspective. It has been suggested that 'the genesis of disability resides solely within linguistic, discursive and cultural practices' (Thomas, 2004: 23). Disability is seen as being socially constructed by those who can exercise power through 'authority confirmed on them by the status and legitimacy of their forms of knowledge' (Thomas, 2004: 23). This includes doctors and legislators. Moreover, the split between 'impairment' and 'disability' is criticised on the grounds that this dualism, and both sets of categories, are also socially constructed.

## Psychotherapy

In the 1970s Oswin drew attention to the plight of people in long stay hospitals who had suffered repeated losses, and who faced what we would now describe as a systemic denial of their feelings. She recommended changes such as sympathetic listening by staff, and participation in family rituals (1991). These are now taken for granted in most care settings, and also marked a step towards the development of psychotherapeutic interventions for people suffering abnormal grief reactions. But until quite recently, mainstream psychotherapy ignored the needs of people with learning disability.

With the development of Community Mental Handicap Teams in the 1990s, clinical psychologists began to see more able people who could discuss their feelings, difficulties and aspirations. In 1993 Bender wrote of the '*therapeutic disdain*' towards people with learning disability and suggested that they had a right to access to psychotherapies. Since then clinicians have begun to adapt psychotherapies for use for people with learning disability. Ground-breaking studies have occurred in the field of psychodynamic psychotherapy (Waitman and Conboy-Hill, 1991), cognitive behavioural therapy (Kroese et al, 1997) and systemic therapy (Baum and Lynggaard, 2006).

And sometimes what people need is mainly the empathy, warmth and sensitivity of a therapeutic relationship.

### Sarah

Sarah is aged 23 and lives in a residential home. Since she was quite a young child she has suffered from temper tantrums, and has physically attacked other people. She has had a lot of therapeutic help, and has learnt to use a 'traffic light' system to let staff know when she is starting to feel angry. Despite this, outbursts persist, often aimed at other residents.

The psychologist asks Sarah what she would like help with and is told that she wants to make friends. One week Sarah arrives looking very tired and says she is not sleeping well. This is because of 'weird' things that are happening at night time. At first Sarah does not want to talk about these weird things because she is afraid they will get her into trouble. Gradually she lets the psychologist know that they involve dreams or fantasies about attacking other people in very gruesome ways. This happens because the people are pushing her out of the way.

Have people ever pushed Sarah in real life? She starts crying and tells the psychologist this happened when she was at junior school. People called her nasty names, cut her out. She became SO ANGRY! She attacked anyone who came her way.

This is the first step for Sarah in making the link between her feelings now and the way others treated her in the past.

## Conclusion

The role of clinical psychologists in relation to people with learning disability was born in the murky waters of eugenics and intelligence testing. Behaviourism was similarly open to the charge of ignoring the humanity of its subjects. Psychotherapy began by ignoring people with learning disability altogether. However, behaviourism has now evolved into Positive Behaviour Support, and a whole range of psychotherapies are being adapted for use with learning disabled people. Therapeutically, these are hopeful times.

## Recommended reading

Brown H and Smith H (eds) (1992) *Normalisation: A Reader* London: Routledge
Murdoch S (2007) *IQ: The Brilliant Idea That Failed* London: Duckworth Overlook
Waitman A and Conboy-Hill S (1991) *Psychotherapy and Mental Handicap* London: Sage

# 5   The legal context

## Capacity and consent

In this chapter I will focus on the issue of capacity to consent to treatment, with brief mention of capacity issues in other contexts. When I first meet a client who is able to speak, I always ask them whether they know why they have come to see me. No-one has ever been able to answer this question except in a most cursory manner. This is not necessarily because carers have not tried to explain the visit to them. Either they lack the confidence to say why they think they have come, or else they are unable to understand or remember what they have been told. When I meet someone who is unable to speak, and possibly unable to understand most of what I am saying, then I am particularly aware of the imbalance in power that has resulted in this person sitting in front of me, in a strange and not particularly welcoming environment.

This problem involves the legal issues of capacity and consent as well as the ethical issues of respect and empowerment. It is important that a person is given the choice of whether to interact with us, particularly bearing in mind the possibly intrusive nature of the assessment process, as well as the implications of assessment results.

### Valid consent

The legal position with regard to consent to treatment in England is established in common law and underpinned by the Human Rights Act, 1998. It is summarised in the *Reference Guide to Consent for Examination or Treatment* and the *Good Practice in Consent Implementation Guide*, both published by the Department of Health in 2001. The BPS guidelines on consent to treatment (that go beyond the legal requirements) are contained in the *Generic Professional Practice Guidelines* (2008), and the particular issues relating to learning disability are given in *Seeking Consent: Working with People with Learning Disabilities* (DH, 2001d).

These documents all use the concept of *valid consent*. The BPS describes this as: 'the client's right to choose whether to receive psychological services or to take part in research, and to make this choice on the basis of the best information available' (BPS, 2008: 2). Without such consent, if a patient suffers harm as a result of treatment, this could become a factor in a claim of negligence against the psychologist.

## Voluntariness

Gelsthorpe (1995: 36) distinguishes between consent, compliance and coercion. Whereas consent exists 'when a client agrees to participate in a joint venture with a therapist which we could label as treatment', compliance exists 'when a client does as the therapist requests'. Coercion 'is the process of getting the client to do as the therapist requests by saying that something unpleasant will happen if the request is not followed'. Coercion may be explicit, through the possibility of compulsory detention, or implicit, in the underfunding of services. Where therapeutic decisions are determined by resources rather than clinical need, then it is important that these decisions are discussed both with clients and with managers and documented.

People with mild learning disability have been found to be both more suggestible and more acquiescent than non-disabled respondents (i.e. more susceptible to leading questions and more likely to say 'yes' to yes/no questions) (Clare and Gudjonsson, 1993). It is likely that both cognitive and psychosocial factors underpin these tendencies. The massive imbalance of power and status in the relationship between psychologists and their clients involves issues such as resources, knowledge, cognitive function, self-confidence and self-esteem. There is also a possibility of pressure coming from family members, support staff or other professionals, though it may be subtle and well-intentioned.

In the therapeutic relationship we can attempt to address possible issues of compliance and coercion, through the way in which information is conveyed, questions asked and interviews conducted. It is good practice to give people time to go away and think about the decision to proceed. They may then talk it over with someone they trust, and make their choice free from the pressure of face to face contact with the psychologist.

## The Mental Capacity Act, 2005

The requirements of the Mental Capacity Act, 2005 apply to all people aged 16 or over unless they are subject to the compulsory treatment provisions of the Mental Health Act, 1983. A cornerstone of the Act is that capacity is assumed unless it can be shown otherwise. Capacity is both issue-specific and time-specific. We need to establish at an early stage whether the person has capacity to consent to our involvement in a particular assessment or treatment at a particular point in time. There is a two-stage test of capacity. The first stage involves assessing capacity by asking:

- Does the person have an impairment of the mind or brain, or is there some sort of disturbance affecting the way their mind or brain works?

- If so, does that impairment or disturbance mean that the person is unable to make the decision in question at the time it needs to be made?

> (MCA 2005 Code of Practice, Department for Constitutional Affairs, 2007: 41)

The impairments referred to in stage one of this test include 'significant learning disabilities', as well as 'conditions associated with some forms of mental illness'. This means that most, if not all, of our clients would meet this threshold test.

The second stage involves assessing the ability to make a decision by asking:

- Does the person have a general understanding of what decision they need to make and why they need to make it?
- Does the person have a general understanding of the likely consequences of making, or not making, this decision?
- Is the person able to understand, retain, use and weigh up the information relevant to this decision?
- Can the person communicate their decision (by talking, using sign language or any other means)? Would the services of a professional . . . be helpful?

> (MCA 2005 Code of Practice, Department for Constitutional Affairs, 2007: 41)

If we incorporate this guidance with that given on consent, then we may summarise the requirements on capacity to consent to treatment, as shown in Figure 5.1, p. 54.

## Giving information

According to the BPS Professional Practice Guidelines, a whole range of information should be given to our clients, much of which would be more confusing than enabling for a person with learning disability (BPS, 2008). So maybe the guidelines on the giving of information are to be observed in the spirit rather than the letter.

Information can be delivered gradually, at a pace and in a manner appropriate to the client. Moreover, we also need to respond in a sensitive way to the fact that people often arrive to meet us with a story that they urgently want or need to tell. We do not need to bombard people with information as soon as we meet them. However, we need to bear in mind that at our first meeting, or soon afterwards, we should aim to give some basic information about the assessment process, including:

- the reason for their referral to us
- our professional identity, and what that means

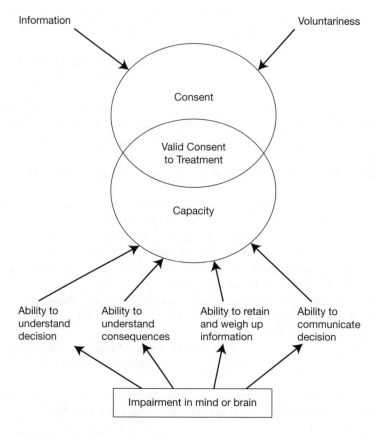

*Figure 5.1* Elements of capacity and consent.

- what assessment will involve, in broad, simple terms
- what help or other outcome may follow from the assessment
- any alternative assessment or treatment options
- any foreseeable risks
- confidentiality, and its limits
- what is likely to happen if the person decides not to proceed with the assessment
- the person's right to refuse, or later to withdraw consent.

## Confidentiality

The obligation to maintain confidentiality, and its limits, are outlined in the BPS Generic Professional Practice Guidelines (2008). However, the situation is complicated by our work as part of multi-professional teams, often with shared access to notes. I usually tell people that I work in a team, and other people in the team may need to have information about them. Apart from team members, I will generally not tell people things they tell me *but* I may have to tell other people if I find out that they are at risk of harm from others, or likely to hurt themselves or other people.

## Influences on capacity

Both physical and cognitive impairments may affect a person's capacity to make a decision. Physical health needs include sensory impairments, fatigue and pain. Cognitive function, including limitations in communication, memory, comprehension and inferential reasoning, have all been implicated in medical decision making (Arscott et al, 1999; Morris et al, 1993). The nature of decision-making tasks suggests that there are also a whole range of executive functions involved, including attention, reasoning, 'theory of mind', information processing, abstract thinking and the ability to conceptualise future events.

'For psychologists, one of the key areas will be to gain an understanding of how the individual's neuropsychological and cognitive functioning affects the psychological processes involved in decision making' (BPS, 2006: 22). A detailed cognitive assessment is unlikely to be needed in assessing capacity to consent to psychological intervention, though awareness of the cognitive functions involved could well contribute to that assessment.

## Enhancing capacity

There is an obligation on us to enhance capacity as far as is possible. 'A person is not to be treated as unable to make a decision unless all practicable steps to help him to do so have been taken without success' (MCA 2005 Code of Practice, Department for Constitutional Affairs, 2007: 19). Clare (2005) suggests that capacity may be viewed in terms of the match between the demands of the decision-making task and the person's functional abilities. Both these aspects may be modified to enhance capacity.

In order to help enhance the person's communication, it will be helpful to know how they communicate, how they indicate 'yes' and 'no', what alternative and augmentative forms of communication they use and how we can best present information to maximise comprehension. This may involve simplifying language, and using visual aids such as symbols and photos, objects of reference, talking mats, signing and social stories. Memory may be enhanced by simplifying language; breaking information down into small chunks; asking for recognition rather than recall of information; writing things down; and recording information. Decision-making abilities may be enhanced by use of a simple, visual problem-solving format. In addition, the interviewer should speak slowly, giving time for the client's responses, and should make efforts to help the person feel at ease. This could involve, for example, choosing a time of day when they are alert, or meeting them in a familiar place or one where there are no distractions.

People with extensive support needs are likely to lack the capacity to consent to the overall assessment or care plan, but may well have the capacity to communicate consent to, or refusal of, actions involving their immediate environment. Observation of their behaviour will indicate whether they are happy to sit in a room with us, sit still for a certain period of time or listen to other people talking about them. In interpreting their behaviour, we need to rely on the knowledge of those who know the person well and understand their idiosyncratic ways of communicating consent.

## Understanding and retaining information

It is not enough for the person to give their assent when we ask them if we may proceed with the assessment. We also need to check their understanding, and we can do this by asking them to repeat back to us the information we have been given (for example, '*Can you tell me about . . .* (the proposed treatment) *. . .? What would happen if you had . . .?*). The Code of Practice states that the person should be able to give a rough explanation of the information they have been given. We can simplify this process by breaking down the information-giving into small sections, and checking on the person's understanding at each stage. The person only needs to be able to retain the information for long enough to use it to make a decision. In the case of people who are nonverbal we can use other methods, such as the observation of behaviour, ability to indicate 'yes' or 'no' or ability to respond to objects or pictures.

## Seeking consent as a process

As time goes on, and the psychologist's knowledge of the client improves, then it is possible for the assessment of capacity to consent, and its enhancement, to become more individualised. 'Giving and obtaining consent is usually a process, not a one-off event' (DH, 2001c: 27). Throughout, it is important to be sensitive to the possibility of fluctuations in understanding and retention, as well as the changing feelings and opinions of clients.

## 'Unwise' decisions

'People have the right to make decisions that others might think are unwise. A person who makes a decision that others think is unwise should not automatically be labelled as lacking the capacity to make a decision' (MCA 2005 Code of Practice, Department for Constitutional Affairs, 2007: 19). This can be very difficult for carers (and ourselves) to accept. However, if the person makes a decision that is out of character, or repeatedly makes decisions that put them at significant risk, then this suggests the need for further investigation (MCA 2005 Code of Practice, Department for Constitutional Affairs, 2007: 25). Moreover, where a person with capacity does make a decision considered by others to be unwise, it may be possible to tackle the issue therapeutically.

## Sally

Sally is aged 25 and has had health and behavioural problems throughout her life. Sally has a longstanding phobia relating to dental treatment. Consequently, her teeth are rotten and she has a lot of dental pain. Attempts to desensitise her to dental treatment have failed. It is decided that a member of staff at her day centre will carry out a capacity assessment. With the support of the psychologist, this staff member talks through with Sally a graphic story about dental treatment. They then establish, with a series of simple questions, that Sally does understand the issues involved. Sally explains for the first time that she is afraid, not so much of the visit to the dentist, but of her own anxiety symptoms.

In a meeting it is agreed that Sally does have capacity to make her own decisions about dental treatment. The psychologist suggests that the problem might be tackled by helping Sally cope better with her underlying anxieties. An anxiety management group was set up at the day centre, and Sally is invited to take part by helping to prepare the visual aids each week. She does this enthusiastically and soon begins to participate in the group, and discuss her own anxieties.

## Best interests

If a person fails the two-stage test described earlier, resulting in a 'reasonable belief' that they lack capacity, a decision as to whether the assessment should proceed must then be made on the basis of their *best interests*. It is the responsibility of the professional who is to carry out the assessment to make the best interests decision, based on all the information available to them. Where it is practical and appropriate to do so, they should consult other people for their views. This consultation is often carried out in a meeting, which includes significant others, relevant professionals and possibly an Independent Mental Capacity Advocate (IMCA). A recommended procedure for conducting a best interests meeting is given in the BPS guidance (2007).

However, this is often not practical and a decision on capacity to consent to treatment has to be made at the first meeting with the client. For this reason, steps may be taken prior to meeting the client to prepare for a best interests decision to be made by canvassing the views of other professionals and carers involved. The fact that another professional has made the referral may be taken to imply that they regard the assessment as being in the person's best interests. It is also good if a carer, advocate or other professional is present during the initial meetings so that they are able to give their view as to whether proceeding with the assessment will be in the client's best interests.

Best interests decisions involve weighing up a range of factors, and deciding what is, on balance, the best for the person both now and in the future. Factors considered include any stated or implied wishes or preferences of the person, as well as the views of their families and carers (BPS, 2007). We also need to bear in mind 'any other factors the person themselves would be likely to consider if they were making the decision or acting for themselves' (MCA 2005 Code of Practice, Department for Constitutional Affairs, 2007: 65). In making a best interests decision, the 'least restrictive alternative' must usually be chosen (MCA 2005 Code of Practice, Department for Constitutional Affairs, 2007: 27). For example, if it were judged in the best interests of a person to have a baseline dementia assessment, and they appear unhappy to meet us, then it might be decided that an abbreviated form of assessment, based mainly on observation and carer reports, should be carried out.

## Record keeping

Wong et al (1999: 444) provide a helpful flow chart that takes the clinician through the decision-making process involved in establishing capacity, and this may be used in record keeping. The Department of Health has produced model consent forms for use with people with and without capacity to consent to treatment (DH, 2001c). However, the guidance makes it clear that capacity to consent is not established by a signature on a form. It needs to be recorded in the person's notes in terms of the procedures followed to establish capacity or best interests, and the evidence collected.

## Independent Mental Capacity Advocate

Capacity to consent to treatment is only one aspect of the lives of people with impairment or disturbance of the mind or brain that is covered by the Mental Capacity Act, and psychologists may be involved in other capacity assessments. If involved in a broader area of decision making, and particularly if a best interests decision is to be made, then it is likely to be important that an IMCA is involved. The purpose of this service, which was created under the Act, is to 'help particularly vulnerable people who lack the capacity to make important decisions about serious medical treatment and changes of accommodation, and who have no family or friends that it would be appropriate to consult about those decisions' (MCA 2005 Code of Practice, Department for Constitutional Affairs, 2007: 178).

## Policy context

As we progress into supervisory or managerial positions, we need to be aware of our responsibility to ensure that policies regarding valid consent are in place and implemented by supervisees and employees. Such policies should include the enhancement of capacity in general, not just at the point of making decisions on treatment. Hillery et al (1998: 117) suggest that 'theoretical and experiential training in decision making should become part of the life-plan for every person with learning disability'. If this happens, they are more likely to develop the ability to give or withhold their consent to treatment and in other matters.

## Capacity decisions not covered by the Mental Capacity Act

There is a range of personal decision making that is excluded from the Mental Capacity Act. This includes the capacity to consent to sexual relations, civil partnership, divorce, or to a child being placed for adoption. In several areas, tests of capacity have been established in common law. These cover the capacity to make a will or gift, enter into a contract, litigate and enter into marriage (BMA & Law Society, 2004). Under Sexual Offences Act 2003, Section 7 a person is said to consent to a sexual relationship 'if he/she agrees by choice and has the freedom and capacity to make that choice'. A person is said to lack capacity if they 'lack sufficient understanding of the nature of the act or the reasonably foreseeable consequences of what is being done or for any other reason'. The potential for a plethora of different capacity tests to be applied in different circumstances presents problems for the psychologist who wants to contribute to the process of appropriate decision making for their clients. The ongoing contribution of case law serves to compound this complexity with uncertainty.

## Capacity and support

There is an interaction between capacity and level of support, since there are some decisions that a person with learning disability may make but only be able to implement if the necessary level of support is available. And support needs funding, which is not always available. In such a case, if the psychologist frames the assessment result in terms of lack of capacity, this may legitimise putting in place protective measures that restrict the person's autonomy. If they fail to do this, then the person may come to harm, or even face life-threatening risk. In such cases it is important that capacity decisions are made in the context of broader multi-disciplinary care planning. Reports need to highlight the broader issues and possible systemic ways of enhancing capacity.

## Limitations of the Mental Capacity Act: real-life complexity

Brown and Marchant carried out a study of 60 cases of complex decision making and found a number of problems in implementation of the Act. For example, it is framed in relation to single, discrete decisions when instead many clients 'presented with cumulative concerns and intertwined decisions' (2011: 35). This means that it may be difficult for carers to judge the appropriate threshold for intervention.

A further difficulty is that the Act assumes a linear, rational model of cognitive decision making, which does not reflect how decisions are often made in real life by a person thinking things through independently. Cultural, systemic and interpersonal factors may also affect the decision-making process (BPS, 2006). Many decisions are influenced more by emotions and previous experience than information (Brown and Marchant, 2011). Depression is 'well recognised as affecting decision making and problem solving ability' (BPS, 2006: 26). Anxiety may affect the weighting given to different factors in arriving at a decision.

Brown lists a number of circumstances where we struggle to apply a rational model of decision making as it is set out in the Mental Capacity Act:

- where decision making is biologically driven, as in the case of Prader Willi Syndrome;
- where 'fractured selves may make contradictory or fragmented decisions', as in Borderline Personality Disorder;
- where 'disorders of thinking lead to stuckness' as in some cases of autistic spectrum disorder;
- where learned helplessness 'leaves the person open to hidden but undue influence';
- where complicated family or community dynamics result in compromised decisions.

Brown suggests that in such cases the psychologist faces, not a balance between autonomy and care, but a 'decision about which to prioritise'. Brown concludes that a person's emotional state, their personal history and family dynamics

> should be taken into account in the evaluation of their 'mental capacity' rather than screened out of the assessment process. . . . Extremes of impulsivity or avoidance disrupt decision-making just as much as cognitive impairment and should not be lost in these deliberations . . .
>
> (Brown, 2011: 201)

This conclusion has implications for our assessments. For example, in relation to 'Sally', the person whose dental phobia was described earlier, it could be that Sally's anxiety was cutting across her ability to make an informed decision about dentistry, and this should have been weighed up as part of the capacity assessment (Brown, personal communication, 24 November 2011).

## Court of Protection

Even with appropriate procedures in place, it is not always possible to arrive at a best interests decision. An example could be where a parent of a person with severe learning disability wants them to be sterilised, and there is no medical reason why this should be carried out. Such decisions should always be referred to the Court of Protection, which may first make a declaration on the person's capacity (MCA 2005 Code of Practice, Department for Constitutional Affairs, 2007, 8.22). If it is decided that the person does lack capacity, the Court may make a declaration as to whether an act relating to the person's care or treatment is lawful. If there is a need for ongoing decision-making powers, the Court may or appoint a deputy to make future decisions in a specified area. An example of a case where this could apply would be where a person with severe learning disability and lacking capacity to protect themselves is at ongoing risk of harm or abuse, and this cannot be resolved by a one-off decision.

## Vulnerable adults

In situations that lie outside the scope of the Mental Capacity Act, even if a person is judged to have capacity, the High Court may intervene to impose a decision on the basis that they are inherently or situationally vulnerable. Since such a decision may be made without reference to the person's own views, it could have deleterious cultural or other consequences (Dunn et al, 2008).

## Conclusions

In complex cases, I think it would be helpful to have, in each health district, a small committee of experts in psychology and law, with whom we could discuss these complex cases and be helped to arrive at a decision. But, as Brown points out, we also have recourse to the Court of Protection.

Legislation cannot cover every eventuality, and the details of the implementation of the Mental Capacity Act are still being established through case law. In this ethical and legal minefield, it is perhaps reassuring that, in making our decisions about capacity, the standard of proof required is not 'beyond reasonable doubt', but 'the balance of probabilities' (MCA 2005 Code of Practice, Department for Constitutional Affairs, 2007, 4.10).

Wong et al (1999: 438) suggest that capacity is the 'pivotal issue' in the difficult ethical dilemma of 'balancing the right to freedom of decision-making and the right to protection from harm'. The clarification of law that has come about with the Mental Capacity Act has helped clinicians negotiate this difficult territory. But the *Good Practice in Consent Implementation Guide* reminds us that this is not just a legalistic issue. As long ago as 1997, this was stated simply in *Signposts for Success*: 'Decisions are made with people, not for them. Good practice involves investment in time and communication with the person concerned and his or her carers' (DH, 1997: 32).

## Recommended reading

BPS (2006) *Assessment of Capacity in Adults: Interim Guidance for Psychologists* Leicester: BPS

BPS (2007) *Best Interests: Guidance on Determining the Best Interests of Adults who Lack the Capacity to Make a Decision (or Decisions) for Themselves (England and Wales)* Leicester: BPS

Brown H and Marchant E (2011) *Best Interests Decision-Making in Complex Cases* London: Office of the Public Guardian

DH (2001) *Consent: A Guide for People with Learning Disabilities* London: Department of Health

# Part II

# Understanding the person

Eight Domains

# 6 Starting to understand the person

> ## John
>
> John is aged 35, and his parents have requested help in relation to his obsessional behaviours. When the psychologist visits him, she is treated to cups of tea, biscuits and conversation about the weather. There is nothing in his appearance or demeanour to suggest that he could be learning disabled.
>
> But in his assessment sessions, the psychologist finds that John is unable to express his feelings, and she suspects that he is also unable to recognise them. She feels she is facing an impasse, and decides to interview his parents.
>
> John's mother says: 'All his life, he has never been able to express his feelings. I just know from his behaviour that something is wrong, and then I have to try and work out what the problem is. For the past 35 years I have been playing Miss Marple'.

People without cognitive impairment can generally be relied upon to work out the source of their distress for themselves, at least in general terms, and to communicate that. This is likely to be problematic for people with learning disability. More often than not, we cannot just ask them what their problem is and receive a coherent reply, and nor can we necessarily rely on our normal understanding of body language to help us interpret their feelings. Getting to know the person with learning disability is a long-term process, a piece of detective work. We are constantly looking for clues, putting together hypotheses, looking for evidence.

## The journey from pre-assessment to intervention

Figure 6.1 summarises the steps that are usually assumed to be involved in progressing from the pre-assessment stage to intervention and review.

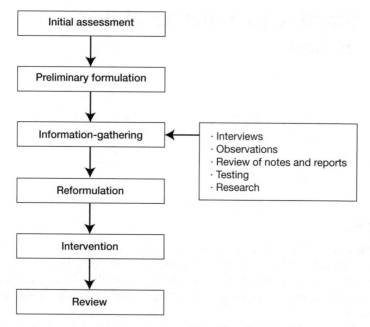

*Figure 6.1* From pre-assessment to intervention and review.

This sort of neat progression is often represented in care pathways, which can be used to ensure that service delivery meets an acceptable standard. It may be applicable in some simple cases, such as where our only remit is to carry out a cognitive assessment, but it ignores the recursive and relational nature of the therapeutic process.

## The recursive nature of the assessment process

In most complex cases, assessment feeds into possible explanatory hypotheses and these hypotheses serve to guide the future shape of the assessment (see Figure 6.2). Similarly, the results of our initial interventions will help us to reshape and refine our formulation and maybe point to the need for further assessment. For example, a defined number of counselling sessions may be offered in order to help both the psychologist and the client better understand the reasons for the person's distress, and the outcome of these sessions may result in further assessment of family background and refinement of the formulation.

Often the linear, care pathway model is better seen as a tool for us to conceptualise the different processes in which we are involved rather than an account of a sequence of events.

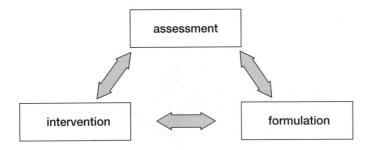

*Figure 6.2* The fluid therapeutic process.

## The relational nature of the assessment process

The word 'assessment' has scientific overtones associated with professionalism and objectivity. It implies that we can engage in this activity in much the same spirit in which a scientist sets about examining the properties of an inert substance. We aim not to bring our preconceptions to the situation, or to change it inadvertently. But the object of our assessment is not an inert substance but a person, and our involvement with them is that of person to person. We form part of the situation that we are assessing. From a humanistic perspective we need to respect the person's subjectivity. From the social interactionist perspective, the 'self' that the person presents to us emerges from our relationship with them.

Relationship-building and relationship-sharing is therefore central to our work. In Gestalt Counselling this is referred to as 'good contact': a 'full and complete authentic meeting between . . . two people' that 'opens the gateways to change' (Clarkson, 1989: 16). Relationship is also pivotal in person-centred counselling, and person-centred counselling skills form the foundation of all other therapeutic work. Similarly, cognitive behavioural therapy is seen as an interpersonal, collaborative process, taking the person into the 'zone of proximal development' where change may be achieved (Jahoda et al, 2009).

In considering how this might be represented visually, the image that comes to my mind is one of a spiral, with the relationship providing the central core to the process, and assessment, formulation and intervention being constantly revisited, at increasing levels of complexity. This is given in Figure 6.3.

Our first meeting with the client marks the beginning of this relationship. As we are assessing the other person, they are also assessing us and adapting their behaviour accordingly. From the moment they see us (or even before then) they will be summing us up, and making decisions as to how to behave on the basis of the judgements they make. Some of the information on which they make these judgements are personal characteristics that are beyond our control, for example relating to age, sex and ethnicity.

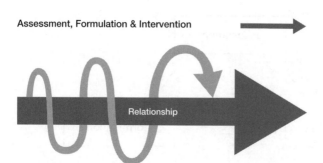

Assessment, Formulation & Intervention

Relationship

*Figure 6.3* The progression of the therapeutic relationship.

## The service context

It appears self-evident that the needs of the client should be the focus of the assessment. However, we are easily sidetracked into meeting the requests of the referrer or the needs of the service we work for. A referral for 'challenging behaviour' may mask the client's needs for improved quality of life. Alternatively, sometimes the referrer has made their own assessment and decision on intervention, which might or might not be appropriate (e.g. a request for 'counselling for bereavement' when the presenting problem is challenging behaviour). Generally, the information we are given in the initial referral is inadequate, and the referrer's ideas as to what the person needs are also often unhelpful. Therefore we should usually carry out a thorough assessment, and make up our own minds as to a possible formulation and the person's needs. However, if funding issues are involved we may need to return to the referrer to re-negotiate our involvement.

The situation is more tricky where we are asked (or directed) to meet institutional needs, e.g. for assessment of learning disability in order to determine eligibility. Our refusal to do this could result in the person being denied a service. If we agree to carrying out the assessment, it is important that the client understands its implications, and also that we produce a report that is clinically meaningful and useful to them and their carers whatever the decision on eligibility. This may well mean extending the cognitive assessment beyond intelligence testing to more detailed assessment of functions such as communication and executive function.

## Pre-assessment

The BPS Guidelines for Challenging Behaviour (2004) suggest that a person's assessment should be preceded by a pre-assessment phase for preliminary gathering of information. This seems to me to be good practice for all referrals. Review of the client's files may give valuable historical information that is not necessarily available to either the client or their carer. Pre-assessment may also include telephone interviews with carers or other professionals. As mentioned earlier, information about the person's communication should be sought, as well as more general information about their level of cognitive function and likely capacity issues. In collecting this background information, the psychologist will already begin to make some preliminary hypotheses as to what is going on for that person, and this will include ideas about what theories are likely to be relevant in understanding the person's problems. The pre-assessment phase will therefore to some extent guide the content and structure of the first interview.

The pre-assessment phase is also the time when the client should be given information about their coming meeting with the psychologist. This can be done in the form of a short, simple written account of who the psychologist is and what the meeting will involve. Makaton symbols or photos may be used, including a photograph of the psychologist. A carer or relative may be asked to go through the leaflet with the client to talk it over and answer any questions.

People with learning disability are often discussed as if they are a homogeneous group, whereas in fact their level of function varies enormously, and this has implications for the way in which assessment is carried out. It makes sense to distinguish between those people with verbal skills with whom we are able to work directly, and those people with largely nonverbal skills, with whom our work needs to be largely observational and/or channelled through third parties. However, this is not a hard and fast distinction. Moreover, people who are largely nonverbal often still appreciate being seen, taking part in a respectful conversation, and having someone take an interest in them.

## The first meeting

### What information do you give your client about yourself?

Do you make a phone call or send a letter? Is the letter from you or from a secretary? Is it written to the client or the carer? Is it written in language the client can understand? Does it include visual aids, such as a photo of yourself? Is the waiting area welcoming? Is the receptionist friendly? Are drinks offered? Is the interview room cheerful/calm/clinical/shabby/comfortable ... ? Is there a coffee table or a desk? What is the relative height of the chairs?

In your appearance and manner, are you friendly or unfriendly? Smart or scruffy? Easy or difficult to understand? Easygoing or demanding? Distant or empathic? Do you smile when you meet your client? And is your smile genuine? Do you explain why you are taking notes? Or ask permission?

All these aspects and many others will affect the client's expectations of us, their assumptions or guesses as to what we expect of them, and their motivation to continue the relationship. They also reflect, in one way or another, the power imbalance that exists between ourselves and our clients. The likelihood is that the person we see will have little understanding of the situation in which they find themselves. They may feel confused and anxious, and attempt to make sense of what is going on using the current concrete and relational aspects of the interview.

I find that the initial assessment interview with a verbal client is best conducted with a colleague, who may be a psychologist or another professional, depending on the presenting problems. This allows one person to engage with the client and gather information, without the obstacle of note-taking. It also allows for an alternative clinical perspective. Towards the end of the interview we leave the room and briefly discuss our preliminary formulation and intervention plan. We then return and talk over with the client and carer the way in which we understand their problems. We aim to arrive with them at a shared preliminary formulation. We then discuss what we can offer, and whether this is acceptable to them. If further assessment or intervention is to take place, a care plan is drawn up and given to the client and carers. A client-accessible copy of the care plan is either made at this time, or given later to the client.

### Conducting an initial assessment interview

1. Ask the person if they know why they have come to see you.
2. Explain why (what the problem is, who is concerned about it, who you are, and how you hope to be able to help).
3. Check understanding and consent.
4. Decide on capacity/best interests.
5. Explain what will happen during the interview and how long it will last.
6. Explain why you will want to make notes, and ask permission for this.
7. Explain that the person may refuse to answer any questions, ask for a break, or end the interview at any time.
8. Ask whether they want their relative/carer to stay in the room.
9. Feed back what the client says at regular intervals, to check understanding and encourage them to elaborate on their answers.
10. Once the interview with the client is complete, ask if they agree to their carer answering some questions.
11. At the end of the interview, recap with client and carer and ask if they want to add anything.
12. Discuss preliminary formulation and draft care plan.
13. Document this, and give the client a copy.

The first meeting is a time for us to begin to gain a sense of the person. In this process the attempt at objectivity must be balanced with sensitivity, empathy, intuition and curiosity. What are your immediate impressions of the person? What is their chief concern? What are their likes and dislikes? What are the strengths that have helped them cope with their problems? What is their history (apart from their problem history)? This can be helpful in setting up from the start a narrative that is not problem-saturated. At other times, this conversation may have to wait, since the person or their carers have arrived desperate to talk about a particular problem and, in this case, it is important to give them time to tell their story and express their feelings. It is also important that the person comes away from the interview with a sense of acceptance and hope.

## Use of language

It is our responsibility to adapt our language to the needs of the person we are interviewing. Trainees often worry about how to do this, but then when I sit in with them I am amazed by how well they manage it. It seems that their sensitivity and interest in the person they are interviewing results in a natural adaptation of their communication style. But awareness of some basic principles is also helpful, and some are given below. It is important to bear in mind both the way in which you express yourself to the person, and also the way in which you facilitate their expression.

### Helping the person understand

- Use short words and sentences.
- Use words that are concrete rather than abstract.
- Use grammar that is positive rather than negative, and active rather than passive.
- Use phrases that are simple rather than compound.
- Ask one question at a time.
- Use visual aids: pictures, photos, symbol, signs and/or or simple drawings.
- Avoid the use of jargon and idiom.
- Pick up on words and phrases used by the client.
- Check that you have been understood.

### Helping the person express themselves

- Create a comfortable, pleasant space for the interview.
- Give plenty of time for responses.
- Check the meaning of words used.
- Ask for specific examples.
- Prompt if necessary.
- Offer drawing materials.

Some of these recommendations apply to written material as well as verbal interaction. Readability formulae are generally based on word and sentence length and these should be taken into account in any written materials we produce (Ley and Florio, 1996).

Johnstone (1997) has pointed out that much of therapy jargon is metaphorical, for example the use of the terms 'space', 'boundaries' and 'sharing'. We should look for alternatives to such terms, using words and phrases that are short and concrete. For example, rather than raising the abstract and metaphorical issue of boundaries with learning disabled parents, it would be better to ask specific questions such as: *'Have you told them their bedtime? What time is it? Is it the same every night? What do they do each evening before they go to bed? What happens if they go to bed late?'*, and so on. In the case of a person whose support needs are not being met, rather than asking about *'support'* it would be better to ask about the person's daily routine, and who is there at particular times of the day. It can be useful for trainees to role play such client interviews with their supervisors, in order to get a sense of how it feels to use language that is pared down to the simple and concrete.

Throughout the interview it is important to be aware of the issues of acquiescence and suggestibility either as a result of not understanding the question, or in order to provide an answer that they believe will be acceptable to their interviewer (Sigelman et al, 1981). However 'acquiescence' may also be a calculated strategy in the face of a disempowering situation.

> Interviewer:   What happened at the meeting?
> Client:   Just . . . they wanted to know if I'd stay a bit longer here but I (laugh) took a long time to give an answer, till I said the magic word
> Interviewer:   What's the magic word?
> Client:   Which was 'yes'
> Interviewer:   In what way is 'yes' the magic word?. . .
> Client:   (pause, sigh) It was only going to be two days when I started here . . .
>
> (Crocker, 1990: 102)

This highlights the importance of us making efforts to create an interview situation where people feel that their answers will be taken seriously. In the forensic setting it has been found that when people are asked simple open questions, and know that it is acceptable to respond *'I don't know'*, then many of them are as reliable as other witnesses (Murphy and Clare, 2009).

The problem in following this advice is that open questions often result in impoverished answers. One way to deal with this is to progress, if necessary, from open questions to increasingly more structured and concrete questions, maybe with prompts (e.g. *'How do you feel today? . . . Do you feel worried? . . . Can you tell me what you feel worried about? . . . I heard from . . . that you sometimes feel worried about . . . Can you tell me about that?'*). Some of the literature on cognitive interviewing is relevant in suggesting ways of prompting that are not likely to compromise validity, e.g. the use of multi-modal cues to facilitate recall (Conboy-Hill, 2001). Use of summarising and reflection are also helpful. When information gleaned results from prompting, it should, where possible, be checked with third parties or review of notes.

In contrast to those people whose ability to offer information spontaneously is limited, in other people, open questions may result in an outpouring of information. To allow this to continue unchecked is often not helpful for the person, and may even add to their feelings of confusion and anxiety. In this case, it is important for the interviewer to exert some control, albeit in a gentle and empathic way, e.g. by interrupting to summarise and move the interview forward, e.g. *'I'm sorry to interrupt, but that was very interesting. You seem to be saying that . . . Is that right? . . . I would like to ask you now about . . .'.*

In our choice of language, we need to be aware of its possible therapeutic impact. The people we see are more than likely be in a Pre-Contemplative Stage in relation to dealing with their problems, and part of our role is to help them move forward through the Stages of Change (Prochaska and Di Clemente, 1982). Cognitive factors can influence their capacity to achieve this. Ley (1988) suggests various techniques for maximising both understanding and memory, for example by using explicit categorisation. This involves the clinician telling the patient what category of information is to be given before giving it (e.g. *'Now I am going to tell you what you can do to help yourself get better'*). Sessions may also be recorded to aid recall.

Different therapeutic schools suggest different ways that language can be used to promote change. Solution-focused therapy suggests emphasis on outcomes and strengths rather problems from the beginning of our interaction with clients. In the words of one young woman with Asperger Syndrome: 'What Vicky did was remind me and bring to the fore all of the skills and coping strategies I did have . . . no-one had ever focused on that before . . . I went away from sessions feeling like a truly competent individual' (Edmunds and Bliss, 2006: 9).

According to narrative therapy, the language used itself creates the reality, and the way in which we discuss people's problems is particularly important (Morgan, 2000). From the first interview it is possible to adopt an externalising approach (e.g. *'it seems as if the anger is controlling your life'* rather than *'your anger seems to be controlling your life'*). The client may also be asked whether they can picture their problem, and whether they would like to draw it. In approaching the problem in this way, we are assessing the person's ability to externalise, and also setting the scene for a possible future narrative therapy intervention.

## Stuart

Stuart's parents have requested that he receives counselling for anger management. Stuart is a young man who suffers from a genetic syndrome. The two psychologists who are assessing him have not had time to discuss the conduct of the interview, nor research the syndrome. One of them remembers from a neuropsychology lecture that sufferers tend to be sensitive, withdrawn and compliant.

Stuart turns out to be tall and gauche with a shifting gaze and hands that are in constant motion. He talks incessantly, mostly about how he needs counselling for his anger. Stuart's language is peppered with inappropriate personal comments and swearing, which he says he enjoys. The initial interview schedule is abandoned in the face of the outpouring by both Stuart and his parents.

When the psychologists leave the room to consult, they feel over-whelmed and baffled. They have failed to either provide a safe structure for the clients or to control the problem-saturated narrative. When they return to the room, they ask Stuart whether he is able to picture his anger, and whether he would be able to draw it. Without hesitation he draws a chaotic, tangled mass of lines in three different colours. 'That's what it is', he says.

The psychologists and the clients consider the drawing in a moment of silence. It feels as if a connection has finally been made with Stuart and his parents.

This vignette illustrates how easily and unexpectedly things can go wrong in everyday clinical practice, when we will often find ourselves entering the interview room rushed and unprepared. On the other hand, it is also possible for even an initial meeting to have a therapeutic impact.

## Beginning a holistic assessment: the Eight Domains

Our first meeting with the person who has been referred or their carers may be seen as a sort of mapping exercise, sketching out the problems and possible influences. Most people with learning disabilities can only be understood in the context of a holistic assessment. This is first because, as mentioned at the beginning of this chapter, the person themselves will probably be unable to identify the nature of their problems. And the second reason is that *the people we see with learning disability are usually very complicated.* It is very rarely that we receive a referral for someone whose difficulties can easily be understood in terms of one or two sets of factors. As psychologists we pride ourselves on our ability to work at what has become known as 'Level 3'. This involves having the knowledge and skills to draw on multiple psychological theories in order to develop individually designed therapeutic strategies. (Mowbray, 1989).

A theoretically eclectic approach requires a structure for collecting and making sense of a broad spectrum of information. This structure I propose is provided by the model of the Eight Domains. These Domains are designed to cover every area of the person's life. Each Domain is linked to a body of theory, which will help to guide the questions we ask. However, the division into domains is a pragmatic one. There are also links between the Eight Domains, and this will be reflected in our formulation.

The Eight Domains and associated theories are shown in Table 6.1, p. 76. The right-hand column suggests the content of the Domains, and the left-hand column indicates some of the theories, concepts and issues that we may bring to bear in understanding each of them.

The order of the Domains is given in the order in which they might be approached in the interview situation, beginning with behavioural issues and the person's social circumstances, and going on to discuss the factors that could be contributing to the presenting problems, such as cognitive impairment and health issues. The Eighth Domain I have called the 'Inner World'. This is probably the most important of the Domains, but I have put it at the end because the person's Inner World is influenced by all the other Domains, and because it may be hard to assess this earlier on. However, the Inner World should of course be considered throughout the assessment.

It is only after the early meetings that we will decide on our initial formulation and on which of the Eight Domains will be the subject of more detailed assessment. For example, we may decide to focus on the individual's thoughts and feelings (CBT approach); on the way their behaviours are reinforced (behavioural approach); on their pattern of relationships (social approach); on the interaction between individual and environmental factors (Challenging Behaviour Guidelines); or on the nested systems in which the person's life is embedded (ecological approach). Or maybe a combination of these theories appears to be relevant.

Information to complete the assessment may be collected from the client, carers, other professionals and notes, and may take several weeks. If the person is living with professional carers, then it will probably be necessary to arrange a separate meeting with the person's parents or other relatives who have some knowledge of their history.

When we link a person's feelings or behaviour into a theoretical network this allows us to predict possible outcomes (see Chapter 2). It helps both to make sense of the behaviour and to suggest possible routes for intervention. For example, if we carry out an assessment to establish whether a person is autistic, we generally do so in the belief that the diagnosis (through its theoretical link to other signs and symptoms) will help us understand and predict their behaviour. We might hypothesise that a person with a diagnosis of autism would have difficulties in coping with change, and would therefore benefit from an intervention that introduced routine and predictability in their

*Table 6.1* The Eight Domains.

| Dominant theories and influences | Domain content |
| --- | --- |
| **The BEHAVIOURAL DOMAIN**<br>Learning theory<br>Positive Behaviour Support | Antecedents and consequences<br>Quality of life |
| **The SOCIAL DOMAIN**<br>Systemic/narrative therapy<br>'Getting to Know You'<br>Person-centred planning | Current intimate/close/distant relationships<br>Language |
| **The PHYSICAL DOMAIN**<br>Models of health behaviour<br>Health promotion<br>Access to healthcare and screening | Pain/sensory issues<br>Medication<br>Physical illness |
| **The NEUROLOGICAL DOMAIN**<br>Genetic/developmental causal modelling<br>Neurodevelopmental/transactional | Research evidence on neurological<br>conditions and child development |
| **The COGNITIVE DOMAIN**<br>Deficit measurement model<br>Developmental model<br>Criterion-oriented model | Cognitive functions, as shown in<br>Appendix 3 |
| **The ATTACHMENT DOMAIN**<br>Attachment theory<br>Emotional regulation | Early relationships<br>Loss/abuse/trauma |
| **The ECOLOGICAL DOMAIN**<br>Historical/political/social context<br>Values and attitudes<br>Social institutions/legislation | Money/poverty/resources<br>Inclusion/access<br>Stigmatisation |
| **INNER WORLD**<br>Subjective quality of life<br>The Responsive Environment<br>Intervention as assessment | Feelings and beliefs<br>Self-awareness/identity/self-esteem/<br>self-efficacy<br>Resilience<br>Sense of safety, self-determination and<br>belonging |

environment. An explanation of behaviour in terms of learning theory will lead us to predict changes in behaviour that are likely to follow changes in reinforcement contingencies.

## An assessment schedule

The Eight Domains are repeated in Appendix 1 as part of a prompt sheet for initial assessment. This includes a preliminary risk assessment, which will be completed on the basis of information from all the domains. A summary form for clients is given in Appendix 2. This should be augmented with pictures or symbols appropriate to the person. It can then be worked through with them, so that the process is transparent, and they are given the opportunity to consent or otherwise to each step of the assessment process. These forms are given as examples, and you will probably want to adapt them to reflect your own approach.

## Integration

Where we refer to more than one theory to explain the person's behaviour, we will need to draw on an integrative model to create a coherent story. This will be addressed in Chapter 15.

## Conclusion

Our relationship with the person we seek to help is at the heart of our ability to understand them and of their potential for change. From the moment of first contact with the client we need to be aware of the impact of our own behaviour on the client. In order to be effective, it is important that our scientific expertise is underpinned by interpersonal skills and a genuine concern and respect for the person we are assessing. Assessment, formulation and intervention, though conceptually distinct, are not discrete processes, but continue in parallel throughout our involvement with the client.

Our understanding of people with learning disability needs to be multidimensional and theoretically eclectic. For the trainee, the range of possible influences on the person may seem daunting. The Eight Domains Model provides a structured format for handling a wide range of possible aetiological variables emerging from different theories. In the following chapters, I will expand on each of these domains and then suggest a way of bringing them together in an integrative model of formulation.

## Recommended reading

Carr A, O'Reilly C, Noonan Walsh P and McEvoy J (2007) *The Handbook of Intellectual Disability and Clinical Psychology Practice* London: Routledge

Emerson E, Hatton C, Dickson K, Gone R, Caine A and Bromley J (2012) *Clinical Psychology and People with Intellectual Disabilities* Chichester: Wiley-Blackwell

Hogg J and Langa A (2005) *Assessing Adults with Intellectual Disabilities* Oxford: BPS Blackwell

# 7    The Behavioural Domain

The BPS has produced guidelines on the treatment of challenging behaviour, which broadly follow the approach of Positive Behaviour Support (PBS) (BPS, 2004). This was earlier described as referring to: 'those interventions that involve altering deficient environmental conditions (eg activity patterns, choice options, prompting procedures) and/or deficient behaviour repertoires (eg communication, self-management, social skills)' (Carr et al, 1999: 7–8). Helping people achieve an improved quality of life is central to this approach (Carr et al, 2002). It represents a fusion of the scientific rigour of behaviourism with a humanistic concern to meet the needs and rights of people, particularly with those described as having 'challenging behaviour' (see, for example, Clements, 2002; Emerson, 2001; La Vigna and Willis, 2005).

However far we may stray from the behavioural fold, we need to retain a good grasp of behavioural theory and methodology. It is important for us to understand the meaning of terms such as intermittent reinforcement, establishing operations and discriminative stimuli, and to be able to use this understanding in our assessments and interventions. The ABC of functional analysis provides the framework for understanding within this model. It involves a detailed analysis of the Behaviour, its Consequences and its Antecedents (Setting Conditions and Triggers).

Getting to know the person is the first step in a behavioural analysis. This will help us to identify those antecedents and consequences that are significant for them. Also, the importance of learning theory should not blind us to the fact that challenging behaviour may take place for other reasons. It may be rule-governed behaviour, result from a loss of inhibitory control or be related to their neurological condition (Clements, 2002).

## Behaviour

In order to get to know the individual we need to seek out those carers and family members who have known them for many years. Their insight into what is going on can be invaluable. At the same time, we must always seek evidence for their views. Sometimes, when I read reports written by trainees, I can pick out the words that have been spoken by carers. Examples are: 'he can hear when he wants to'; 'he has mood swings'; 'she looks forward to her mother's phone call'; 'she is wound up when she comes back from visiting her family'; 'he gets jealous of other residents'; 'she has become very aggressive', and so on. All these may on the surface seem to be reasonable descriptions, but they tell us little and may be misleading. We need to find out the exact behaviours that give rise to descriptions such as those given above. What does the person actually do? Hit? Scream? Push? Moan? Sit motionless in an armchair? Run around the house? For the purposes of obtaining a baseline so that we can evaluate the intervention, we also need to know the frequency, severity and duration of the behaviour. And we need to know the evidence for or against the inferences that carers have made about the possible or likely reasons for the behaviour. It is only by finding out the conditions under which the behaviour takes place that we are able to formulate our initial hypotheses about aetiology, which will enable us to plan an intervention.

## The Consequences of Behaviour: reward and punishment

And the Lord God called unto Adam. . . . Hast thou eaten of the tree, whereof I commanded thee that thou shouldest not eat? . . . Because thou hast . . . eaten of the tree . . . cursed is the ground for thy sake; in sorrow shalt thou eat of it all the days of thy life. . . . In the sweat of thy face shalt thou eat bread, till thou return unto the ground . . .
(The Holy Bible, St James Version, Genesis, chapter 3,
verses 9, 11, 17, 19)

And he opened his mouth, and taught them, saying,
Blessed are the poor in spirit: for theirs is the kingdom of heaven.
Blessed are they that mourn: for they shall be comforted.
Blessed are the meek: for they shall inherit the earth . . .
(The Holy Bible, St James Version, Matthew,
chapter 5, verses 2–5)

Whether we see these stories as literal truth, metaphor or mythology, there is no denying their archetypal nature. Punishment and reward are woven into the fabric of our being. It is impossible to get through a day or even an hour without being exposed to one or the other. We know this so well and so deeply that it barely merits thinking about. And perhaps we would rather not, since the ubiquity and significance of reward and punishment seem such a challenge to our cherished ideas of free will. When we analyse reward and punishment we are entering into a discourse about power relationships. Treatment of people by behavioural methods inevitably involves the use of our privileged, powerful positions to change people's behaviour, albeit for benign purposes.

## Kevin

Kevin has a diagnosis of autism and shares a house with a number of other people. He appears to get on well with his keyworker Terry, and enjoys the days they spend going into town together. This is his only allocated one-to-one time with staff.

Kevin has a habit of urinating on the bathroom floor, sometimes in public places. He has signed a contract to say he will not do this again, but it still happens and he cannot explain why. Terry thinks Kevin does it when he is worried, but cannot offer any evidence for this. He agrees to keep more systematic records of the incidents, and they find there are no clear triggers. They discuss the fact that Kevin enjoys one-to-one attention, and maybe his urination is a way of ensuring that staff spend time with him.

After discussion with Kevin it is agreed that each full day that he urinates appropriately he will be 'rewarded' with a 15-minute card-playing session with Terry in the evening. This is backed up with a 'sticker' chart completed by Kevin. In the two weeks following implementation of this plan, the frequency of the behaviour goes down from three incidents to one incident per week. But one month later incidents of urination have returned to their previous level. When the psychologist examines the records, she discovers that one-to-one time has been delivered only occasionally, and not in a way that is consistent with Kevin's behaviour.

In this case it seems that the intervention was initially effective because the hypothesis as to the environmental contingencies was correct. But implementation failed to take into account the systemic issues involved in maintaining implementation. Inconsistent environmental contingencies can place the person on an intermittent reinforcement schedule, which is extremely reinforcing of behaviour.

There is also an ethical issue involved in 'rewarding' people or withholding from them things that they ought to have by right (e.g. 15 minutes of one-to-one interaction in the evening). This is why simple behavioural interventions should usually be just a first step towards helping improve the person's life experience.

The use of punishment is usually both unethical and ineffectual, and should not be included in a treatment plan. However, the distinction between reward and punishment is less clearcut than first appears. Loss of an expected reward may well be experienced as punishment by the person on the receiving end.

### The functions of behaviour

I have talked about Kevin as being 'rewarded' with one-to-one time by his keyworker. Alternatively, I could say that the 'function' of his behaviour was to gain 'attention' from Terry. This sort of reconceptualisation marked the evolution of Behaviour Therapy into Applied Behaviour Analysis. Seven broad classes of behaviour function have been identified:

- to avoid or escape from demands
- to gain social attention
- to access activities or objects
- to gain sensory feedback
- to reduce arousal and anxiety
- to exert choice or control over the environment
- to express emotion.

(see RCP et al, 2007)

Historical analysis, detailed observation and behaviour monitoring can all help us generate hypotheses as to the function or functions of the behaviour. Once these have been identified, it is then possible to consider alternative ways for the person to meet their needs, so that they are less likely to resort to challenging behaviour. For example, if the function of the behaviour is 'demand avoidance', then consideration can be given towards modifying the demands that are made, the conditions under which they are made, or the way in which they are made. In Kevin's case it appeared that the function of his behaviour was to spend time with people he liked.

If the functions served by the behaviour are not understood, carer responses can have unforeseen consequences. When Terry spent time discussing Kevin's behaviour with him immediately after it took place, he may have been simply reinforcing it (i.e. making it more likely to take place in the future). On the other hand, there would have been no point in 'rewarding' Kevin for 'good' behaviour with one-to-one time if he found contact with certain people aversive.

The difficulties of achieving consistency in administering rewards in real-life situations means that, like Kevin, many people treated in this way do not maintain behavioural change. When we see behaviour in terms of its functions, we shift attention to the extent to which people's needs are being met by their living conditions. This involves an analysis of the antecedents of the behaviour.

## The Antecedents

Emerson (2001: 102–103) distinguishes between:

- environments in which challenging behaviour is more likely to occur;
- establishing operations, which 'may either activate or abolish the contingencies maintaining the person's challenging behaviour'; and
- the contingencies themselves.

For example, in a person who is sensitive to temperature, an environment that the person experiences as too hot or cold may raise their level of arousal, so that it will take only the small trigger of someone brushing past them for them to react with challenging behaviour. In this case the analysis would be:

| | |
|---|---|
| *Environment*: | internal: sensory sensitivity |
| | external: day centre |
| *Establishing operation*: | temperature/arousal level |
| *Contingency*: | somebody brushing past. |

Any of these three sets of factors could be targeted for intervention.

Clements (2002) describes the establishing operations as 'motivational'; they generate the wants or needs that the person will act upon. A wide variety of conditions, both internal and external to the person, may act as establishing operations (see Emerson, 2001). Gathering information on conditions under which the behaviour does and does not occur can suggest to us what the establishing operations may be. Changes in antecedent conditions are often relatively easy to implement and can be highly effective (Emerson, 2001).

Kevin may be seen as someone whose needs were not being met, and who was attempting to communicate those needs, albeit in a way that was socially inappropriate and not entirely effective. Our involvement is likely to include assessing the extent to which the person's environment meets their communication needs. Where it fails to do so, this can have serious, and occasionally catastrophic, consequences. Ephraim (1998: 218–23) half-jokingly comes up with a series of laws:

'Where there is denial of the other's uniqueness, there is no conversation.'
'Where there is no conversation there is a struggle for control.'
'Where there is a struggle for control there is exotic communication.'

We might add to this that where there is exotic communication, this fuels the denial of the other's uniqueness, trapping the person and their carers in a vicious circle of animosity and problematic behaviours.

The most significant relationships that many people have are with their paid carers. Many people exist in an emotional desert, where the majority of interaction is short-lasting and task-focused. In our assessment we need to consider questions such as: what is the level and quality of their interaction with carers? Is it all directive, or is there time for non-purposeful communication? Is there regular, allocated time for one-to-one interaction? Is communication adult-to-adult or parent-to-child? How do carers respond to the person's attempts at communication? And how do the feelings and perceptions of carers affect this interaction?

## Quality of Life

Positive Behaviour Support incorporates the systematic assessment of a person's environment through the concept of Quality of Life. This shifts the focus of assessment and intervention from the behavioural control to environmental enrichment, and from remediation to prevention.

The 'objective' quality of life is generally agreed to include several broad dimensions. For example, Felce (1997) suggests Physical, Material, Social, Productive, Emotional and Civic Wellbeing. More recent conceptualisations include dimensions with more explicitly ethical flavour such as self-determination, inclusion and rights (e.g. Schalock et al, 2004). Quality of Life also has a 'subjective' as well as an objective aspect, and both should be considered. It has been found that subjective quality of life is remarkably consistent across different populations, and may not reflect real deficits in a person's environment (Hensel et al, 2002). Moreover, the problems inherent in assessing subjective quality of life with people who may have difficulty in either evaluating it or communicating that evaluation, have never been entirely resolved (though Cummins, 2005a and 2005b does give some helpful recommendations). A recent development has been the conceptualisation of Family Quality of Life, which is seen as an indicator of the adequacy of services received by the family (Samuel et al, 2012, 2012b).

The assessment of Quality of Life may provide one of the first clues as to the functions of the person's behaviour. For example, if the person is living in an environment that is impoverished in terms of interpersonal relationships and interesting activities, then we might hypothesise that two of the functions of the behaviour are to attract interaction from carers and to self-stimulate. We can investigate this by inviting carers to go back to specific events and 're-run' them in some detail. When were the specific behaviours seen? And, equally importantly, when were they not seen? And what happened as a result? Interventions flow from the various foci of the assessment, including for example, environmental manipulation, individual skills training and changes to reinforcement schedules.

## The carers' experiences and perceptions

It is extremely stressful to be given responsibility for dealing with challenging behaviour, and negative feelings towards the person concerned affect carers' behaviour (Mitchell and Hastings, 1998). According to Attribution Theory, how carers manage their own feelings and deal with the client is likely to depend on their beliefs about the causes of the behaviour – their 'causal attributions'. It has been suggested that carers tend to underestimate the influence of external factors on people's behaviour. When carers see behaviour as being under the control of the individual, they are unlikely to acknowledge their own part in instigating that behaviour, and will probably be resistant to interventions that require that they change their own practice. However, the evidence on attributions is variable (e.g. Weigel et al, 2006; Whittington and Burns, 2005). Internal and external attributions may be mixed and also influenced by gender stereotypes (Wilcox et al, 2006).

Carer responses both to clients and to proposals for change reflect service organisation issues such as role ambiguity, control, support, emotional exhaustion and organisational ideology (Devereux et al, 2011). Mansell (2007) highlights the macro-level organisational change that needs to underpin effective services, including proactive commissioning; individualised services; good management; family support; staff training; and a range of supporting mainstream services.

## Sequences of interaction

Carers often tell us that a person's behaviour takes place 'out of the blue'. The ABC analysis suggests that Antecedents, Behaviour and Consequences occur in a discrete temporal sequence. The reality is more complex, often involving an escalating sequence of feelings and behaviour that are punishing for both the client and the carer. The carer's role in this is often disguised or forgotten under the rubric of 'Consequences'.

The Assault Cycle may be used to conceptualise and visualise this process (Hewett, 1998). It involves the breakdown of incidents into the four factors of *trigger, escalation, crisis* and *recovery*. A key question to ask is: *What are the early signs of distress?* And from this it is possible to track the preceding and subsequent sequence of internal and external events involving both client and carers.

### Suzie

When Suzie comes to see me, she seems anxious and unhappy. She tells me repeatedly that Ben is nasty to her and she does not like being with him. She says she likes to be on her own. On the other hand she asks me about the local day centre, and says she would like to go there.

When I visit Suzie I find her wandering around aimlessly, still with that anxious look on her face. It is her birthday in three days' time and she has received a present, which the staff have put in the office. Suzie is very worried that it will get lost, and begs to be able to put it in her bedroom. Every few minutes she goes into the office to ask about it. The staff address her from behind their desks, telling her she cannot be relied upon to keep the present in her room.

Then it is tea time. All the residents go into the dining room for tea and cake. Suzie does not want to go in there, because Ben will be there and she thinks he will say nasty things about her. She sits miserably at the table, her mug of tea in one hand and cake in the other, both untouched. The member of staff in the kitchen calls out to her that Ben is not doing anything, and she needs to settle down.

Eventually Suzie starts to scream and bite her hand. The manager then calls out from the office that she can go to the sitting room. There she stops screaming and has her tea and cake.

This sad little scene demonstrates the way in which institutional practices can percolate into life in a so-called community home, creating a setting that is ripe for the emergence of challenging behaviour. Viewed in terms of the Assault Cycle, the escalating sequence of events is as follows:

| | |
|---|---|
| *Trigger*: | Suzie is refused access to her birthday present |
| *Escalation*: | for Suzie – distress at being ignored, and then having to sit at the table with Ben; for staff – increased irritability at Suzie's demands and the noise she is making |
| *Crisis*: | Staff call to Suzie from the kitchen, telling her to settle down |
| | Suzie starts to bite her hand and scream |
| *Recovery*: | Suzie is allowed to take her tea and cake to the sitting room |

In the midst of this repeated pattern of escalation, Suzie's feelings and needs have been ignored. In the absence of enjoyable daytime activity, Suzie's life was filled with obsessive worries, which were dismissed by staff. It was also assumed by the staff that they had the right to make decisions on Suzie's behalf – to the extent of keeping control of a present that rightfully belonged to her, and insisting that she share every mealtime and teatime with someone she disliked. Suzie was not afforded the respect of having someone come to talk to her face-to-face, and interaction was all in parent–child mode. Despite her diagnosis of autism there was also no attempt to meet Suzie's specific communication needs, through the use of visual aids. Her feelings were ignored, so that her behaviour escalated to the point of self-injury. These carers were untrained and badly managed rather than callous or cruel, but this sort of organisational malpractice can easily slip over into neglect and abuse.

## Agency in behavioural work

Traditionally, behavioural work is implemented without involvement of the person concerned. Environmental contingencies are manipulated without the person's consent, in the hope that this will result in behavioural change. This presents the risk of a dehumanising objectification. Sometimes a person's level of impairment is such that there is no alternative. In this case, decision on intervention will need to be made on the basis of their best interests, following appropriate procedures. But where people have some verbal understanding and expression, we should try to negotiate with them and engage them in the planning and implementation of behavioural work.

## Richard

Richard rarely speaks at normal volume. His speech varies from normal shouting to a sort of guttural screech when he is distressed. It is painful to hear and has alienated his carers and fellow residents. It has also resulted in his exclusion from day services, and he now spends most of his time isolated in his residential home. Behavioural programmes have been tried in the past, but have proved ineffective.

There is little historical information on Richard, other than the fact that he was severely abused over many years by his parents. Is his shouting a way for him to insist on being heard? Is he aware of his own shouting?

Much of Richard's conversation is tangential, referring in a random and unintelligible way to distant and recent events. But occasionally real communication breaks through, like a shaft of light: 'I do want to work on it . . . we can do something about this . . . haven't I done well?'

The psychologist helps Richard to practise speaking at normal volume. With prompting, he is able to achieve three short sentences, much to his delight. In collaboration with both Richard and his carers a programme is set up whereby he is offered five minutes one-to-one time with carers each hour to practise speaking at normal volume. Richard is to record his own progress on a chart with ticks. It is hoped that this practice will raise Richard's self-awareness, so that he is better able to control his voice volume at other times.

### Assessment tools

A central component of the formal assessment is the careful gathering of evidence by means of observations, traditionally done through the use of ABC charts. In principle, these should tell us everything we need to know about the Behaviour, its Antecedents and Consequences. The difficulty is that in order to collect good quality information, the people who complete the charts need to be trained to know what to look for, what to record and how to record it. In the absence of such training, the completed charts tell us little. Moreover, they annoy hard-pressed staff who see form-filling as just another demand on their time.

When asking staff to monitor incidents, I try to use forms that make minimal demands on both their time and their judgement. The approach I use is as follows:

i.   Carry out detailed behavioural interviews with carers (both parents and support staff, if applicable).

ii.   Spend some time informally observing the person, preferably in at least two settings.
iii.  Produce a draft formulation as to the likely behavioural contingencies (e.g. the triggers for the behaviour, the things staff do in response).
iv.   On the basis of this information, work with staff to construct a 'tick box' observation chart, which names the factors thought to be relevant. The chart should also include space for a staff signature next to each incident, so it is possible to see who has been involved.
v.    Agree on a time frame for recording.

Each record form is different, since it is personally designed. The design of the form is always a trade-off between the volume of information requested and the cooperation of the carers, and is produced in collaboration with the staff. A section from a hypothetical record form is given in Table 7.1. The results can be analysed quantitatively, and qualitative analysis can emerge from discussion with carers.

*Table 7.1* Section from behaviour monitoring form.

| Mandy's behaviour: 4.9.12 | | | | | |
|---|---|---|---|---|---|
| *Time* | *What Mandy did* | | | *What was happening* | |
| | *Shouted* | *Hit staff* | *Hit herself* | *Refused a drink* | *Asked to clear up* |
| 8.00–9.00 | | | | | |
| 9.00–10.00 | | | | | |
| 10.00–11.00 | | | | | |

Assessments should cover service issues as well as individual issues. The Institute of Applied Behaviour Analysis produces a whole range of assessment and training materials, including the wide-ranging Behaviour Assessment Guide, the Aide to Functional Analysis and the Periodic Service Review (LaVigna et al, 1994), which is a total quality assurance system, designed for the evaluation of service settings. The Behaviour Explorer Assessment System (Clements, 2002) is a package of assessment materials, which covers the ABC of functional analysis, but puts this in the context of a broader understanding of the individual and their social context. The Functional Analysis Screening Tool (FAST, Iwata and DeLeon, 1996), and the Motivation Assessment Scale (Durand and Crimmins, 1992) are both designed to help the clinician tease out the possible functions of behaviour.

In 2012 the BPS carried out an evaluation of challenging behaviour outcome measures (Morris et al, 2012). The criteria used included the sensitivity of the measures to change following intervention, ease of use and acceptability to clients. Based on returns from eight UK services, they recommended the use of the Behaviour Problems Inventory (BPI-01) (Rojahn et al, 2001); the Maslow Assessment of Needs Scale (MANS-LD) (Skirrow and Perry, 2009); the Challenging Behaviour Interview (Oliver et al, 2003); and the Health of the Nation Outcome Scales (available at http://www.rcpsych.ac.uk/crtu/healthofthenation.aspx). The BPI-01 and the MANS-LD are available to download from the Learning Disability Faculty website: http://dcp-ld.bps.org.uk/dcp-ld/ld_members_area/outcomes.cfm. Of these the MANS-LD is the only self-report measure, and a more accessible version for use with people who have more significant learning impairments (the miniMANS-LD) has also now been produced (Raczka et al, 2013).

Evidence on Quality of Life may be based on formal assessment, using one of the many schedules available (see Cummins, 2005c for an overview). Perry and Felce (2003) give a useful list of the tools used in their study. There is also the Family Quality of Life Survey (Brown et al, 2006). One difficulty with this questionnaire approach to Quality of Life is that the construct has both universal and culture-bound properties (Schalock, 2004). Also, standard questionnaires may fail to capture the person's idiosyncratic needs.

## Conclusions

During the decades since the birth of behaviourism, our understanding of people with learning disability, and of our own responsibility towards them, has been transformed. In 1996, Herb Lovett made a blistering attack on services that define certain behaviours as problematic, when those behaviours are a perfectly understandable expression of people's needs. We are now interested in people's inner world, and the meaning of their actions. *The Clinical Practice Guidelines for Challenging Behaviour* suggest that the applied behaviour analytic approach 'needs to be interpreted broadly and should include the cognitions and emotional responses of people with learning disabilities, families and carers as well as strictly observable behaviour in the traditional behavioural sense' (BPS, 2004: 61).

Ephraim suggests that we replace the term 'challenging behaviour' with that of '*exotic communication*', which, he says, is 'the communication of the desperate', of 'the pained, the unheard and the unloved' (1998: 216). Our role as psychologists is to try to hear, to understand, to communicate the message these people are trying to convey, and to act on it.

## Recommended reading

Clements J (2002) *Assessing Behaviors Regarded as Problematic for People with Developmental Disabilities* London: Jessica Kingsley

Emerson E, McGill P and Mansell J (eds) (2001) *Severe Learning Disabilities and Challenging Behaviours* London: Chapman & Hall

Hewett D (ed.) (1998) *Challenging Behaviour: Principles and Practices* London: David Fulton

# 8 The Social Domain

However divergent our ways of life and beliefs, we are all alike in trying to make sense of the existential dilemmas involved in human existence. The nature of the relationship between the individual and their social world lies at the heart of these dilemmas. In the Buddhist culture this is understood in terms of the law of dependent origination.

> The Buddhist approach is neither to build nor to abase the self. It is to recognize the reality of our existential position in relationship with the world. . . . Who we are depends on the context in which we live. . . . Non-self theory places people in dynamic encounter with one another and with the environment they inhabit. It acknowledges the ever-unfolding social process and the ways in which people provide conditions for one another.
>
> (Brazier, 2003: 138)

It is believed that all phenomena exist in mutually interdependent cause and effect. We are therefore linked indissolubly with our fellow human beings through their actions and our own.

Western psychological theory tends to focus on the individual as the unit of understanding and intervention. But the theme of interdependence has been expressed in systemic theory, which affords primacy to the social above the individual. Indeed, the very existence of individual identity is called into question. The unit of understanding and intervention is the nexus of social relationships that serve to define the person, and the beliefs that underpin these relationships. This is particularly apposite in the case of people with learning disability, whose lives are so intimately bound up with the actions and feelings of others.

> In the traditional view of a person, one thinks that what a p--- --- does comes from inside the person. . . . If, however, one view of what a person is, namely that what one says and are answers to what others said and did to the person, the of expressions and answers shapes who the person beco

we can ask: With whom does the person become incompetent or weak? . . . With whom does the person become competent and strong? What does that other person do?

(Andersen, 2006: xvi)

There are many versions of systemic theory, some of which have been applied in relation to learning disabled people. Here I shall focus on systemic narrative therapy.

The narrative metaphor 'refers to ideas we hold about ourselves that come to shape the way we organize our lives and approach new experiences . . . the stories we live and tell ourselves guide how we think, feel, act, and attribute meaning to new experiences' (Scior and Lynggaard, 2006: 103). Narrative therapy emphasises the validity of the individual's experience and its meaning to them, and the therapeutic endeavour of helping to facilitate that expression. It provides us with a way of opening up conversation and hence the possibility of transforming perspectives and relationships.

The voice of the therapist is not the voice of authority, but just one voice among many, subject to the influence of the system in the same way as anyone else (Dallos and Draper, 2000). The therapist is a 'collaborative explorer . . . working alongside a family to co-create new and hopefully more productive ways of viewing their situation' (Johnstone, 2010: 41). The therapist consciously takes a 'not knowing' position from which they are able to explore multiple viewpoints by means of techniques such as hypothesising, circular questioning and reframing. Observation also plays a part, since the narratives may be expressed nonverbally. This process of exploration is itself therapeutic, meaning that assessment, formulation and intervention may merge into a single process.

A key aspect of narrative therapy is *externalisation*. Or, in Michael White's oft-quoted words: *the person is not the problem, the problem is the problem.* This location of the problem outside the person is achieved by the language in which it is described (e.g. *'how does anger get the better of you?'*). It is also aided by techniques such as visualisation and drawing. Externalisation allows the person to distance themselves from the problem, gain a fresh perspective on it and develop new, empowering narratives relating to their own lives. Similarly, it allows the people around them to see that the problem is not an expression of individual pathology, but is located in relationships and conditions.

Narrative therapy has shifted 'away from a focus on interaction patterns within families per se, to a focus on the effects of cultural beliefs and practices on interactions among family members' (Tomm, 1998: 409). The challenge to dominant discourses allows the therapist to 'open space for marginalized perspectives' (Scior and Lynggaard, 2006: 104). These include diversity issues, as summarised in the GRRAACCEESS model (gender, race, religion, age, ability, class, culture, ethnicity, education, sexuality and spirituality) (Burnham et al, 2008). Narrative therapy can be carried out at the level of the individual or the group.

# Systemic narrative therapy and people with learning disability

## *Working with the individual*

Narrative therapy techniques can be adapted for people with learning disability, for example by allowing extra time for the person to express themselves, putting forward ideas in a concrete, visual way, and checking on both our understanding of the person and their understanding of us.

If we pick up on the words and phrases used by the person this is validating for them and means they are more likely to understand what is being said. It is also important to build on concepts and experiences that are meaningful to the person. Leaning, for example, describes working with a person who has anger problems by externalising his coping techniques as members of a football team (Leaning, 2007). In therapy, people may struggle to create coherent personal narrative, or may relate a very thin, problem-focused narrative that is based on comments they have heard from others. They may be described as lacking narrative competence (Dallos and Vetere, 2009). This may be because they have a limited capacity for spontaneous self-reflection, or lack the ability to articulate their ideas in the therapeutic situation. Part of the role of the therapist is to help enhance their narrative competence. The therapy provides way of understanding the person, helping them understand themselves and helping them address their problems.

Here I shall give some examples of the use of narrative therapy, used as a form of both assessment and intervention.

---

### Thomas

Thomas is a young man who has been diagnosed as suffering from Obsessive-Compulsive Disorder. He fears contamination, and a large proportion of his life is spent washing either himself or his clothes and bedding. He agrees to a programme of desensitisation, which proves unsuccessful. Then the psychologist tries helping Thomas to externalise his fear. Thomas pictures it as a large round, sad face, with a 'softe sad voice', saying to him: 'This dirt and unclean. You have to wash your hands'. The fear is called 'Mr Sad'. The psychologist discusses with Thomas how he might deal with Mr Sad, rather than just doing what he says. Thomas writes in tiny letters: go away. The psychologist says telling the fear to go away is a good idea, but maybe the message needs to be a bit stronger. Thomas thinks for a bit, then writes in huge letters that fill up a whole page:

SERIOUSLY GO AWAY

Later, Thomas describes how he feels about his therapy. Underneath a brightly smiling face he writes:

'Pleased with myself. The fear gose away because I'm not think about it. It more nicer when I'm calm'.

---

During the therapeutic conversations, the therapist tries to 'listen out for actions and intentions that do not fit within the dominant, problem-saturated story' – for 'unique outcomes' or 'sparkling events' (White, 2007: 232). These can be picked up on and discussed with the person, who has probably considered themselves in an entirely negative light up to this point. This new, capable story may be 'thickened' through the development of alternative storylines. An example is Fox's description of his treatment of a boy with traumatic memories, whose was helped to develop a 'thick' story of himself as a good citizen (Fox, 2009).

Those qualities and resources that help the person resist the externalised problem can also be externalised, and then drawn upon in future situations when strength is needed to overcome the problem. Deborah Lee uses the image of the 'Perfect Nurturer' to generate warmth and self-acceptance in people with feelings of shame, inadequacy and self-loathing (Lee, 2005).

---

### Melanie

Melanie suffers from incapacitating anxiety, which she has externalised as 'Mr Nasty'. She is overcoming him with 'Mr Brave', who 'looks like calm water', and sprays Mr Nasty when he puts in an appearance. Mr Brave 'has a light bulb over his head because he is always thinking of new ideas to help me'. These include behavioural strategies (keep hugging your animals), cognitive strategies (we can beat him!) and use of externalisation (keep on top of the spraying!).

---

In addition to externalisation, the person can be invited to 'bring other people into the room', by discussing their likely points of view. This can help the person to step outside their own frame of reference, consider alternative possibilities and begin to take into account other people's perspectives.

Consolidation and maintenance of progress in therapy can be helped by making a visual record of the weekly sessions and by writing letters, which re-conceptualise the presenting problems in relational terms (Haydon-Laurelut and Nunkoosing, 2010). If the person agrees, a session may be arranged with their carers to talk to them about their new narrative and how they may be helped to maintain their progress outside the consulting room.

People are likely to be successful in maintaining therapeutic progress if they have a close relationship with carers who are able to prompt them to use the strategy they have learnt, consistently and over an extended period. Unfortunately, Thomas did not have this. He lived in a shared house with high staff turnover, and no-one was able or prepared to take on a close supportive role. Within a few months, he was referred back for additional psychology input. Duncan was more fortunate.

## Duncan

Duncan is aged 23 and has a bad temper. He shouts, slams doors and occasionally hits people. His parents alternately make demands on him and reject him. He now lives in a foster family placement and says he is happy there, but his behaviour is putting this placement at risk.

Duncan feels terrible that his behaviour is upsetting his carers. He pictures his temper as 'horrible green snot'. Mr Snotty has lots of tricks that he uses against Duncan. Among these are: 'to hide in a corner'; 'to shout at me'; 'to tell me I'm a horrible person'; 'to tell me I should jump out of the window'; 'to tell me not to eat'.

Duncan draws Mr Snotty as an ugly big green lump. The psychologist then asks him to think about how he might get the better of Mr Snotty. Duncan is gleeful. He draws a fresh picture, this time with a huge boot kicking a much shrunk Mr Snotty firmly through the cat flap.

Afterwards, Duncan's carers are invited in. He proudly shows them his picture and explains to them how he is going to deal with Mr Snotty in the future. At home, the carers encourage him to continue to be aware of Mr Snotty and to kick him out when necessary.

Most people feel bad about their 'problem', and it is a great relief for them to hear that someone else appreciates the efforts they have made to overcome it, and can help them find some entertaining ways of dealing with it. This has the effect of transforming a therapeutic session that could otherwise feel difficult and shameful into a shared time that is engaging, validating and fun.

Care must be taken to ensure that the person understands that the externalised problem is not 'real', but is just a helpful way of thinking. All the people I have worked with have been able to understand this distinction, but it could be an issue with a person who had difficulty in distinguishing between fantasy and reality.

### *Working with the group*

Rather than working individually, it may be more effective to work directly with the group to which the person belongs. Narrative therapy 'creates a forum in which people's voices can be heard in a different way and where their stories can be witnessed and acknowledged' (Cardone and Hilton, 2006: 86). Use of a reflecting team may help the group to hear alternative perspectives, and help individuals feel that their voice is being heard. However, people may also find this an uncomfortable and excluding experience (Petrie, 2011). If it is used, therefore, the reflecting team needs to be introduced in a collaborative, sensitive and possibly modified way. Haydon-Laurelut and Nunkoosing (2010), for example, used a 'chat show' format to introduce the reflecting team.

Where people are unable to express themselves verbally, the technique of *interviewing the internalised other* may be used (Tomm, 1999). The group may be asked: 'If X could choose someone to speak for them, who would they choose?' From the experience of being interviewed 'as if' they were the other person, 'conversations that began with internalising and denigrating descriptions developed . . . quite a different tenor . . . staff have begun to notice barriers clients face; felt pain they may have experienced' (Haydon-Laurelut, 2011: 9). I found this approach helpful in making a best interests decision on surgery for a woman who lacked capacity. Both parents and carers agreed that the person best able to 'speak for' the woman concerned was her keyworker, who proved able to give a thoughtful and powerful account of the person's feelings and wishes.

### *Understanding carers*

A recurrent theme in the literature on staff consultation has been the difficulty in engaging their cooperation. This can lead to a negative cycle of inaction, mutual blame and animosity. It has been attributed to a number of factors, including lack of staff training, poor management procedures and (as described in Chapter 7) staff attributions. Whatever the reason in any particular situation, we need to move beyond frustration and inefficacy to try to understand what is going on from the point of view of the staff. In terms of the Stages of Change Model (Prochaska and DiClemente, 1982), we may see staff as being in the Pre-Contemplative Stage. According to the theory of Motivational Interviewing one of the 'essential ingredients' for helping move people through the stages of change is empathy (Miller and Rollnick, 1991). Our empathic understanding of the staff situation, feelings and opinions can help them move on to the Contemplative Stage of Change.

---

### Stephanie

The psychologist has prepared carefully for the training day, which is to focus on Stephanie, a woman with autism and challenging behaviours. She arrives armed with PowerPoint displays and interactive exercises. But when she greets the staff members, she is met with folded arms, pursed lips and avoidance of eye contact. After a few hapless attempts at conversation about Stephanie, she asks the staff how they feel about coming to this training day. Two of them make it clear they are not at all happy. They have been required to attend after working a night shift. They have had no sleep at all. It does not take long for other staff to add their list of grumbles to the general dissatisfaction with management. Once time has been allowed for this discussion, the staff engage thoughtfully in the training.

If staff feel that we are passing judgment on them or blaming them for the behaviour of their clients, we will get nowhere with them. . . . What is it like for them to spend hours on end with a person who is unable to speak, where all the normal rules of social interaction are overturned? They need to feel that we appreciate their goodwill and hard work, understand their difficulties and are there to support them.

(Webb, 2011: 26)

### *Working integratively*

Where the formulation of the person's problems is complex, then it may be helpful to combine a systemic approach with other interventions. For example, where there are significant relationship problems, Rhodes (2003) has suggested the use of family therapy alongside behavioural interventions in families. Daynes et al (2011) report a successful application of this approach. Jenkins (2006) has developed a model for working with a person's whole support network that she calls 'Network Training', and which involves a combination of systemic practice, education and problem-solving.

In Attachment Narrative Therapy (ANT), the attachment narratives of the family are explicitly incorporated within the systemic sessions. They are dealt with according to the principles of systemic narrative therapy, but with a focus also on the emotional content of people's stories, using a range of nonverbal techniques. Formulation 'attempts to explore how the expectations that people hold and the stories that they have about their childhood experiences are being played out in their current relationships' (Dallos and Vetere, 2009: 23).

## Other approaches to working with the system

It is possible to work *with the system* of which the person forms a part, without necessarily working *systemically* in the sense of implementing systemic theory. Other approaches may also have systemic implications. I give four examples here.

### *Cognitive behaviour therapy in the family*

Where it is clear that family members or other staff are contributing to the person's problems, then engaging the person in cognitive behaviour therapy alone is unlikely to have lasting benefit. In this case the formulation needs to be set in a systemic context and understood by significant members of the person's network.

---

### Simon

Simon is aged 19, and has a lifelong history of violent and sometimes cruel behaviour. He is keen to talk to the psychologist, and expresses his mortification at his own behaviour, which he experiences as being completely out of his control. The psychologist talks to his father, and finds that they are daily locked in an escalating battle of misunderstanding, hurt and anger. Yet he too means well, and is at a loss to know how to improve matters.

Part of the formulation for Simon's behaviour is the hypothesis that they are both unwittingly caught in the Assault Cycle (see Chapter 7). The psychologist sees them together and begins by acknowledging the fact that they both mean well and want to learn better ways of relating to each other. She explains the Assault Cycle, and they discuss cognitive and behavioural techniques for extricating themselves from this. After their work comes to an end, Simon writes to the psychologist:

'Thank you ever so much. Last year you turned my life round. . . . It's made a real difference at home. . . . I will forever thank-you for all your help and hard work.'

---

### Cognitive Analytic Therapy

In its collaborative approach and emphasis on the ways in which problematic relationships are expressed in dysfunctional patterns of behaviour, Cognitive Analytic Therapy (Ryle, 1990) is intrinsically systemic. It also acknowledges the way in which people's 'sense of self' develops through their early social experiences. Breckon and Simpson (2011) suggest that, since it focuses on the relational aspects of people's lives, it may be particularly helpful in exploring issues of marginalisation and labelling.

This approach may also be used as a consultation model for staff teams. This involves a 'shared experience of describing and mapping out what the typical patterns are that have developed between the client and staff teams . . . from our position of realistic humility and empathic validation of staff experiences' (Lloyd, 2011: 27).

### 'Getting to Know You'

In the 1990s, practitioners were encouraged to just go and spend time with one individual, to share their lives and think themselves into the shoes of that person. Gaining this understanding remains crucial for us. When trainees arrive with me one of the first things I suggest they do is go and spend at least a morning or afternoon in a service delivery setting, and think imaginatively about what life is like for the service users. In a workshop run by John Clements that I attended in about 1992, he used *Getting to Know You* as a way of helping a staff team deal with someone with challenging behaviour. Its therapeutic core is the gathering of information by the whole staff team and the fostering of their empathic understanding. I first tried it out for myself in connection with a young lady called Gay, who was habitually pushing people in her day centre. Towards the end of the afternoon I gave the participants pencils, paper and drawing materials and asked them to express in whatever way they wanted what they felt life was like for Gay. Here is part of a poem one staff member produced.

*I am happy*
*The bus picked me up*
*We drive and drive*
*My vision is a blur . . .*
*At last the Centre*
*All is quiet, I hang up my coat,*
*I know the corridor*
*I walk awkwardly down it*
*'Hello Gay', 'good morning Gay'*
*I'm taken unaware*
*I push away blurred images*
*and head towards safe areas*
*I visit the Art room, looking all the time*
*Looking for people I recognise . . .*
*people I like . . . people who are blurs . . .*
*people I don't like*
*I feel bored. I push people away . . .*
*they are invading my space . . . I am being intimidated*
*I push them away . . . they return . . .*
*again I push them . . . they annoy me.*
*I stand my ground and they retreat.*
*I feel more safe, secure*
*I am being left alone now*

(thanks to the anonymous author)

At a second workshop people shared their letters, poems and works of art. For the first time they developed a care plan based on Gay's feelings and needs. During the following year, there were no further incidents of pushing.

I have since discovered that *Getting to Know You* has an effect that is both intangible and incalculable. It involves the co-construction of an alternative narrative in which blame, anger and hostility are replaced by shared knowledge and empathic understanding. Once this happens, staff are ready to take on board further training or consultation, which will vary according to the person's needs. This may include, for example, training on communication, the Assault Cycle, positive reinforcement or the needs of a person with autism. And sometimes it is not necessary at all. It seems that *Getting to Know You* works its own magic, resulting in a subtle shift in staff behaviour that is reflected in the feelings and behaviour of the client (Webb, 2011).

### Person Centred Planning

Person Centred Planning refers to a group of interventions originating in the work of John O'Brien and including PATHS, MAPS and Circles of Support. These are based on shared principles, including:

- recognising the aspirations and capacities of the person
- emphasising the authority of the person's voice
- mobilising the person's networks, both natural and professional
- providing the support required to help the person achieve their goals.
                                    (Mansell and Beadle-Brown, 2005: 20)

> ### Amanda
>
> With her shabby clothes, missing teeth and dyed hair, Amanda is instantly recognisable for any English person as someone who is struggling at the bottom of the social hierarchy. As a child she was subject to multiple rapes by friends of her father. She has already had three children taken into care. Her relationship with child services is full of animosity. She is also involved with several other services, none of whom communicate with each other.
>
> The psychologist suggests to Amanda that they work together to set up a Circle of Support. Amanda is excited. She has no friends, and has never been offered any sort of control by services. She thinks of some people that she would like to have in her Circle and decides she would like to meet for morning coffee in a local pub. The Circle meets six-weekly for a period of about a year. During this time, Amanda starts to be able to discuss her own needs and what she would like from services. Professionals start to liaise with each other, and also to see Amanda as a needy person deserving of their respect and support. Amanda starts to develop a more assertive relationship towards the son she has remaining at home with her. Her physical health problems and debts are addressed for the first time.

Person Centred Planning emerged from normalisation and was advocated in *Valuing People* (2001a). It is a collaborative approach, encouraging the development of alternative narratives, and allowing the person's voice to be heard. In addition, the process itself is designed to empower the person. For example, when a person-centred planning meeting is held, it is the person who decides who is to be invited, sends out invitations, decides on the venue and refreshments, and so on. This sets a completely different set of relational dynamics to those experienced in the usual multi-disciplinary meeting. There are tools for structuring person-centred planning meetings, such as PATHS, and MAPS (see O'Brien, 2004; O'Brien and O'Brien, 2000; Towell and Sanderson 2004). Circles of Support provide a further empowering process by which the person may be helped both to meet their need for belonging, and to develop their capacity for self-determination.

In 2005, Chamberlain et al asked rhetorically whether psychologists would strangle person-centred planning at birth. And, indeed, in many places it has not survived the test of time. Person-centred planning does not easily fit into a service-driven delivery of care, nor is it easy to implement with people who lack verbal skills. But properly conducted, it can be an inspiring process.

## Conclusion

I began this chapter with a contemporary Buddhist quotation, designed to demonstrate the universality of the assumptions underlying systemic narrative therapy. And I end with a 17th-century quotation that illustrates a similar point.

No man is an island entire of itself; every man
is a piece of the continent, a part of the main;
if a clod be washed away by the sea, Europe
is the less, as well as if a promontory were, as
well as a manor of thy friends or of thine
own were; any man's death diminishes me,
because I am involved in mankind.
And therefore never send to know for whom
the bell tolls; it tolls for thee.

John Donne

## Recommended reading

Baum S and Lynggaard H (2006) *Intellectual Disabilities: A Systemic Approach* London: Karnac Books
Morgan A (2000) *What is Narrative Therapy?* Adelaide: Dulwich Centre Publications
*Clinical Psychology & People with Learning Disabilities*, 2012, *10*(2)

# 9   The Physical Domain

We believe that Mark died unnecessarily. Throughout his life, we encountered medical professionals who had no idea how to deal with people with a learning disability or what it is like to be a parent of someone with a learning disability – to know their suffering, to see their distress. If only they would listen.

(Mencap, 2007: 1)

Alan's son Mark died in hospital of bronchopneumonia. In the report *Death by Indifference* Mencap presented the stories of six such people who they believe to have died unnecessarily. This formed part of a stream of literature that began to emerge towards the turn of the century documenting the fact that people with learning disability were not only at increased risk of poor health but also likely to suffer institutional discrimination in access to healthcare (e.g. Mencap, 1997, 2004). The government responded to these concerns with several reports and policy initiatives.

Nevertheless, it seems that access to adequate healthcare remains problematic for many people. To be learning disabled is to be at higher risk of physical ill health than those who are not learning disabled. Risks include sensory impairment, mobility problems, heart conditions, epilepsy and early death. The Disability Rights Commission reported in 2004 that in the UK four times as many people with learning disabilities died of preventable causes as people in the general population. Glover and Ayub (2010) studied death certificates over a five-year period, and found a relatively high level of deaths from causes that were to some extent preventable, such as epilepsy, or lung problems caused by solids or liquids going down the wrong way. On 3 January 2012, Mencap and the Guardian jointly published a report that accused the NHS of causing or contributing to the deaths of at least 74 people during the previous decade (www.mencap.org.uk/guardian_investigation).

Physical health is the foundation of the person's wellbeing, a basic level of Maslow's hierarchy of needs as well as an essential component of all indices of quality of life. There is little point in us implementing sophisticated psychological therapies with someone and ignoring the fact that they are in chronic pain, or obese to the point that puts their health at risk. If we are to help improve people's access to physical wellbeing, then we need to understand the factors that contribute to the current situation. These range from macro-economic factors such as the distribution of wealth in society, to individual communication skills. They are addressed in the remainder of this chapter.

## Individual issues

### *Conditions with health implications*

Many conditions that result in cognitive impairment are also associated with risks to physical health. Some examples are given in Table 9.1.

*Table 9.1* Health risks associated with some syndromes.

| Syndrome/condition | Health risks |
| --- | --- |
| **Down's Syndrome** | Endocrine disorders, e.g. hypothyroidism<br>Cardiac defects<br>Obesity<br>Visual and hearing impairment<br>Respiratory tract infections<br>Leukaemia<br>Gastrointestinal problems, e.g. coeliac disease<br>Diabetes<br>Skin conditions<br>Muscular/skeletal problems/juvenile arthritis<br>Infertility in men<br>Early onset dementia |
| **Fragile X Syndrome** | Recurring ear infections<br>Epilepsy<br>Scoliosis<br>Connective tissue disease leading to joint laxity and cardiac abnormalities |
| **Lesch-Nyhan Syndrome** | Self-injurious behaviour |
| **Williams Syndrome** | Sleep problems |
| **Prader Willi Syndrome** | Strabismus, myopia<br>Hypogonadism<br>Hyperphagia<br>Hypotonia<br>Obesity<br>Diabetes |
| **Angelman Syndrome** | Ataxia<br>Hypotonia<br>Epilepsy |

### Sensory impairment

Sensory impairment or disorder is widespread and under-recognised in people with learning disability (Warburg, 2001). It can involve both sensory receptors and those brain areas that process this information. People with extensive/pervasive support needs are particularly at risk for sensory impairment, as a result of defects in their sight and hearing. Carers will often fail to take this into account and assume that hearing is intact, or that people 'choose' what they want to hear.

Vision has been described as a uniquely 'coordinating and integrating sense', which gives a 'direct, precise and effortless awareness of the whole spatial context. . . . It is through vision that the very core of reciprocal human relationships begins' (Webster and Roe, 1998: 68, 73). Routines such as mutual gazing, joint attention and turn-taking serve as a foundation for secure attachment, sense of self, interest in exploring the environment and cognitive development. Deprivation of these early experiences can result in infants who are passive, lacking in motivation, in understanding of causal relationships in the material and social worlds and in theory of mind (Hobson et al, 1999: 55). Visual impairment may also result in eye-poking, sometimes used as a form of sensory stimulation (see www.lookupinfo.org/eye_care/eye_care_factsheets/). These difficulties continue into adult life.

A person's ability to take part in formal testing of visual acuity is likely to be limited. Functional assessments are observational, and involve asking questions such as: at what distance do they start to show an interest in an object? Is this affected by the side at which the object is presented? Do they track the movement of objects, or shift gaze from one object to another? If they are mobile, are they able to negotiate spaces without bumping into things? Do they become anxious in new settings? Is their vision affected by levels of lighting?

It is helpful to involve carers or others within the person's natural environment in this assessment, and this may include collecting video material.

The Vision for Doing assessment (Aitken and Buultjens, 1992) involves observational assessment of each area of visual perception (e.g. visual field, object size, face perception) in relation to five levels of response to visual stimuli. SeeAbility also provides a downloadable functional vision assessment (http://www.seeability.org/eyecare_hub/carersandsupportersinfo/eye_problems/functional_vision_assessment_fva.aspx).

Results of such an assessment can serve as a basis for a care plan designed to enhance the person's perception as well as their control over their environment. They will benefit from carers creating situations in which they are able to learn that their actions do have effects – what Ware (2003) terms a 'responsive environment'.

### Sensory sensitivity

People with autism are at risk of abnormal sensory responses, in any of the sensory domains. This sensitivity may result in behavioural responses that appear bizarre and baffling to carers. For example, one young man I met used to routinely tear down the blinds in his bedroom, and it transpired that he was sensitive to their vertical lines. Some people with autism may fail to demonstrate that they are in pain, or to realise that they are satiated with drinks. In these cases risk assessments must be made and procedures put in place to ensure people's safety. Sensory sensitivity may be assessed by observation and questionnaire (Bogdashina, 2003).

### Pain awareness

Pain is very often the first sign of medical problems, so its early identification, diagnosis and management are crucial. For people with learning disability, the recognition of pain, the ability to tell others about it and knowledge of how to deal appropriately with different types of pain, can all be problematic. For example, Beacroft and Dodd (2011) found that out of a sample of 40 people described as having good verbal abilities, a high proportion had difficulty in describing pain, locating pain and telling others about it. At the same time one-third of staff interviewed considered that people with learning disabilities have a higher pain threshold than other people. This illustrates the way in which a superficial facility with language may well mask a limited vocabulary and difficulties with language use, some of which interact with other cognitive deficits. Failure to deal appropriately with acute or chronic pain can result in failure to treat medical problems, as well as anxiety, depression and deterioration in daily living skills (Singleton and Kalsy, 2008).

Visual aids such as a body map and coloured analogue scales may be used to aid self-report of pain. However, people's ability to use them may be compromised, particularly as ageing takes its toll. Observation is often the main tool we have in pain assessment. This is dependent on knowing the person's baseline behaviour, and ways in which this is likely to change if they are in pain. Such an intimate knowledge of the person can only develop in a close relationship over a long period of time, and we should draw on family members' understanding of the person's pain-related behaviour. It is also important to challenge assumptions staff may have about sensitivity to pain, to work with them on behavioural observation and ensure that pain assessment and management is included in the person's health action plans (Mackay and Dodd, 2010).

Structured assessment of pain and discomfort may be carried out using the DisDAT (Disability Distress Assessment Tool; Regnard et al, 2007). The Paediatric Pain Profile provides a format for gathering information on the idiosyncratic expression of pain, and this may be adapted for adults (www.ppprofile.org.uk). Pain assessments designed for the elderly may also be used (see Abbey et al, 2004).

### Challenging behaviour

Where people are unable to communicate pain and distress, this may be expressed in challenging behaviour. De Winter et al (2011) found evidence of specific associations between challenging behaviours and physical problems such as urinary incontinence, chronic sleep problems and pain related to cerebral palsy.

In some cases, challenging behaviour may result from the functioning of neurotransmitter systems. People with Lech–Nyhan Syndrome, who all exhibit self-injurious behaviour, 'show a significant deficiency in dopamine pathways . . . and decreased levels of dopamine and its metabolites' (Emerson, 2001: 52–53). Serotonin has been implicated in both aggressive and self-injurious behaviour. The optoid peptides are involved in pain control systems, and are also thought to influence self-injurious behaviour in some people.

Understanding such relationships may influence carers' perceptions of those whose behaviour is challenging. It may also suggest treatment strategies, through the use of medication and diet. For example, clozapine has dopamine and serotonin receptor binding properties, and may therefore be used to treat self-injurious and aggressive behaviours.

## *Medication*

The use of medication can have far-reaching effects on people's physical condition and cognitive function. For example, anti-psychotics can result in a horrifying list of side-effects, including sedation, nausea, weight gain, seizures and parkinsonism, and culminating in possible death through neuroleptic malignant syndrome (Emerson, 2001). Serotonin reuptake inhibitors are used in treatment of depression, but their use can result in headaches, diarrhoea, anxiety and sexual dysfunction. Other anti-depressants affect memory. Lithium, which is used in treatment of bipolar disorder, can be toxic, resulting in diarrhoea, vomiting, drowsiness, muscular weakness and blurred vision. Added to all this is the fact that many of the people we see are on cocktails of medication, with unknown interactive relationships. There is little information on the specific cognitive effects of different forms of medication and this creates difficulties of interpretation when we carry out cognitive assessments (see James' vignette, p. 105).

There are guidelines on the use of medication: for example, the Cochrane Review on use of antipsychotic medication in people with learning disabilities (Brylewski and Duggan, 2004); and the Quick Reference Guide produced by the Royal College of Psychiatrists and Mencap (Deb et al, 2006).

## *Cognitive impairments associated with learning disability*

Healthcare in the UK, as elsewhere, is based on a reactive model of provision. It relies on people being able to identify their own healthcare needs and pursue treatment. It assumes their ability to understand time, use a phone, read information, express themselves verbally and cope with a crowded waiting room. All these may be lacking in people with learning disability.

## James

James is aged 45 and has a near-lifelong history of challenging behaviour. Recently, his behaviour escalated and changed in character, with loss of motivation, social withdrawal, paranoia and apparent experience of visual and auditory hallucinations. This culminated in James pulling out one of his own teeth. His carers have requested inpatient admission for assessment. The psychiatrist believes James is simply continuing in his pattern of challenging behaviour.

When the psychologist studies James's notes, she finds a detailed description of James's behaviours written by his parents two years previously. This makes no mention of paranoia or hallucinations. These new behaviours began one month after a change in James's epilepsy medication. This medication has now been stopped, and since then James's new symptoms have started to subside. The psychologist concludes that James was suffering from a psychotic episode, superimposed on existing challenging behaviours, and apparently associated with his medication change.

These problems can result in a high level of anxiety, exacerbating the person's difficulty in communicating their healthcare needs.

### *Health risks associated with lifestyle*

When we are given a choice as to whether to avoid exercise, consume an unhealthy diet, go to bed late or consume addictive substances, many of us choose to do these things. However, our indulgence is usually tempered by an understanding of consequences, and ability to reason and to resist impulsive behaviours. In many learning disabled people, this is not the case. Nevertheless services expect that even people with serious cognitive impairments can live 'independently', 'in the community', with minimal preparation and support. The consequences for health include obesity, substance abuse and chronic tiredness, all resulting in reduced quality of life.

Harmful lifestyle choices are often defended by carers and the people themselves on the grounds that they have the right to make that choice (which of course they do). Once entrenched, this pattern is very difficult to change, particularly in people with autistic spectrum disorder. In our assessments we need to take into account the impact of such lifestyle choices. When people are being considered for 'independent living' we also need to try to ensure that such change is preceded by thorough assessment and preparation.

## Capacity issues

In relation to both lifestyle choices and the need for medical treatment, there may be a conflict between a person's wish to make their own choices, and their capacity to understand the longer term implications of those choices. In this case, interventions are needed both to provide the person with the support they need and to enhance their decision-making abilities (Keywood and Flynn, 2006).

Where serious risks are involved, caregivers are understandably likely to feel protective towards a family member who may be making what appear to be unwise lifestyle choices. Paid staff, on the other hand, may be confused as to where their responsibilities lie, between duty of care and the person's right to self-determination. Keywood et al challenge the 'tolerance of people's choices and . . . the ways in which these can be distorted to justify non-interference in people's lives' (1999: 57). They make it clear that a person's refusal of treatment does not absolve health providers of a duty to provide some healthcare. Health may become the crucible in which the issues of rights, self-determination, quality of life, parental love, staff guidelines and capacity all smoulder.

---

### Sam

Sam is aged 24 and has a diagnosis of Down's Syndrome. He lives in a small flat in a building designated for supported living and loves his independence. He likes to go alone to the local shop to buy fizzy drinks and ready meals. He also likes to stay up late at night watching TV and playing computer games. Often he is too tired to get up for his daytime activities, and he is putting on weight.

The support workers say Sam has the right to make his own choices, and they have no authority to dictate to him what he should do. On the other hand, his parents are sick with worry. They see their son's health and quality of life deteriorating, and blame the support workers for being too laissez-faire.

A capacity assessment of Sam's ability to understand the health implications of his diet is carried out by the clinical psychologist, using photos of different types of food, and a set of simple questions. It is established that Sam does understand the relationship between diet and weight, but does not know about the health problems associated with Down's Syndrome, or understand the potential impact of increase in weight on his health.

In order to enhance Sam's capacity in relation to his diet, a series of health education sessions are held between Sam and the Community Nurse. Following this, a second capacity assessment is carried out, which establishes that Sam still lacks capacity in these areas. A series of meetings are held with Sam and his carers to discuss helping him maintain his health in ways that are respectful of his autonomy.

# Service delivery issues

## *Access*

Despite their legal responsibilities under the Disability Discrimination Act (1995), services rarely cater for the needs of people with learning disability. Emerson and Baines (2010) mention the issues of physical access; failure to make 'reasonable adjustments' to people's communication abilities; diagnostic overshadowing; disablist attitudes among staff; and failure to understand consent and capacity issues. Barriers to access may be a deliberate feature of the organisation (e.g. eligibility criteria) or an inadvertent result of ignorance or inattention to the needs of vulnerable people.

GPs generally have only about 40 people with learning disability within their practice, and they are unlikely to be able to devote time to studying the particular needs of this group (even assuming opportunity for such training is available). They are likely to lack an understanding of the communication needs of their patients or how to respond to them. And their learning disabled patients are often accompanied by a support worker who barely knows them. They may have limited knowledge of syndromes and their associated health conditions. Webb and Stanton (2009) carried out an assessment of staff knowledge in three primary care practices. None of the nurses and only 9 per cent of GPs felt adequately trained in learning disability.

Problems exist at the level of secondary care as well as primary care. A review found that factors such as poor communication and failure to take into account individual needs could result in people becoming bored, distressed, anxious or angry when they visited hospital (Backer et al, 2009).

## *Health promotion*

In view of the health risks faced by people with learning disability, it seems self-evident that they should be the focus of proactive programmes for health monitoring, education, screening and health checks. However, screening programmes introduced for the general population may fail to reach people with learning disabilities, for example, if notification is given in writing, without follow-up by phone. Screening procedures should be adapted and targeted and cover those areas for which people with learning disability are known to be at increased risk or that if undetected could result in serious problems. It may need to be personalised to allow for people's idiosyncratic needs (Taggart et al, 2011).

There is little evidence that health education campaigns are effective in changing people's behaviour and this has resulted in the development of various theories that seek to explain health-related behaviours (e.g. the Theory of Planned Behaviour, Ajzen, 1991; the Health Belief Theory, Harrison et al, 1992; and the Health Action Process Approach, Schwarzer, 2008). These theories typically refer to a range of factors that include self-efficacy, motivation, beliefs, values and expectations, including perceived threat.

External constraints on health-related behaviours figure less prominently. Schwarzer's model suggests a Motivation stage and a Volition stage, with the latter being divided into planning, action and maintenance phases. Barriers and resources are seen as having an ongoing influence throughout the process (Schwarzer, 2008).

Some attempts have been made to apply such theories in the case of learning disability. For example, Barr and Shields (2011) investigated physical activity among children with Down's Syndrome, and found there were both 'external facilitators/barriers' and 'internal facilitators/barriers' to physical activity. They concluded that their results were compatible with the Health Belief Theory. On the other hand, Martin et al (1997), in a study of care staff, found that the Theory of Planned Behaviour, in particular perceived behavioural control, was helpful in predicting physical activity of the people being supported.

Most of the components of these models are problematic for people with learning disability, who frequently have a low sense of self-efficacy, inadequate knowledge, difficulties with planning and impoverished social and material resources. We need to include such factors in our formulation of what appear to be self-harming health-related behaviours. But we also need to go beyond this to work pro-actively with people in order to enhance their understanding of health issues. This could involve groupwork (Swaine et al, 2011), the development of user-friendly health educational literature (Taggart et al, 2011) and health education programmes focused on carers (Hanna et al, 2010).

## Economic and political factors

### *Inequality*

The difficulties that people face in achieving physical wellbeing are under-pinned and exacerbated by more general social inequality. The risk factors for poor health include poverty, poor housing and unemployment, all of which are suffered disproportionately by people with learning disability. They are experienced at an individual level through institutional factors such as the structure of the labour market and the welfare system (Graham, 2005).

> It has been estimated that increased exposure to low socio-economic position/poverty may account for 20–50% of the increased risk for poorer health and mental health among British children and adolescents with learning disabilities and 32% of the increased risk for conduct difficulties . . . among a nationally representative sample of 3 year old British children with developmental delay.
>
> (Emerson et al, 2011: 12)

These astonishing statistics reflect not just the distribution of wealth in society but the norms and values that underlie that distribution, the macro-economic policies that serve to uphold it and the relative powerlessness of people with learning disability (see Chapter 13). They are particularly likely to be at risk if they belong to more than one vulnerable and disempowered group; for example, if they are also elderly or belong to a racial minority.

### Policy context

Any policy that penalises those who are unable to earn a living wage, will place learning disabled people at risk, and this means that the broad policy context is important in addition to specific health-related policies. There is a need for policies that actively support access to healthcare, through education, training and development plans (Keywood and Flynn, 2006). In England the government has produced a range of targeted policy initiatives. *Once a Day* (DH, 1999) aimed to explain to GPs the access needs of people with learning disability, and how they might be met. *Valuing People* introduced Health Action Planning and Health Facilitation (DH, 2002a). Liaison Nurses have been appointed in hospitals, and Hospital Passports introduced.

Even where policies aim to be facilitative, there may remain problems in ensuring implementation. In this case *targets, protocols, standards* and *indicators* may all be used to try to achieve change (Leeder and Dominello, 2005). In Scotland a set of six quality indicators was developed and used as a basis for service review. In England, doctors were given targets regarding the establishment of registers of patients with learning disability and annual health checks. Financial incentives may back up targets, as in the Directed Enhanced Service offered to primary care for establishing registers and making annual health checks.

## Scaffolding access to healthcare

The factors described up to now may all combine to undermine the person's access to physical wellbeing. In order to achieve such access, scaffolding is required at each stage of the process of accessing healthcare, and at both individual and systemic levels. The resources required are summarised in Table 9.2, p. 110. This provides a framework within which we can assess the point at which the person's access to healthcare is breaking down.

Detailed assessment of these factors can probably only be made in the context of an intervention programme. In 2004–05, with the help of two psychologists and two nurses, I carried out such a programme in Essex (Webb and Stanton, 2005). It involved assessment and intervention both with individuals and with the GP surgeries that they visited. We used health stories and targets to help enhance people's physical self-awareness and awareness of the difficulties they had in accessing healthcare. We combined this with role play relating to people's own GP practices, for example, involving the participation of the practice receptionist. A health supporter was involved throughout to aid generalisation and maintenance (Webb and Stanton 2008).

*Table 9.2* Resources needed to achieve access to physical health and wellbeing.

|  | *The person* | *Care environment* | *The Health Service environment* |
| --- | --- | --- | --- |
| **Lifestyle choices** | Knowledge of links between lifestyle and health; ability to defer gratification; ability to resist peer pressure; resources to pursue healthy leisure activities | Support to engage in healthy leisure activities; carers who understand the impact of lifestyle choices on health, and who understand capacity issues | Health promotion and screening programmes targeted at people with learning disabilities and delivered in an accessible way |
| **Awareness of ill-health** | Awareness of physical sensations; ability to interpret physical sensations; knowledge of own health issues | Carers who can interpret signs of pain or discomfort; knowledge of health issues associated with particular conditions; use of visual aids | Policies that take into consideration and actively promote health of learning disabled people |
| **Making an appointment** | Ability to use phone; communicate with receptionist; understand time | Adequate carer support | Primary care registers that identify people with learning disability; training for administrative staff in communicating with people with learning disabilities |
| **The consultation** | Ability to cope with anxiety in the waiting room; ability to describe symptoms and to understand what the doctor is saying | Presence of carers who know the person's history and understand their current problems | GPs with knowledge of syndrome-related health risks, and training in communi-cation; physical access to surgery; systems that do not rely on literacy skills; provision of extended appointments |
| **Treatment and follow-up** | Ability to remember how and when to take medication | Carers who follow up treatment recommendations | Use of visual aids; liaison between primary care and Community Teams |

Some of the group participants described their communication needs and their understanding in the following ways:

**Pre-group**
(The waiting room) is the hardest bit . . . I feel anxious, a bit uptight
If you ask me a question there might be a long pause before I answer it. I'm . . . just trying to think of the right answer
It's hard to tell him how I feel – to put it into words
He didn't explain what was wrong. He doesn't talk to me. I don't like it.

**Post-group**
Pain is telling us something is wrong, like a car light telling us there is something wrong with the car
In a medical examination they listen to your heart, look in your ear, take your temperature . . . You need to have them check you are healthy
I wanted to feel better, for my weight to come down and to lower my blood pressure. The health story helps you sort these things out.
I enjoyed the group work with the others and it boosted my confidence that I can do things for myself

(Webb and Stanton, 2008: 119–21)

Training of GP practice staff was based on their identified needs, and resulted in the production of Practice Development Plans, designed to improve access. This included measures such as the use of visual aids in the consulting rooms, an easy-read practice leaflet, a flexible appointment system and an identified quiet waiting area. A liaison system between GP practices and the CTPLD was set up. Staff reported that they were 'more aware', had 'a more positive attitude towards people with learning disabilities' and were more aware of local services that they could call on for support (Webb and Stanton, 2009: 225).

## Conclusions

The 2008 report by the Joint Committee on Human Rights highlighted the failure of *Valuing People* to ensure better healthcare for people with learning disability. Part of the reason for this lies in the fact that health is affected by broad socio-economic factors such as inequality, social disadvantage and marginalisation (Braveman and Gruskin, 2003).

As psychologists we are rarely able to address these broad issues. Also, we do not often involve ourselves in the physical health of our clients, since this is considered the province of the medical members of the multi-disciplinary team. However, we are uniquely placed to understand both the individual and the structural factors that contribute to poor health. If we consider both in our assessment of the individual, we are then in a position to help promote both agency and access in delivery of their healthcare. Similarly, in our understanding of both the psychological and structural factors underlying access to healthcare, we have much to contribute to a strategic role in its delivery.

## Recommended reading

Emerson E, Baines S, Allerton L and Welch V (2011) *Health Inequalities and People with Learning Disabilities in the UK: 2011* Manchester: Learning Disabilities Observatory
Michael J (2008) *Healthcare for All: Independent Inquiry into Access to Healthcare for People with Learning Disabilities* London: Department of Health

# 10  The Neurological Domain

The extreme complexity of brain structure, together with the long period of post-natal brain development, is such that there are many ways in which healthy growth may be compromised, both pre- and post-natally. These are listed in Table 10.1.

*Table 10.1* Developmental disorders (based on Spreen et al, 1995).

| Type of developmental disorders | Examples |
| --- | --- |
| Genetically transmitted disorders | Neurofibromatosis, phenylketonuria |
| Chromosomal disorders | Turner Syndrome |
| Structural abnormalities present at birth | Fragile X Syndrome |
| Anoxic episodes | |
| Prematurity and low birth weight | |
| Infections | Rubella, meningitis |
| Toxic damage | Foetal alcohol syndrome |
| Nutritional disorders | Kwashiorkor |
| Traumatic brain injury during childhood | |
| Focal neurological disorders | Tumours |
| Convulsive disorders | Epilepsy |

The relationship between neurological and other factors may be represented by a unidirectional or by a transactional model.

## Developmental Causal Modelling

Developmental Causal Modelling was put forward by Morton (2004) as a way of clarifying the relationship between the causal factors involved in autism and other developmental disorders. It comprises three levels of explanation, namely: organic factors (genes and brain); cognition (including affect); and behaviour. These are represented vertically on the page, with the environment by their side, able to exert its influence at any of the three levels. Morton suggested that the direction of these causal relationships was from brain to cognition and cognition and behaviour (O → C → B).

Many people with diagnosed syndromes suffer from severe/profound learning disability, with widespread brain damage, affecting physical health as well as intellectual function. This results in increased risk of mortality with factors such as immobility, tube feeding and epilepsy (Chaney and Eyman, 2000). Health risks are associated with many syndromes and conditions (see Chapter 9).

There is a growing literature on cognitive function in particular syndromes. To take just a few examples, Baker et al (2011: 19) found: 'a generalised deficit in working memory in young boys with Fragile X Syndrome, with a specific disproportionate impairment in the phonological loop'; Whittington and Holland (2011) found deficits in recognition of emotion in facial expression by people with Prader–Willi Syndrome; Lanfranchi et al (2010) found deficits in executive function in people with Down's Syndrome; Numminen et al (2000) found that whereas verbal working memory is deficient in people with Down's Syndrome, visuo-spatial working memory is deficient in Williams Syndrome. But, despite such studies, the research on the cognitive impact of most developmental neurological conditions is often limited in the extent to which it can help to us understand the individual client.

## *The localisation of cognitive function*

In the early days of neuropsychology, studies of brain-injured patients revealed the localisation of different aspects of language and other cognitive functions. As research has revealed the interconnectedness between brain areas, it has confirmed Luria's early contention that we can no longer assume a one-to-one correspondence between localised neurological abnormalities and cognitive function (Luria, 1970). Nevertheless, knowledge of brain areas can alert us to the likely impact of abnormalities. Understanding this can help us to make sense of clinical issues. For example, a person suffering from dementia may nevertheless be able to dress himself because autobiographical and procedural memory have different organic substrates.

Here I will consider just the localisation of executive functions. I have chosen this because impairment in this area is proving to be so important in the lives of those people judged able to live independently or semi-independently.

## *The frontal lobes and executive functions*

If learning disability is viewed in terms of developmental delay, then we might expect that later developing executive functions would be more compromised. From another point of view, since the frontal lobes constitute such a large part of the brain, this might also lead us to expect that executive functions would be particularly affected. In terms of people's ability to lead a normal life and meet their needs, executive function is of critical importance.

There is evidence that different executive functions are differentially located in the frontal lobes. A summary of these suggested relationships is shown in Table 10.2.

For clinicians the significance of the posited localisation lies in the need to separately identify and assess different aspects of executive function, as suggested by the neuropsychological evidence. These functions include

*Table 10.2* Executive functions associated with the frontal lobes (based on Driver et al, 2007; Siegel, 2007; and Spreen et al, 1995).

| Area of frontal lobes | Function | Lesion in area or pathways results in |
|---|---|---|
| **Dorso-lateral pre-frontal cortex** | • Working memory<br>• Temporal memory<br>• Planning act<br>• Concept formation | • Difficulty in remembering and planning sequential actions |
| **Orbito-medial pre-frontal cortex (linked to limbic system including amygdala, reticular activating system, motor areas of frontal lobe and posterior association cortex)** | • Emotional processing and guidance of behaviour<br>• Perceptions given 'emotional' tone via direct links with limbic system<br>• Inhibition of inappropriate responses especially in the social domain<br>• Energisation in social behaviour | • Pseudo-psychopathy<br>• Reduced spontaneous behaviour<br>• Problems in episodic memory because of reduced emotional value of sensory stimuli<br>• Devaluation of reinforcers<br>*Difficulty in:*<br>• initiating actions (e.g. neglect of personal hygiene)<br>• terminating or amending behaviour once started (perseveration)<br>• inhibiting first response (stimulus-driven behaviour)<br>*Lesion-specific effects:*<br>• Medial lesions – pseudo-depressed syndrome, emotional blunting<br>• Orbital lesions – euphoric behaviour, disinhibition, disregard of others' feelings |
| **Anterior cingulate cortex** | • Focusing and supervision of attention to external events and internal thoughts/plans<br>• Selection of appropriate responses | |

working memory, planning, ability to understand abstract concepts, ability to initiate activities, impulsivity and ability to self-monitor.

Executive function deficits can exist in people who are otherwise capable and this can make their behaviour hard to understand. For example, it may be well within the person's abilities to buy a calendar on which to mark their appointments. But the process of buying it, finding somewhere to put it, remembering to record appointments and remembering to look at it each morning, may take weeks or more to achieve. Where this level of support is not available, people may be criticised for their lack of motivation and summarily discharged from care.

A distinctive pattern of executive dysfunction can be seen in people who have suffered traumatic brain injury with, for example, marked disinhibition or apathy. In this case the head injury service should be involved in their care, since they have the necessary expertise. This applies even where the person has been injured in late childhood, having previously had no cognitive impairments. Though they may technically be labelled as learning disabled, their clinical presentation falls more appropriately within the brain injury service.

### Three conditions

The three conditions that trainees are most likely to encounter are Down's Syndrome, epilepsy and autistic spectrum disorders. I shall briefly consider each of these.

### Down's Syndrome

Down's Syndrome is the most common of the conditions causing learning disability. People with Down's Syndrome have an extra chromosome 21, which affects the brain during the second half of foetal development and post-natally. Clear differences in the brain, cognitive function and physical health of infants with Down's Syndrome begin to emerge when they are about six months old, but become more prominent by early adolescence. Consequently, the gap between chronological age and cognitive function increases with age, a fact that must be very hard for parents to witness.

Characteristic brain abnormalities include: reduced neuronal density; delayed myelination; reduced synaptic density; abnormal cortical lamination and reduced dendritic arborisation. Areas particularly affected are: the hypothalamus; the temporal lobe in general; the pre-frontal cortex; the visual and auditory cortices and the cerebellum and brainstem. In people over age 35, neuropathology resembling that seen in Alzheimer's disease is common (Rondal and Perera, 2006; Rondal et al, 1996).

Abnormalities of cognitive function include aspects of: language and pre-linguistic communication skills; learning and memory; motor function and executive function, including working memory. However, there is a wide range of ability in people with Down's Syndrome, and there may also be a wide range of abilities within individuals. Cognitive assessment can help parents and other carers understand these puzzling inconsistencies.

---

### Trevor

Trevor is aged 25 with a diagnosis of Down's Syndrome. He recently moved into a flat, with carers coming in each day to offer support. His carers have expressed concern about Trevor's lifestyle. He seems to act 'on the spur of the moment', changing arrangements at the last minute and spending excessive amounts of money. His flat is chaotic and he often loses things. When carers discuss their concerns with him, Trevor seems to understand and agree with what they say, but nothing changes.

In carrying out an assessment the psychologist considers the hypothesis that a contributory factor in Trevor's behaviour could be the cognitive deficits associated with Down's Syndrome. She carries out a neuropsychological assessment that confirms impairments of executive function in areas such as planning and impulsivity. When she feeds back the results of the assessment, she is able to present them in the context of a broader understanding of Trevor's behaviour. This helps to open up different approaches to working with Trevor and his carers on a solution to the problems.

---

Certain personality or temperamental characteristics may be evident, e.g. sociability, passivity, stubbornness and low motivation, even in infants. Rondal and Perera suggest that this profile may be attributable to the interaction between early strengths in social functioning and deficits in means–end thinking, conditionability, problem-solving and instrumental communication.

People with Down's Syndrome also sometimes show obsessive traits. In a study of children with Down's Syndrome, Kent et al (1999) found that 7 per cent of children also received a diagnosis of autism.

About 50 per cent of people with Down's Syndrome over the age of 50 have a diagnosis of dementia, and this percentage rises with age. In their case, cognitive function and associated everyday living skills decline, and behavioural problems are also often evident early in the process (Ball et al, 2008). BILD has produced a series of booklets relating to Down's Syndrome and dementia, including information for people with learning disability and their families (see www.bild.org.uk). The BPS (2009b) has produced comprehensive guidance on the assessment, treatment and support of people with learning disabilities and dementia.

*Epilepsy*

Epilepsy is defined as 'recurrent and persisting seizure activity', with a seizure defined as an abnormal electrical discharge of neurons (Spreen et al, 1995: 309). Such discharge is a symptom of an underlying disease that affects neurotransmitter functioning. Examples are Fragile X Syndrome, tuberous sclerosis and Alzheimer's disease. Longstanding seizures can cause brain lesions. Some frontal lesions may cause disinhibition. Mesial frontal lesions are associated with apathy and withdrawal.

Associated cognitive impairments depend on the nature of the underlying pathology. Status epilepticus is likely to be particularly damaging. Temporal lobe seizures can result in a verbal memory deficit, emotional lability and behavioural disturbance. Frontal lobe epilepsy may result in disorganisation and impairment of executive functions such as motor control, processing speed and inhibition.

In generalised tonic–clonic seizures there may be a prodrome; that is, a period of change in mood and behaviour in the minutes or days prior to the seizure. Symptoms may include poor concentration, headache and altered mood and sleep pattern. Following the seizure there can be a period of confusion and agitation. Post-ictal psychosis can occur for up to three months following complex partial seizures.

Anti-epileptic medication can have adverse effects, both cognitive and behavioural. These include sedation, mood change, allergy, weight change, reduced processing speed, ataxia and psychosis. These effects can be expected to multiply if a person is taking a cocktail of drugs, as is often the case for people with learning disability (Espie et al, 2003). In view of the difficulty people are likely to have in describing their symptoms, careful record keeping over a period of months may be necessary to establish the likely impact of an individual's drug regime.

Epilepsy is a uniquely challenging condition. It can strike without warning; is largely out of the control of the individual; can result in progressive cognitive impairment and can cause serious injury. It can also be socially stigmatising. The history of other people's response to their condition is critical in setting the scene for a person's adjustment. These factors must all be considered and disentangled in the assessment of a person with epilepsy.

The British Epilepsy Association is a source of further information (www.epilepsy.org.uk).

*Autistic spectrum disorder (ASD)*

The diagnosis of autism is based on Wing's 'Triad of Impairments' (socialisation, communication and imagination; Wing and Gould, 1979), and various diagnostic tools have been developed to help clinicians apply these criteria. However, people may exhibit such problems due to other conditions. A behavioural diagnosis is necessarily imprecise and this affects our understanding of the underlying organic pathology. Nevertheless, there is evidence that people with ASD suffer from widespread abnormalities in the limbic system, cerebellum, brainstem, corpus callosum, amygdala, frontal cortex, mirror neuron system and dopamine system (see, e.g. Baron-Cohen et al, 2000; Happé and Frith, 1996). Associated cognitive impairments exist in the areas of language (comprehension, expression and pragmatics); memory (verbal and autobiographical) and executive functions (e.g. sequencing, planning). Presenting behavioural problems have been explained in terms of cognitive theories (executive function; central coherence; extreme male brain theory); social theories (theory of mind) and perceptual theories (abnormalities of sensory processing). Any or all of these may be relevant in the case of particular individuals.

The National Autistic Society is a source of further information (www.autism.org.uk).

### *Limitations to Developmental Causal Modelling*

The assumption of a one-to-one correspondence between brain, cognition and behaviour is both an oversimplification and overly deterministic (Spreen et al, 1995). Any behaviour has multiple causes, and the same antecedent conditions may contribute to different behavioural outcomes. In the case of genetically determined conditions, there may be variations in the way the gene is expressed, resulting in wide variability in cognitive function. For example, Fragile X Syndrome may be manifest in multiple patterns of cognition and behaviour (Morton and Frith, 1994).

The reasons for this are not fully understood, but there is evidence that the way genetic syndromes are expressed is a product of the individual's interaction with the environment. In the case of children with Down's Syndrome, it has been found that early intervention programmes can help prevent some of the expected decline in intellectual function during childhood (Guralnik, 1996). Their development may even extend to becoming bilingual (Edgin et al, 2011). Didden et al (2009) found that communication in Angelman Syndrome was influenced by medical and environmental factors. In Williams Syndrome, the development of language is intimately associated with environmental changes in the course of the children's lives (Karmiloff-Smith, 2009).

### Transactional theories

Transactional theorists stress the fact that the relationship between brain, cognition and behaviour is not uni-directional (Pennington, 2009). They are associated with the discipline of developmental cognitive neuroscience (Johnson, 2005). By 'transactional' is meant that the theories imply 'an ongoing process of mutual and emergent effects within relationships' (Fogel, 2009: 271). In other words, out of a transaction emerges a process of development that is more than the sum of its parts. Hogg and Sebba describe the clinical utility of this approach in relation to the development of the profoundly disabled:

> The child and the environment mutually affect each other . . . and each in different ways adapts to the other. This view of the developing child as part of a complete system of interdependent people and objects is . . . of relevance to people who are severely and profoundly retarded. . . . By considering their development from an ecological perspective we not only come to understand them in their own right, but can better establish ways in which to intervene in order to enhance their development.
>
> (Hogg and Sebba, 1986: 30)

This interdependence is present even at the cellular level of brain development. Processes such as the proliferation of neurones (synaptogenesis), their pruning and the myelination of axons, are all dependent on environmental input. Transcription genes allow the brain to be shaped by learning (Cozolino, 2006). In the words of Greenough et al (1993), neurological development is both *experience-expectant* and *experience-dependent*.

*Experience-expectant* development is development that, though it may be genetically pre-programmed, is dependent for its manifestation on environmental inputs that are relatively invariant across time or between groups of people. Neuronal pruning provides the neurological substrate for this process. An example is the dependence of visual system development on time-sensitive periods of visual input. *Experience-dependent* development is that which depends on environment input that is likely to vary between people, resulting in a range of developmental patterns. The development of synaptic connections provides the neurological substrate for this process. Changeux and Dehaene (1993) stress that these two processes involve active experimentation, and a view of the brain, not as a piece of hardware to be programmed, but as a structure that is constantly generating hypotheses on the outside world.

This transactional process continues post-natally. Our knowledge on this comes from studies of processes such as mother–infant gaze patterns and the early imitation of facial expression. Experimental evidence on both auditory and visual processing suggests that an enormous amount of learning takes place post-natally, in response to environmental input. The infant is predisposed to orient its attention to particular classes of input and actively participates in the 'progressive restructuring of their brain into increasingly specialised circuitry' (Karmiloff-Smith, 1995: 1294). This development takes place through the infant's relationships with others (Cozolino, 2006).

According to the sociolinguistic approach, language and other communication skills and cognitive abilities emerge from the interaction of the child with their caregiver. At birth the child's behaviour is reflexive, but in time reactive and then proactive behaviours emerge. The caregiver ascribes communicative intent and meaning to the child's proactive behaviours, so that the child learns that it can act on its environment to achieve desired outcomes. This takes place at the age of about ten months, and marks the birth of the critical watershed of intentional communication. It can involve the child wanting something (proto-imperative communication) or the child wanting to share something (proto-declarative communication). Once intentionality is established, then the normally developing child will go on to develop formal means of communication (e.g. words) and internalised representations of the world.

The relational environment is thus critical for the development of both intellectual and social function. This means that genetic or other organic condition does not fully determine people's potential. Understanding the mutual influence of organic and social factors can be important in helping us understand the presentation of our clients, and also how we might help them.

## *The social brain*

Cozolino suggests that there is a functional system in the brain that is specialised for social understanding and behaviour. This 'social brain' is a highly connected circuit that includes the orbito-medial pre-frontal cortex (OMPFC); the somatosensory cortex; the cingulate and insula cortices; amygdala; hippocampus and hypothalamus (Cozolino, 2006: 51). These areas regulate neurotransmitter and endocrinal systems. The OMPFC is 'the executive centre of right hemisphere networks of attachment, social relationships, affect regulation and higher level input to bodily homeostasis'. These include the functions of empathy and emotional regulation.

## *Emotional regulation*

The Hypothalamic–Pituitary–Adrenal Axis is 'a central component of the body's stress response system'. Sensitive and appropriate parental responses to the child's distress are the foundation for the development of adaptive systems of emotional regulation, both cognitively and neurologically. The development of the social brain thus depends on the quality of interactions with caregivers, in particular their responsiveness to the infant's distress (Cozolino, 2006; Gerhardt, 2004; Schore, 1994). When failure in the development of the social brain results from early abuse or deprivation, people may suffer disordered early attachment and profound, lifelong distress. They are likely to find it difficult to regulate their emotions and to maintain stable relationships.

In people with learning disability, the failure of emotional regulation may be exacerbated by 'frontal' cognitive deficits such as impulsivity and inflexibility. Some people with such problems (often young men) are referred for 'anger management'. Others (often young women) are referred with a diagnosis of Borderline Personality Disorder.

## Theory of Mind

The late development of the pre-frontal cortex and other critical areas has implications for the social functioning, including Theory of Mind, or the capacity to imagine what others are thinking and feeling. It is suggested that this capacity has different components, and its organic substrate involves a complicated neural network, including mirror neurons, spindle cells and an inhibitory mechanism of the prefrontal cortex (Decety and Jackson, 2004).

In a detailed review of Theory of Mind, Saxe et al suggest that 'understanding other minds follows a characteristic developmental trajectory' (2004: 115). This begins, during the first two years of life, with attribution of goals, perceptions and emotions to others. At about the age of four, children go on to develop the ability to attribute beliefs to others. However, this is an ongoing process. It has been found that perspective-taking and intention understanding develop during adolescence, possibly in parallel with underlying neurological changes (Blakemore, 2007). This raises the question of how such capacities function in people with learning disability, who, in terms of cognitive development, are far from reaching the level of a typically functioning adolescent. Investigation is confounded by deficits in language ability, and the fact that language itself may contribute to Theory of Mind development (Abbeduto et al, 2004). There is evidence of Theory of Mind deficits, not only in autism, but also, for example, in Fragile X Syndrome (Garner et al, 1999) and Down's Syndrome (Abbeduto et al, 2001), though there may be qualitative differences in these deficits.

## Intellectual development

In addition to its role in contributing to our capacity for healthy relationships, the development of the Social Brain is a necessary precursor to learning in general. It is the cornerstone of our intellectual development, including the development of language, self-regulation and consciousness (Schore, 1994).

Vygotsky suggested that it is through their personal relationships, which give expression to the society and culture in which they are living, that children learn. It is this that distinguishes us from animals: 'human learning presupposes a specific social nature and a process by which children grow into the intellectual life of those around them' (1978: 88). He identified the critical period in child development as being the 'happy moment' when speech develops. From this time, the child's actions are freed from the present, concrete, visual situation. They also become less stimulus-driven and less impulsive. They 'acquire the capacity to be both the subjects and objects of their own behaviour' (1978: 26). At a later stage, as social speech becomes internalised, children develop their capacity to use language as a problem-solving tool. Speech then starts to precede action and acquires a planning function. It also serves to focus and extend the field of attention, and is the vehicle for coherent memories. This description highlights the difficulties faced by people whose linguistic and pre-linguistic ability is severely impaired.

### The socio-historical environment

Neurological and intellectual development may be affected, not just by interpersonal relationships but by the broader social and cultural environment. Vygotsky's pupil Luria, in a unique blend of Marxist analysis and scientific experimentation, explored the thinking patterns of people at various stages of social, educational and economic development. On the basis of his findings, he put forward the theory that neurological and cognitive development are a product of socio-historical conditions. Concrete thinking is likely to prevail in societies where practical activity (such as peasant agriculture) is dominant; in contrast, in more 'advanced', technological societies, abstract thought, involving processes such as generalisation, deduction and reasoning, are more likely to be found (Luria, 1976).

Sue Gerhardt (2004) has linked the development of the social brain with the demands of Capitalist society, arguing that we will need to rethink our materialist ideals in order to return to a more empathic style of child-rearing, with the attendant benefits we will achieve, both socially and psychologically.

Both Richardson (2002) and Sternberg et al (2001) argue that academic achievement is a function of many non-cognitive factors that are associated with social class. These include teacher and parent expectations, academic orientation, self-efficacy and anxiety.

## Conclusions

It has been suggested that people with learning disabilities fall into two groups. The first are those with organic pathology and severe/profound/ multiple disabilities. The second are those with mild learning disability that is often assumed to be the result of socio-economic and familial factors (Iarocci and Burack, 1998). But research developments over the last decade suggest that this distinction is less clearcut than was once thought. Even in genetically determined conditions, development may be affected by environmental factors. And even where there is no identified organic impairment but early infant–caregiver relationships are problematic, both intellectual and social development are likely to be compromised.

## Recommended reading

Cozolino L (2006) *The Neuroscience of Human Relationships* London: Norton
Rondal J A, Perera J, Nadel L and Comblain A (1996) *Down's Syndrome: Psychological, Psychobiological and Socio-educational Perspectives* London: Whurr
Spreen O, Risser A H and Edgell D (1995) *Developmental Neuropsychology* Oxford: Oxford University Press

# 11 The Cognitive Domain

Where a person has relatively intact cognitive functions, this will contribute to their ability to make their own decisions and implement them. But where there are cognitive impairments, agency is also likely to be impaired, and this will be expressed in difficulties with everyday living, emotional distress and challenging behaviour. Understanding of deficits will enable us to scaffold the person's performance in order to support their access to physical and social wellbeing. For example, if we know they have difficulty with sequencing, planning and remembering, then we can arrange for carers to spend time with them each morning going through the planned events of the day, and entering this on a visual timetable.

## The process of assessment

Assessment of cognitive function should not be equated with testing. It involves gathering information from a range of sources. Interviewing the client and significant others, taking a detailed clinical history, studying past reports and records, making observations and researching known organic factors, are all at least as important as test administration. Through this we can explore the answers to questions such as:

- What does the person perceive of the world?
- How much do they understand of what is said to them?
- How do they interpret the actions of others?
- What do they understand of social conventions?
- What do they need or want to achieve in everyday life?
- What cognitive functions are involved in this?
- How may they be helped to function more effectively?

We need to consider the answers in the context of a broader understanding of the person, their circumstances, and the cognitive, social and emotional tasks facing them at their stage of their life. Evidence for hypotheses relating to the impact of cognitive function will then be set against evidence for other possible alternative or complementary hypotheses.

## Anna

Anna is aged 18 and has a rare genetic syndrome, about which little information is available. She has problems in controlling her anger, and has asked for 'counselling' to help her with this. In the interview, she talks at great length, with a sophisticated vocabulary. Her mother declares her despair at the impact that Anna's behaviour has on the family. When she is assessed, Anna's behaviour is impulsive, distractible and stimulus-driven. At one point she throws water over the examiner. Her mother sits passively throughout this incident.

The psychologist feels that Anna's behaviour may be explained in terms of either executive dysfunction, behavioural or systemic factors – or maybe a combination of all three types of factors. In order to explore each of these three possibilities she arranges:

i.   to carry out a more comprehensive cognitive assessment
ii.  to ask her parents to monitor her behaviour for an agreed period
iii. to interview Anna's college tutor, to find out whether her behaviour varies across different settings
iv.  to carry out a family interview, in order to explore the experiences and perceptions of family members, and arrive at a better understanding of family relationships.

## Formal cognitive assessment

Being on the receiving end of a formal cognitive assessment can be an intrusive, time-consuming and anxiety-provoking experience for our clients. It is inevitably an unequal process, in which we run the risk of undermining both the client's confidence and our relationship with them. It is helpful if time can be allowed for us to get to know the person, and them to get to know us, before formal assessment begins. It is important to explain in ways the client can understand the reasons for the assessment, what it will involve and ways in which it could prove to be helpful to them. Issues of consent should be revisited throughout the assessment procedure, and the assessment should proceed at a pace and in a manner that suits the person.

The nature of most psychological tests excludes people who are non-verbal, and in their case assessment is more likely to be based on observation and structured carer interviews than on face to face testing. However, even the ability to indicate 'yes' or 'no', or to use communication aids, can contribute to cognitive assessment (Sabbadini et al, 2001).

## Models of cognitive function

Tests are based on one of three models: deficit measurement, developmental or criterion-referenced. The choice of model affects not just the choice of test but the conceptualisation of the person's difficulties.

### Deficit measurement model

Use of a deficit measurement model involves comparing the person's performance with what would normally be expected at that person's age, based on performance of a standardisation sample. Scores are converted into a scale derived from the normal curve and based on the standard deviation unit. The individual's score may then be compared with the distribution of scores derived from the standardisation sample, and evaluated for statistical and clinical significance. Differences of two or more standard deviations are seen as statistically significant. On the other hand, clinical significance is ascertained by referring to the frequency of difference in scores in the general population.

The standardisation sample should be appropriate to the client, scores should be normally distributed in the standardisation sample and test conditions should equate to those applied during standardisation. These are hard conditions to meet. In any case, it is by no means clear what would constitute an appropriate standardisation sample for people with learning disability. Moreover, the person's limited understanding of the test situation may well preclude the possibility of meeting standard test conditions.

So why attempt to test people at all? The justification is that sometimes the clinical value of a test may to outweigh its statistical weaknesses (Lezak et al, 2004). But test results should always be treated cautiously, and interpretation made with appropriate caveats. It may be more useful to report on test results in a qualitative manner, drawing out their implications for real-life performance.

### Developmental model

For people with PMLD the important issue is often for others to understand the level at which they are functioning, and how they may be supported to function at that level, or progress to a higher level. A developmental model provides a structure for such understanding. It involves conceptualising a person's difficulties in the context of normal child development, with analysis of test results in terms of deviation from this norm. Tests are often in the form of checklists, involving observation of the person and questioning of those who know them well.

Piagetian theory may help us better understand this group of people (Hogg and Sebba, 1986). For example, it has been suggested that people with deficits in object permanence are in a 'permanent state of separation distress', and this may account for some challenging behaviours (Janssen et al, 2002: 450). If a person is unable to tolerate waiting to leave the house, and starts to hit his carers, then this could be because he has not reached the stage of understanding the temporal sequence of events.

Nevertheless, the BPS has cautioned against using a developmental model in cognitive assessment and suggests avoiding the use of the term 'mental age' (BPS, 2001). Such terminology may infantilise the person in the eyes of carers.

It also ignores the person's social and emotional development, and their lifetime's experience. In using the developmental model it is important to put assessment results in the context of the person's overall experience, development and adult needs.

### Criterion-referenced model

In some cases we are interested in a person's behaviour or cognitive function per se, not in how it compares with that of other people. The only comparison made is to a set criterion (e.g. can the person put on all their clothes unaided? Can they recognise family members?). Such assessments may be used where it is important to monitor change through repeat testing, for example, in the case of dementia, or where intervention is being carried out. If I am working clinically with someone and discover that he does not know his own address, it does not much matter how many other people in the population do not know where they live. However, it is important for me to understand the effect this disorientation may have on the person's quality of life, and on the risks they face. I will want to explore the possible cognitive, emotional and social reasons for the problem, and the steps that may need to be taken to compensate for the deficit.

## A functional approach to cognitive assessment

A framework for cognitive assessment is suggested in Table 11.1. In view of the extent of connectedness and complexity of cognitive functions, the functional areas suggested here should be regarded as conceptual constructions used for the purpose of helping us understand our clients' behaviours (Lezak et al, 2004). We can use this functional framework from initial history taking through test selection to report writing.

This framework is summarised in the form of a checklist for assessment in Appendix 3. What follows is a brief account of these functions, together with

*Table 11.1* A framework for cognitive assessment (based on Lezak et al, 2004).

- General intellectual ability
- Orientation and attention
- Sensory processing
- Visual-spatial perception
- Communication
- Memory
- Motor function
- Concept formation and reasoning
- Executive function
- Educational abilities
- Social understanding

suggestions as to tests that might be relevant. The list of tests is not by any means exhaustive. They are mostly those of which I have personal experience. Space precludes giving source details of all these tests, but most are readily accessed online.

### General intellectual ability

The Wechsler Adult Intelligence Scale is based on a deficit measurement model. A 'spikey' subtest profile can indicate areas of strength and difficulty, and suggest which cognitive functions need further exploration. However, if the WAIS is used in this way, as a sort of screening tool, it should be supplemented by some tests of areas that are poorly represented in the WAIS, including tests of memory, executive function, reading and drawing. Moreover, we need to bear in mind the wealth of evidence on the poor reliability of the WAIS and its lack of ecological validity in relation to people with learning disability (see Webb and Whitaker, 2012 and Chapter 2). This makes its use as part of an assessment of eligibility for services questionable. However, individual subtest results and index scores may be used alongside other assessment results to shed light on discrete cognitive functions. Interpretation of the WAIS is thoroughly dealt with by Lichtenberger and Kaufman (2009) and Weiss et al. (2010).

## Wendy

Wendy is aged 19 and she is pregnant. The psychologist is asked to carry out a learning disability assessment to help ascertain if she is eligible for services. The results obtained on the WAIS and on the Adaptive Behaviour Assessment System are as follows:

Full scale IQ = 68–76

General Adaptive Composite = 68–78

As the psychologist gets to know Wendy she becomes concerned that the test results do not reflect the depth of her impairments. For example, she believes that Wendy's chatty manner may be masking failure to understand much of what other people are seeing. She asks for a Speech and Language Therapy assessment. It is found that Wendy has difficulty in understanding negatives, plurals, comparatives, complex sentences and abstract or meta-phorical expressions. She is reluctant to say she does not understand, and her conversation is tangential.

The psychologist has also discovered the problems Wendy has in coping with everyday life. She asks for an Occupational Therapy assessment, and an Assessment of Motor and Process Skills is carried out. Wendy achieves a score of <51 on this test, and the Occupational Therapist remarks on her difficulties in motor coordination as well as her distractibility, disorganisa-tion, poor problem solving and inability to learn from experience.

The results of these additional assessments suggest that those available to the psychologist were inadequate to reflect Wendy's real-life problems. In other words they appear to lack ecological validity. So how are the IQ results to be interpreted? How is the reporting of these results to be negotiated, when statement of Wendy's psychology test results will undoubtedly lead to her exclusion from services, and probably the loss of her child? And, more generally, why are we using IQ tests at all in these circumstances?

Lezak is scathing about the use of composite scores:

> 'IQ' as a score is inherently meaningless and not infrequently misleading as well. 'IQ' has outlived whatever usefulness it may once have had and should be discarded. . . . Combined scores such as the 'Index Scores' in Wechsler batteries may also obscure important information obtainable only by examining discrete scores.
>
> (Lezak et al, 2004: 22)

Lezak's view must be set against the wealth of statistical evidence for the existence of a factor *g*. However, this is more properly seen as 'an overview of each person's diverse abilities' rather than as a theoretical construct (Lichtenberger and Kaufman, 2009: 37).

An alternative test, appropriate for people with extensive/pervasive support, is the Draw a Person test. It may be used to estimate their developmental level (Barrett and Eames, 1996). The figures people produce may also provide visual-perceptual information and other information on their view of themselves and others.

*Other tests:*

Ravens Coloured Progressive Matrices
Leiter Performance Scale (which is nonverbal)
Leicestershire Intellectual Disability Tool
Kidderminster Curriculum: for children and adults with PMLD

### Orientation and attention

Orientation, 'the awareness of self in relation to one's surroundings, requires consistent and reliable integration of attention, perception, and memory' (Lezak et al, 2004: 337).

Questions relating to orientation of time, place and person may be asked in the context of collecting standard personal information during the process of test administration. They are also included in some memory tests. *Time orientation* involves knowing the date and time of day, and having a sense of time passing and the temporal continuity of events (e.g. *How long have you been living at* . . . ?). Difficulty in estimating the passing of time or anticipating the length of time before an event will occur in the future can contribute to behavioural problems. For example, a person may be told that their parents are going to visit the following Sunday, but have no way of understanding the length of time that this involves. As time goes by, they are likely to become increasingly agitated and frustrated. However, they may well be able to grasp a sequence of events taking place in time and represented pictorially and may therefore be helped by the use of a sequence strip.

*Orientation for place* involves awareness of current location, direction and distance. *Topographical orientation* involves the location of objects and places in space and memory for familiar routes. Disorientation may be a lifelong problem, or may arise in the context of dementia.

Problems with *attention* may involve deficits of *focused attention* (concentration); *sustained attention* (ability to track external events, or to track internal events, as in problem-solving); *divided attention* (i.e. ability to deal with more than one task at a time) or *alternating attention* (i.e. ability to shift focus between tasks). In the case of divided attention, deficits may reflect slowed processing speed (Lezak et al, 2004). Carer reports that clients lack concentration inevitably mask complex attentional issues and should always be explored further through observational assessment. Formal tests of attention tend to be too difficult for learning disabled people.

### Sensory processing

*Sensory impairment* and *sensory disorder* are under-recognised in people with learning disability. Up to date checks of sight and hearing should be requested before starting the cognitive assessment (see Chapter 9).

### Communication

Communication comprises *understanding, expression* and *pragmatics*. People who are able to understand language and express themselves verbally may be assessed using standardised tests. The focus of assessment may be grammatical, involving, for example, the extent to which the person understands and is able to use negative or passive constructions. But communication skills also involve understanding the nuances of communicative behaviour, custom and meaning that arise in diverse social situations. Examples are being able to maintain a normal rhythm of turntaking, take an appropriate interest in their conversational partner or keep discussion of a topic going. The *Manchester Pragmatics Profile* (Coupe O'Kane and Goldbart, 1998) provides a structured format for recording the kind of behaviours that the person shows in different social situations. Use of video material can be a helpful resource in making these observations.

In assessing less able people, it is important to understand the developmental stages of communicative abilities. In particular, the development of intentionality is a critical watershed in communication. The Revised Triple C: Checklist of Communication Competencies provides a structured format for assessing what stage of communication the adult has reached (Bloomberg et al, 2009).

For people functioning at a pre-intentional stage, Coupe O'Kane et al (1985) have designed the *Affective Communication Assessment*. This allows us to explore the person's idiosyncratic responses to a range of stimuli. How do they show they like something? Or dislike something? Or want to move? Their behaviours may just be reactive, but once carers interpret them as if they are communicative, then this may set the scene for the emergence of intentional communication.

In carrying out such an assessment it is important to bring together and share the information and understanding of all those who know the person well. *See What I Mean* (Grove et al, 2000) provides a structure for this, and can be used as a guide to decision making with and for people with PMLD.

In addition to assessing the individual's communicative abilities, it is important to assess their *communicative environment*. This includes the approach used by their communication partners in the various contexts in which they function (Bunning, 2009). Are they aware of the different ways in which the person communicates their likes and dislikes? Do they allow time for the person to respond? Do they use nonverbal forms of communication, such as signs, symbols and other visual aids? It has been found that staff consistently over-estimate the communication skills of people with learning disability. Many staff will tell you *'They understand everything I say'*, unaware of the way the person is using contextual cues to interpret the language. In addition, staff may fail to see that communication is two-way, and clients also need to be able to express themselves.

If a detailed communication assessment is needed, then referral should be made to a Speech and Language Therapist.

*Other tests:*

Communication Assessment Profile
Pre-Verbal Communication Schedule
British Picture Vocabulary Scale (for receptive language)
Vocabulary subtest from the WAIS (for expressive language) Test of Reception of Grammar Token Test

### Memory

There are several different memory functions, and each should be assessed separately, since the person is unlikely to function equally well in all areas. For example, it is common for people who are learning disabled to have a better memory for visual information than for verbal information.

- *Immediate memory* may be assessed using the Digit Span Forward subtest from the WAIS.
- *Working memory* refers to a person's ability to hold information in their mind whilst performing a mental operation on it (Lezak et al, 2004). It involves Executive Function as well as Attention and is of crucial importance in the performance of a wide range of real life tasks (see the case study in Webb and Whitaker, 2012). It may be assessed using the Digit Span Backward and Digit Span Sequencing subtests from the WAIS-IV.

- *Prospective memory* (memory for events in the future) also involves Executive Function and can be assessed using the 'appointment' subtest from the Rivermead Behavioural Memory Test (RBMT).
- *Declarative Memory* divides into *Semantic Memory* (delayed verbal memory and delayed visual memory); and *Episodic Memory* (for events/autobiographical memory).
- Tests of delayed verbal memory are the Story Recall test, e.g. from RBMT or BIRT Memory and Information Processing Battery (BMIPB); and the list learning test from the California Verbal Learning Test (CVLT).
- Tests of visual recognition and recall may be found in the RBMT, Middlesex Elderly Assessment of Memory Scale (MEAMS) and the BIRT. People will often approach visual memory tasks in a confused or fragmented manner that indicates possible executive dysfunction. This can be recorded by giving them different coloured pens at different stages in their drawing. Systems for qualitative scoring of the Rey Complex Figure Test are given in Lezak et al, 2004: 544 and 546.
- *Episodic* or *autobiographical memory* is best assessed in interview, by asking questions about recent events, for example '*Have you had a good morning? Did you go out? What did you do?*' It is important to be aware of answers that may represent semantic rather than episodic memory. For example, the person may tell you that they had cornflakes for breakfast because they know that is what they have every day rather than because they remember the event. Answers may be checked with carers.
- *Procedural memory* is involved in memory for everyday living activities, such as dressing. Though they are likely to have impaired autobiographical memory, people who are in the early stages of dementia may have relatively intact memory for practical procedures. It is important for carers to establish routines for personal care and domestic activities, so that these can become routine.

### Visual-spatial perception

This involves both *object* and *spatial perception*. Problems may arise in the eyes or within those parts of the brain that process visual input. Cortically based visual impairment will not be helped by wearing glasses. Tests of object perception are given in the Visual Object and Space Perception Scale (VOSP). A simpler alternative is given in the Middlesex Elderly Assessment of Memory Scale (MEAMS). The VOSP also includes tests of spatial perception.

New problems with visual perception may first be expressed in behavioural changes such as an uncharacteristic reluctance to go out, unwillingness to join in activities or loss of skills. For example, depth perception is often affected in dementia, resulting in people being hesitant to cross thresholds or go up and down stairs.

Where there are doubts about visual perception, the person should be referred for specialist assessment, which will cover areas such as visual field and acuity, colour vision and binocular coordination. However, within the limits of the everyday environment, it is possible to carry out a functional assessment of vision that can be helpful in directing carers as to how to input information to the person (see Chapter 9).

*Other tests:*

Drawing or copying tests, e.g. house, clock, square, star. [Scoring systems for drawings of a bicycle and a house are given in Lezak et al (2004: 552–553).]
Colour matching and space matching tasks
Vision for Doing
Rivermead Perceptual Assessment Battery
Object Assembly, Block Design and Matrix Reasoning subtests from the WAIS

### Praxis

Conditions such as impaired mobility and spasticity are sometimes tolerated in people with learning disability, whereas they would be questioned in others. *Praxis* refers to learned voluntary *fine* or *gross movement*. Control over movement depends both on primary motor skills such as muscle tone and coordination, as well as on brain function. In order to successfully carry out a movement, a person needs to:

i.    formulate an idea of the movements needed to achieve a goal, initiate activity, sequence and coordinate actions
ii.   carry out the movements
iii.  have proprioceptive feedback so that they can adjust their movements appropriately.

A person may lack ability in any of these three areas, giving rise to what are termed *ideational, constructional* and *kinetic apraxia*. The possibility of apraxia should be considered in relation to people described as 'clumsy', or with a diagnosis of dementia or Asperger Syndrome.

Deficits of spatial perception may be involved in constructional ability disorders, and this may be assessed using drawing tasks involving copying or free drawing. The Developmental Test of Visual Motor Integration involves copying 24 geometric figures, which are arranged in developmental order. Adult norms are given in Beery et al (2010). Competence in reproducing the Bender-Gestalt drawings may also provide information on developmental level. Performance on these and other drawings also reflects deterioration in Alzheimer's disease. Where movement is clearly impaired or diagnostic clarification is needed, consideration should be given to referral to a physiotherapist.

*Other tests:*

Western Aphasia Battery, Apraxia Scale
Luria Nebraska Motor Functions Scale

### Executive functions, concept formation and reasoning

These functions are neurologically distinct, with executive function being associated with the frontal lobes and concept formation and reasoning being attributes of the whole brain (Lezak et al, 2004). But in real life they tend to merge, and are usually assessed concurrently.

Executive functions, concept formation and reasoning are the 'higher order' abilities that serve to marshal all other abilities to serve the needs of the individual, enabling them to engage effectively in independent and purposeful behaviour. They involve the ability to think abstractly, reason logically, initiate activities, plan, organise, carry out purposeful action, respond flexibly and self-monitor. These abilities begin to develop during early childhood, and achieve maturity in late adolescence or the twenties. They are particularly problematic for people with learning disability, and are much misunderstood or neglected, even by other professionals. It is sometimes assumed, for example, that because a person is capable of washing themselves, cooking or shopping, they are capable of living independently. In fact, these abilities can only be made use of in the context of the executive functions of planning, initiation, organisation and self-monitoring. In other words, they refer to *how* or *whether* something is done, rather than *what* is done (Lezak et al, 2004). These and other executive functions all need separate assessment. A useful simple test of planning abilities is the Key Search Test from the Behavioural Assessment of Dysexecutive Syndrome (BADS). Free drawing can sometimes demonstrate perseveration.

Deficits of executive functions can be elusive on formal assessment, since the structured assessment procedure itself tends to compensate for the deficits. Indeed, even a person with quite severe deficits of executive function may perform at a normal level when they take part in a psychometric assessment. Sometimes, only real life descriptions of the person's functioning can give an idea of what their problems are. They may include impulsivity, rigidity, inability to initiate activities, self-monitor or show self-awareness.

*Some tests:*

Delis–Kaplan Executive Function Test
Weigl Colour Form Sorting Test
Similarities Letter–Number Sequencing subtest from the WAIS
Observation of test performance and drawings
Embedded Figures Test (for central coherence)
The Frontal Systems Behaviour Scale (FrSBe)
The carer interview from the BADS

### Social understanding

This includes *emotion recognition, theory of mind* (TOM), *empathy* and *understanding of social rules.* Deficits are most commonly associated with people with autistic spectrum disorder, though may be seen in other people with learning disability. Where a person presents with anger problems, this may be at least partly due to difficulties in emotion recognition, particularly in people who are more severely disabled.

TOM is the ability to attribute mental states to oneself and others and to understand that others' mental states may differ from one's own. It is acquired developmentally, with necessary pre-requisites including the understanding of others' intentions, perspective-taking and empathy. First-order TOM involves inferring the thoughts of another person. Second-order TOM involves reasoning about what another person would think about a third person's thoughts. Assessment should be directed towards trying to establish the aspects of TOM that are problematic for the person. A detailed discussion of such tests is given in Baron-Cohen (2001). A more recent development is the Conversational Assessment Tool (Lacey, 2012).

Impairment in TOM can make the world an unpredictable and frightening place, and may contribute to the person's apparent obsessionality. With environmental support, some people with autistic spectrum disorder are able to develop TOM skills as they progress into late childhood and adulthood.

*Other tests:*

Sally Ann Test (false-belief task)
Smarties Test (appearance–reality task)
John and Mary Ice Cream Story
Happé Strange Stories (understanding of misunderstanding, lies, metaphors, jokes, etc)
Dewey test of social reasoning
The Awareness of Social Inference Test
WAIS – Comprehension and Picture Arrangement subtests

### Educational abilities

*Some tests:*

Exam results
Schonell Reading Test (one-word reading)
Neale Analysis of Reading Test (reading and comprehension)
Name writing
Telling the time

## Dementia

The presence of dementia can only be established by comparing the person's performance pre- and post-morbidly. It is therefore good practice to carry out baseline dementia assessments on all people with Down's Syndrome aged 30 or over (see Aylward et al, 1997). Where dementia is already suspected, collecting the person's pre-morbid history provides a retrospective baseline. This can include a retrospective skills assessment.

*Some tests:*

CAMCOG-DS
Down's Syndrome Dementia Scale (DSDS)
Middlesex Elderly Assessment of Memory Scale (MEAMS)
Neuropsychological Assessment of Dementia in Adults with Intellectual Disabilities (NAID)
Severe Impairment Battery (SIB)

### Everyday living skills

We can usually find out about the person's ability to function in everyday life through observation and assessment. Formal assessment may be needed, for example, in the case of suspected dementia, in order to track changes over time. Choice of assessment tool depends partly on the person's level of ability.

*Some tests:*

Adaptive Behaviour Assessment System (ABAS-II)
Adaptive Behaviour Scales (ABS)
Vineland Adaptive Behaviour Scales, 2nd edition

### Interpretation and feeding back

Interpretation of the cognitive assessment is always tentative, taking into account other factors that may have contributed to test performance. These include the person's understanding of the test situation and test instructions; their level of motivation and distraction; sensory or motor factors that may have hampered test performance; medication effects; fatigue and anxiety.

In addition to formal reports to carers and referrers, the assessment result should be fed back to the person concerned in a format and language that is meaningful to them.

## Conclusions

Awareness of likely cognitive determinants of the person's functioning should permeate and inform the whole process of assessment and formulation, whether or not formal testing takes place. In people with extensive/pervasive support needs, it is more appropriate to use a developmental or criterion-referenced model than a deficit measurement model.

Cognitive impairments interact in complex ways with other factors. Understanding this can inform interventions at both individual and environmental levels. These may be designed to help the person to develop their skills, to scaffold their learning or to compensate for their impairment.

## Recommended reading

Kaufman A S and Lichtenberger E O (2006) *Assessing Adolescent and Adult Intelligence* (3rd edition) Hoboken, NJ: Wiley

Lezak M, Howieson D B and Loring D W (2004) *Neuropsychological Assessment* (4th edition) Oxford: Oxford University Press

# 12  The Attachment Domain

> ## Barbara
>
> Barbara is a lively, friendly, talented person. She knits, sews and makes beautiful greeting cards. Sometimes she is cheerful, greeting staff in the morning with a joke and even a song. But at other times a black mood suddenly descends on her. This can last an hour, a day or weeks at a time. Barbara has a diagnosis of Bi-Polar Disorder and has been taking medication for it for the last 15 years.
>
> It seems that Barbara's mood swings are often triggered by her perception that staff are spending more time with other residents than they are with her. Another trigger is Barbara's belief that staff are criticising her. The very long black moods seem to result from a series of such triggers.
>
> Barbara describes her father (now dead), as a nasty, angry man. When she was unable to do her arithmetic homework he would take off his shoe and beat her with it. Staff say that Barbara's mother, who is still alive, constantly undermines her with comments about her weight ('You take up too much space!'). When the psychologist asks staff how they think Barbara feels inside, one says 'empty'.

When a person comes to see us, they bring with them not just their presenting problems but their whole personal history. The nature of their relationship with their primary caregivers sets the scene for the rest of their lives. Since Bowlby put forward his early ideas on Attachment Theory in 1953, its significance has been increasingly recognised and it is now regarded as 'the basic approach for conceptualising child development' (Gilbert, 2005: 30).

People's early experiences result in them developing an internal working model, which 'includes a set of beliefs or expectations about others and the self . . . [that] help a child to make predictions about his or her parents' likely responses' (Dallos, 2006: 2). It is also an internal working model of themselves, telling them how worthwhile and lovable they are. Depending on this, children develop different strategies, both for coping with their own feelings, and for relating to others. These working models and associated strategies, are then applied to all future relationships (Bowlby, 1969).

## Secure attachment

Observations of parent/child interactions, as well as interviews with adults, suggest that there is a constellation of parental behaviours that results in the development of a securely attached child. These involve sensitivity and responsiveness to the child's needs, giving them a sense of '*attunement*', which is the experience 'of being deeply understood by the other, of feeling "felt" by the other' (Hughes, 2009: 1). One of the ways in which this is achieved is through the caregiver reflecting back to the child what they are feeling and how these feelings are related to external events. In this way, the sensitive caregiver helps the child to make sense of their feelings and to develop a sense of self (Mead, 1934). Also, through this unconditional acceptance by the caregiver the child experiences a sense of *validation*, that is, that their feelings make sense to others (Leahy, 2005). The child also begins to develop an understanding of their self and others as intentional beings (Fonagy et al, 1991). This is thought to be the foundation of theory of mind, empathy and secure attachment.

## Emotional regulation

'The infant, as Winnicott says, is all the time on the brink of unthinkable anxiety' (Giddens, 1991: 39). The interaction between the infant and their environment determines how well they learn to cope with that anxiety. According to Gilbert (2010) we possess three systems for emotional regulation. These systems are threat-focused; incentive-focused and affiliation-focused. Reflective, soothing and caring behaviour by a loving adult enables the development of the affiliation/safeness system. Children learn how to cope with feeling threatened or unsafe, and to regulate defensive emotions such as anger. By learning to internalise and use self-calming statements they also learn that their feelings can be brought under control (Leahy, 2005). They are able to explore their environment and develop qualities of compassion towards themselves and others.

## The securely attached adult

The securely attached child grows into the securely attached adult, with an effortless sense of their own identity, self-worth, relatedness and autonomy. Laing's description of ontological security seems apposite: they will experience their own being as 'real, alive, whole; as differentiated from the rest of the world . . . so clearly that [their] identity and autonomy are never in question; as a continuum in time; as having an inner consistency, substantiality, genuineness, and worth . . .' (Laing, 1960: 41).

On the other hand there are people who have suffered horrendous early attachment experiences but have nevertheless gone on to lead fulfilled adult lives. The literature on *resilience* suggests that we can understand this in terms of 'protective factors', particularly the existence of a supportive and stable adult relationship somewhere in their lives (Furman, 1998).

## Insecure attachment

If a child's relationship with their primary caregivers lacks moment-to-moment sensitivity and responsiveness, they are not able to develop a sense of security and safety. In the event of mishap, they cannot rely on a caregiver who would care for them, calm them down and restore them to equilibrium. They do not learn how to self-soothe and can be subject to incapacitating free-floating anxiety. They try to maintain safety by means of strategies such as hypervigilance, prolonged displays of stress and withdrawal. They lack the confidence necessary to explore their environment, with all the learning and development that results from this. They fail to develop a secure sense of self, and their personal relationships may either lack sensitivity or be over-sensitive towards the feelings of others. Instead of effective emotional regulation, they develop defensive strategies such as submission or aggression. Moreover, repeated activation of the threat system may lead to 'permanent changes in brain pathways' (Gilbert, 2005: 32).

### Morris

Morris has a diagnosis of Obsessive-Compulsive Disorder. His life is ruled by a ritualistic regime of checking doors, windows, taps, his dog's water bowl, his key and other things.

It is only when the psychologist has met Morris several times that he tells her about his fear of death. He goes to bed every night afraid that this will be his last. It seems the checking is a way of injecting a semblance of safety into a world that is full of threats.

Morris sees his parents regularly and there is no suggestion that his childhood has been overtly abusive. However, in time it becomes clear that their relationship with him is subtly rejecting and cruel. Morris spends much of his time trying to gain their favour, but nothing he does is ever right. Every meeting with his parents means a renewal of the pain of their disapproval and rejection.

Three forms of insecure attachment are traditionally recognised: Avoidant; Ambivalent/Anxious and Disorganised. The behaviour associated with each is seen in terms of a strategy for maintaining safety in the face of inadequate or inconsistent caregiving. However, where the caregiver is abusive they are themselves the source of threat and the child is faced with an insoluble dilemma (Walker, 2008). In this case, their behaviour will be erratic, disorganised and ineffective in helping them maintain safety. Such children are more likely to develop into adults who feel worthless, powerless and desperately lonely. Their early relationships act as templates for destructive relationships later in life (Steele, 2002).

Contemporary research has led to a more nuanced understanding of attachment theory, whilst not undermining its main tenets. It has been suggested that there other forms of attachment; that various attachment styles should be seen as dimensional rather than categorical attributes; that the child forms distinct attachment relationships with their two parents; that we all have the potential for multiple types of attachment and that attachment relationships may show different forms in different cultures (Gillath et al, 2005; Steele, 2002).

## Attachment in learning disability

People with learning disability are more likely to suffer from insecure attachment in early life (Clegg and Lansdall-Welfare, 1995; Schuengel et al, 2010). In later life they are more likely to have these experiences exacerbated by events and are less well-equipped to develop coping strategies (Fletcher, 2008; Janssen et al, 2002).

### *Early relationships*

As is the case with non-disabled children, parents bring to the relationship with their infant their own history of attachment relationships (Fonagy et al, 1991). Post-natal depression, perhaps more likely after the birth of a child with a disability, can also affect early bonding. In any case, establishing a bond with a learning disabled child can be a difficult process. Problems may involve issues such as the child's responsivity or ability to smile or to engage in mutual gaze. The child may not understand either means–ends relationships or object permanence, and 'lack the cognitive flexibility and planning skills necessary for developing a goal-directed partnership, in which parent and child coordinate each other's wishes and needs' (Janssen et al, 2002: 449). Delayed or unusual responses are likely to inhibit reciprocity and affect caregiving and play routines, diminishing the mutual enjoyment that would normally be expected. These problems are exacerbated where there are multiple impairments involving, for example, impaired mobility or vision. A study of pre-school children with Down's Syndrome found that the majority 'had not developed smoothly functioning secure base behaviour, even by toddlerhood and the preschool years' (Atkinson et al, 1999: 64).

It has been suggested that parents grieve the loss of their anticipated healthy child, and therefore have difficulty in coming to terms with their child's disability. Marvin and Planta (1996) found that mothers who have achieved resolution of the intrapsychic loss of the healthy children were more likely to have secure attachments with them. Fletcher (2008) found that 56 per cent of mothers she interviewed were still experiencing significant difficulties in resolving issues of loss and trauma a number of years after receiving their child's diagnosis. Their grief may be rekindled at key transitions in the child's life, when the child might be expected to move on to new challenges.

But to see this parent/child relationship solely in terms of grief is an over-simplification. More or less conscious feelings of loss, frustration and anger may be accompanied by a most profound love and devotion. These are the words of Domenica's mother, Mrs Monkton: 'it is hard to describe the love you have for a child who is handicapped. It is particularly intense. Your natural maternal protectiveness is much sharper. . . . I am always conscious of her aching vulnerability' (*Daily Mail* 4 November 2005, quoted in Cottis, 2009: 77).

Frances Young is a Christian minister and mother of Arthur, a child with profound disabilities.

> Community and corporateness are essential to human thriving and give us a sense of meaningfulness. . . . There are many passages in the epistles of St Paul which encourage this other perspective. The most obvious perhaps is his image of the church as the Body of Christ . . . it is about honouring the contributions made by others – even the weakest and least presentable. . . . It is too easy to imagine that the divine image is found in the rationality that distinguishes human beings from animals . . . we are the body of Christ, not as individuals but as a community. We are, most truly Christ's Body when, like St Francis we carry the stigmata. Corporately that means, when we are in solidarity with those who live with impairment.
>
> (Young, 2000: 4–5)

So parents' feelings about their disabled children are complex and varied, and the process of adaptation to their situation may form part of their own search for meaning in existence (Stolk and Kars, 2000). Parents' feelings are further complicated by the battle in which they often have to engage in order to ensure that their child's needs are met. Many parents shoulder an enormous and exhausting physical and emotional burden. It has been found that 60 per cent of parents of children and adults with profound and multiple learning disabilities spend more than ten hours a day on basic physical care (Mencap, 2001). These responsibilities can go on for decades, involving a prolonged physical intimacy, sometimes combined with a lurking terror relating to their child's survival.

As parents age, they also face the anxiety of their own failing health, and the impossibility of any other person or service filling the void that they will leave (Cottis, 2009, Chapter 5). It is often at this time that conversations start to take place about their child making a transition to alternative accommodation. Parents can then be torn between their wish to protect their child and what they regard as a moral imperative to foster their 'independence' (Alborz, 2003). This is particularly difficult if their adult child has substantial physical care needs or is not able to achieve independence in everyday living skills.

Support workers may see the parents as *'over-involved'*, *'over-protective'* or even, as I once heard *'cotton wool parents'*. Care managers may be frustrated at their impossible demands or their ambivalence when it comes to discussing alternative living arrangements. The person themselves may exhibit behaviours that oscillate between extreme dependence and frantic attempts at self-determination. We may find ourselves in the position of trying to make the feelings of the person and their parents intelligible to others who are professionally involved.

We also need to remain alive to the possible history of abuse by parents or other caregivers. Studies have found high, though variable, rates of child sexual abuse in people with learning disabilities (Lindsay et al, 2011). Turk and Brown (1993) found that in 95 per cent of cases the abuser was known to the survivor.

### Relationships in adult life

#### Cognitive function

Cognitively, people with learning disability are likely to be poorly equipped to find ways of countering the harmful effects of an insecure attachment history. They are also likely to have a poor understanding of their own experiences and their impact. Their adult experiences may add to these difficulties. Each new adult relationship serves as an arena within which early attachment patterns are played out and often reinforced.

#### Loss

As people they get older, family members die or move away and the person's opportunities for close relationships shrink. At the same time they may lack the resources they need in order to develop alternative relationships. Where people have suffered insecure attachment in relation to their parents, the loss of a grandparent or other close adult can be devastating. The effects of loss can be compounded by the change in lifestyle that often accompanies loss of a family member (Blackman, 2008). Once people enter the world of paid care, relationships are likely to be relatively superficial and transitory. Staff may move, or be moved on, at any time. People are thus exposed to repeated losses, anxiety and grief. Their 'hidden losses', and the nature of their grieving, are often poorly understood by carers.

*Relationships with paid carers*

Some staff are dedicated and caring, but relationships with others can be lacking in warmth, sensitivity and reciprocity. Carers bring to the relationship their own attachment experiences (Schuengel et al, 2010). They may struggle to interpret the person's attempts at communication, particularly when they are themselves tired, stressed or poorly trained. Studies have found that people are given very little opportunity to relate to staff, and when communication does take place, it fails to take account of the person's communication needs (Money, 2002).

From the carers' point of view, there can be confusion about the nature of their role. Is their relationship purely professional? Or are they friends? Or substitute family? Or a little of each of these? How is this perception affected by the service ethos, which may stress the importance of staff maintaining professional boundaries? And how does it reflect their own need to defend themselves against 'the unbearable reality of being unlovable?' (Sarah Boyd, personal communication, July 2012).

As a result of the poverty of their natural networks, many people express their need for belonging and relatedness in relation to their paid staff, and see them as friends (Clegg and Lansdall-Welfare, 1995). On the other hand the support staff may prefer to view themselves as facilitators to these individuals' friendships (Pockney, 2006). And even where the roles are blurred, this 'friendship' may lack the reciprocity and expectations of acceptable behaviour that form part of the usual cultural definition of friendship.

> Michelle . . . talked about her friendship with Susan in two 'languages'. The first is what I call the 'language of love', which Michelle used to express her love and affection for Susan. . . . Michelle used this language when she said that Susan and she were friends 'just like any other friends'.
>
> The other language is the 'language of work'. Michelle used this language when she talked about the work of the friendship . . . the language of work reflected the day-to-day reality of their friendship. This reality was different from the ideal in the literature and was characterized by many of the difficulties which Susan's disabilities brought to the friendship. . . . Some of these difficulties made [Michelle] feel insecure, frustrated and even scared. . . .
>
> (Traustadòttir, 2000: 126)

*Challenging behaviour*

A history of insecure attachment may be expressed in behavioural problems in adult life (Sterkenburg et al, 2008; De Schipper and Schuengel, 2010). Clegg and Lansdall-Welfare (1995) suggest that attachment theory could provide a clinically useful explanation for a range of behaviours that include: expressions of distress out of proportion to the triggering event; resistance to exploring the physical environment and being fixated on a professional or family worker. Clegg and Sheard (2002) found that 34 per cent of students were rated by staff as 'overinvesting in one or a few relationships which become a source of jealousy'. Other suggested signs of attachment problems include lacking normal sensitivity to social rewards (Sterkenburg et al, 2008); being clinging and demanding; hypervigilant; indiscriminately friendly; extremely sensitive to change and rejection and recklessly endangering themselves (Fletcher, 2008).

### Adult abuse and exploitation

Where the person has been subject to abuse as a child, they are likely to display disorganised attachment, with a range of psychological problems and challenging behaviours, including a profound sense of shame and self-disgust (Lloyd, 2009). The combination of impaired cognition and insecure attachment creates a toxic mix, rendering people extremely vulnerable to abuse or exploitation (Peckham, 2007). They may feel a desperate need for a close and affirming relationship, but lack the ability to negotiate and sustain this.

> Mary: 'I don't mind it, but not all the time, not all the time, like every night, because you get fed up . . . when I went out with T he wanted it morning, afternoon, tea time, every night.'
> Lynn: 'I haven't really got anybody that sticks with me long term. . . . Nobody's really interested in what I could say long term . . . nobody can be bothered. . . . A week, maybe two weeks . . . then they sling me in. I have really nobody I can turn to.'
> Maureen: 'They just say "come on, I need you" and they just pull you down and before you know where you are, they're at it. . . . They cover your mouth up somehow, they get a bit brutal and when it's over, you're left there . . .'.
>
> (McCarthy, 2000: 142)

Other factors contributing to this vulnerability are: a habit of acquiescence that makes it difficult for them to resist others' demands; a view of themselves as being worthless or unlovable; lack of coping skills and services that fail both to understand people's vulnerability and to provide them with the level of support they need to ensure their safety. Their emotional dysregulation and erratic, self-defeating behaviours may result in them being labelled as having 'Borderline Personality Disorder', 'Complex Post-traumatic Stress Disorder' or 'Bi-Polar Disorder'.

## Tracey

Tracey has twice been banned from the premises of the Community Team because of her aggressive behaviour. She has also been taken off her GP list for the same reason. She has multiple health problems, including Irritable Bowel Syndrome. She has been threatened with loss of her tenancy because of the unreasonable demands that she makes on her landlord and her abusive language.

Tracey suffered from physical, emotional and sexual abuse at the hands of her father. She says her mother had no interest in her. She was put into foster care, but later returned to her parents. She has a history of relationships with vulnerable men, all of which have ended with her feeling 'abandoned and devastated'.

Tracey is anxious, depressed and sometimes suicidal. She struggles with everyday tasks such as shopping. Most attempts to help her therapeutically have broken down. However, she did develop a stable relationship with the Consultant Psychiatrist. Unfortunately, this Psychiatrist left recently, and Tracey's behaviours have again escalated, threatening her exclusion from the service.

### *People with profound and multiple learning disabilities*

For people with profound and multiple learning disabilities, the development of secure attachment is likely to be an ongoing process. Attachment is the process through which the person not only learns to feel safe, but also learns about intentional communication, cause and effect, the nature of relationships and their own identity (Lacey and Ouvry, 1998). Moreover, it is only through the agency of others that the needs of people with profound disabilities can be anticipated and met. The development of secure relationships is therefore vital to their emotional and physical wellbeing as well as their cognitive development.

If they are referred to us on account of their challenging behaviour we need to ask questions such as: what is the person's developmental level? How are their emotional and physical needs being met? How do they communicate their needs, and how do others respond to that communication? What is the quality of their relationships with staff? Are there any 'special people' in their lives? Observation will give us some answers to our questions, but it is in relationship that we will really get to know the person. *Intensive Interaction* is based on the early attachment behaviours within the infant–caregiver relationship (Nind and Hewett, 2001). Ritualistic behaviours may be used as 'access points' through which the therapist can 'learn the language' of the person so that their needs can be better understood (Jefferies, 2009).

*A stress-attachment model of challenging behaviour*

Janssen et al (2002) suggest that people with severe and profound learning disability are both more vulnerable to stress and use less effective coping strategies: 'frequent and sustained stress may put the biological response systems of these individuals into an almost permanent state of activation' (Janssen et al, 2002: 447). This means that even a low level of stress may evoke challenging behaviour such as self-injury (which is also associated with high levels of cortisol). In terms of the Assault Cycle, we may see the person as habitually functioning half-way up the curve towards crisis. Use of this image can help to make people's sensitivity to low levels of stress understandable to carers (see Hewett, 2001: 152 and Chapter 7).

### Measures of attachment

Three types of attachment measures have been developed for use with people with learning disability: verbal, observational and physiological.

The Adult Attachment Interview (George et al, 1985) includes a number of open-ended questions relating to childhood relationships. It has been found appropriate for people with learning disabilities, with minimal adaptations (Deanna Gallichan, personal communication, 2012). For those less verbally able, Smith and McCarthy (1996) simply asked: *What would you do if you were feeling miserable/worried/frightened?*

For people with extensive/pervasive support needs, observational measures of attachment are the Secure Base Safe Haven Observation list (SBSHO; De Schipper and Schuengel, 2010) and the Manchester Attachment Scale (MAST) (Penketh and Hare, 2011). However, carer report may be problematic and structured video coding provides an alternative (Schuengel, 2011).

## A footnote: whatever happened to *loving*?

Bowlby's seminal work *Child Care and the Growth of Love* includes the word *love* in the title, and it ends by berating 'governments, social agencies and the public' for their 'lack of conviction' that 'mother-love in infancy and childhood is as important for mental health as are vitamins and proteins for physical health' (Bowlby, 1953: 182). However, the concept is largely missing from his later works, in which he describes 'attachment' as a behavioural system, the byproduct of the evolutionary need for physical safety (Bowlby, 1971). And if we look beyond Bowlby, it seems that *love* is a taboo topic. We tend to use proxy terms, such as *attachment, compassion, belonging* and *unconditional positive regard*. This is odd, given the centrality of love to our everyday lives and experience. Of course, the concept of love has been debased in popular culture, and in any case the word is imprecise and varied in its meaning. But by failing to consider the concept, we are in danger of shutting down discussion on a central feature of human existence.

It is through being loved that a child develops a sense of itself as a precious human being. We can observe this process in action in the mutual absorption, sensitivity and sheer delight that is expressed in interaction between parent and baby. And like the rest of us, people with learning disability need to experience such love, both as children and adults.

Fromm, in *The Art of Loving*, suggests that we all suffer from existential loneliness and spend our lives in a vain attempt to compensate for this pain. We find the meaning of love and life in *giving*, which involves care, responsibility, knowledge and respect for the integrity of the other (1985: 21). It seems to me that, where secure attachment develops, it is because the child has received this unconditional love from their parent or parent-substitute. What a precious gift! So mundane, and yet so priceless – an 'internal pot of gold' (Baron-Cohen, 2011: x).

## Conclusions

How many of us would be happy if we did not have sustaining and significant relationships? I suspect that one basic source of contentment for all of us is to know that there is at least one person in our lives who needs us and whom we need. . . . And yet how many of our friends who have been labelled retarded can say another person needs them? And how many know they are needed in an important way?

(Lovett, 1985: 138–39)

Sadly, these questions are as pertinent now as they were in 1985. In place of what should be an internal pot of gold there is just emptiness. Understanding people's attachment history and current needs can help us and others to make sense of their feelings and behaviour.

## Recommended reading

Cottis T (ed.) (2009) *Intellectual Disability, Trauma and Psychotherapy* London: Routledge
Dallos R (2006) *Attachment Narrative Therapy* Maidenhead: Open University Press
Gilbert P (2010) *The Compassionate Mind* London: Constable

# 13  The Ecological Domain

I use the term 'Ecological Domain' to represent the way in which the broader economic, political, social and cultural world impinges on the life of the person and so either facilitates or impedes their capacity for Agency and Access. The influence of the wider world is exerted through a variety of avenues, which include: social institutions such as education, employment and law; economic policies; the possible roles that are open to people and the resources that are made available to enable them to fulfil these roles; and the values, beliefs and practices, both of carers and of members of the wider society. These influences are all experienced by the individual at an interpersonal level. We as psychologists form a part of this at the same time as ourselves being individuals influenced by the ecological domain. These are two-way relationships.

The current economic, social and cultural influences have developed from a particular UK historical context, and are to a large extent understandable in terms of that context (see Figure 13.1, p. 149).

This chapter picks up from where Chapter 3 left off, with the White Paper *Valuing People* (DH, 2001a).

## *Valuing People* and *Valuing People Now*

*Valuing People* marked the culmination of decades of profound change in services for people with learning disabilities. Normalisation, the Disability Movement, the Social Model of Disability, the discourse of Human Rights and the voices of people with learning disability and their carers, all fed into this document. It expressed the principles of Rights, Independence, Choice and Inclusion for all. The personalisation agenda lay at the heart of mechanisms through which these grand aspirations were to be achieved. These included Person Centred Planning, Direct Payments and Advocacy.

*Valuing People* was consistent with broader government policies of the time, including a concern with social exclusion. This referred to 'a range of social, cultural, economic and political contexts to which people were not gaining access' (Hall, 2010: 49). *Valuing People* defined Inclusion more narrowly as: 'enabling people with learning disability to . . . make use of mainstream services and be fully included in the local community' (2001a: 24).

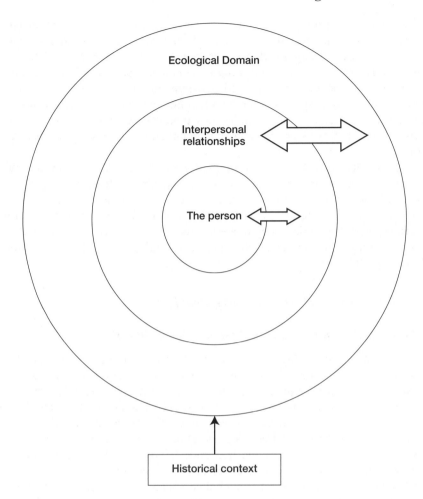

*Figure 13.1* The Ecological Domain in historical context.

Personalisation was also seen as being at the heart of the transformation of adult social care, particularly through the use of Direct Payments (DH, 2009a). *Valuing People* was said to mark the transition from the 'professional gift model' to the 'citizenship model' (Duffy, 2010).

*Valuing People* was initially introduced as a three-year strategy but it was extended beyond this. In 2009 *Valuing People Now* was published, again as a three year strategy. *Valuing People Now* (DH, 2009a) continued in the radical furrow ploughed by *Valuing People*. Its content was influenced by recent reports on the progress, or lack of progress, since *Valuing People*, including those by Michael (2008) on health; the Department of Health (2007) on personalisation; and the Joint Committee on Human Rights (2008). It emphasised the social model of disability and a Human Rights-based approach, and proposed a cross-governmental strategy, which included 'a significant expansion of employment opportunities' (2001a: 15); 'designing and delivering public services and support which meet people's individual needs' 2001a: 2); improved healthcare; a renewed commitment to personalisation and action on hate crime. It looked for 'improved outcomes in terms of social inclusion, empowerment and equality' (2001a: 14). Funding was transferred from the Department of Health to Local Authorities, though it was not ring-fenced (Pitt, 2010). And in 2011, following a change in government, the project was shut down.

Implementation of *Valuing People* and *Valuing People Now* was erratic and in some respects problematic. Similarly, the Consultation Report on *The Same as You?* found that though progress had been set in motion, it was variable (Scottish Government, 2012). Though the portents for this lie partly within learning disability policy, they relate to broader themes. Here I will discuss them in terms of the political, economic, social and intellectual context in the UK since 2001.

## Post-2001: the context of *Valuing People*

### *The political context: neo-liberalism and commodification*

In the post-war years there was consensus around the need to temper the operation of the market by means of government regulation and policies designed to reduce inequality and deprivation. But more recently we have witnessed the steady rise to ascendance of neo-liberalism. This has been defined as the theory that human wellbeing can best be furthered through individual entrepreneurial freedoms and skills, supported by strong private property rights, free markets and free trade (Harvey, 2005). Neo-liberalism has been accompanied by globalisation and increased concentration of wealth and power in the hands of multinational companies. Alongside this there has been the demise of belief in the state as a legitimate agent of wealth production and distribution; the increasing influence of the media, including advertising; the rise of new technologies and the near-obliteration of value systems that might challenge the hegemony of the market.

A market economy rewards those who excel within it and devalues those who are not in a position to sell their labour. Consequences have been increased inequality, an individualistic approach to social policy and a creeping commodification in both public and personal life. *Commodification* refers to the objectification and assignment of a monetary value to people and processes not previously seen in these terms. This can include time, commitment and human relations (Kagan and Burton, 2001). People are judged by their economic worth, or by their ability to live without consuming scarce social resources. Official rhetoric has returned to the Victorian constructs of the 'deserving' and the 'undeserving' poor, placing the responsibility for deprivation firmly in the hands of the people who suffer from it. This justifies policies which focus on employment, even for the severely impaired, and punitive cuts to social and welfare benefits. Consistent underfunding of services appears to be due not just to ignorance or scarce resources, but also to lack of political will.

## *The economic context: inequality and resource starvation*

In 2010 the chief executive of an umbrella group for more than 400 learning disability providers, said £1 billion would be needed to make *Valuing People Now* a reality (Lombard, 2009). Instead, services have been chronically under-funded. The funding attached to *Valuing People* was derisory (Baum and Webb, 2002), and no new funding at all was made available for *Valuing People Now*. In 2010, the Independent Living Fund was closed to new applications (Pitt, 2010).

In July 2011 the National Valuing Families Forum (NVFF) was asked to collect information on how spending cuts were affecting families of people with learning disability in England. They reported on seven areas in which families were affected, including cuts to levels of support, preventative services, staff and staff training and the voluntary sector. The Minister responded that he was disappointed that the NVFF members could not provide examples of good practice, and sent them off to try again (Minutes of the Learning Disability Programme Board Meeting, 2011).

Wood and Emerson (2005) define poverty in terms of the person's inability to share in the typical lifestyles of the society to which they belong because of their lack of resources. There is a close association between poverty and disability. In other words, the poorer you are, the greater the risk that you will suffer disability, and the more severe that disability is likely to be (Emerson et al, 2009). Emerson et al suggest the need for a number of measures to reduce inequality, including a significant increase in Disability Living Allowance (now being cut) and support to cover the disability-related costs borne by families. Instead, there has been a trend towards increasing inequality in the distribution of income (Wilkinson and Pickett, 2010). This has inevitably been reflected in resources available to people with learning disability, and their consequent quality of life, including physical and mental health. The sad consequences of this are illustrated in the case studies given by Simpson and Price (2009). Providing more 'choice' through personal budgets will do nothing to address this underlying deficit in resources.

Person Centred Planning was seen as central to the delivery of *Valuing People*, since it provided an assessment based on what people wanted out of their lives, rather than on professional preconceptions. However, the tool through which decisions are made and scarce resources are allocated is not Person Centred Planning but care management, implementing the decisions on resource allocation made by Commissioners. Even where Person Centred Plans are made, implementation may fail, resulting in concern at their 'debasement' (Osgood, 2005: 59).

An additional effect of the squeeze on resources has been the tightening of eligibility criteria. 'Mild' learning disability has been equated with 'mild' problems, with people deemed to be in this category increasingly being thrown on their own resources; and those who are potentially eligible have to prove ever-higher levels of risk in order to receive social services.

### The social context: values, attitudes and stigmatisation

When I meet support workers and the people they support, I am often impressed by the respect they show for the person, and the conscientious and sympathetic way in which they listen, encourage and try to ensure that the person's voice is heard. In this respect there has been a sea change in the quality of many services. However, this is not universal. Shortcomings range from the subtle abuse of institutional practices to the flagrant abuse of physical violence. Abuse within services did not come to an end with the closure of the large institutions, as the investigation into Winterbourne View demonstrates (CQC, 2011).

Widespread abuse suggests systemic failures, which have been found to include an authoritarian management style, staff shortages and stress, service and client isolation and dehumanising beliefs and processes (White et al, 2003).

But this issue goes beyond service delivery to more general social perceptions. Commodification sets the scene for a more general devaluation of people, which may be manifest in discrimination, stigmatisation and even abuse. 'A new harshness toward minorities has developed' (Kagan and Burton, 2001: 3). If people are seen as having low market value they may thereby be devalued in their social lives and defined as 'other'. People can maintain their own intact sense of self by distancing themselves from others and vilifying them (see Goodley, 2011). This process echoes, and perhaps re-awakens, historical attitudes towards people with learning disabilities.

'Othering' may be expressed in stigmatisation:

> Stigma arises when a person differs from dominant social norms on a particular dimension, and is negatively evaluated by others. Consequently, the person's whole identity is defined by that dimension and the person is dehumanized, to a degree, by those who hold such views.
>
> (Jahoda and Markova, 2004: 719)

Stigmatisation forms one of the roots of abuse. In an extensive survey carried out by Mencap, 88 per cent of people interviewed said that they had been 'bullied' during the previous year. This bullying included: 'kicking, biting, name-calling, . . . stealing . . . hair-pulling, throwing stones, spitting, being beaten up . . .' (Mencap, 1999: 2). A survey in Scotland found that 20 per cent of respondents had been attacked at least once a week (Sin et al, 2009). Such abuse has now received official recognition under the rubric of 'hate crime'. It sometimes involves horrendous violence, as in the shocking murders of

Steven Hoskin (in 2006), Brent Martin (in 2007) and Michael Gilbert (in 2011). The bare statistics fail to convey the terrible suffering behind these events. Fiona Pilkington killed herself and her daughter because they were unable to tolerate the prolonged bullying they had endured.

The Criminal Justice Act 2003 allows for sentences to be increased for disablist hate crimes, and in Scotland the Offences (Aggravation by Prejudice) Bill, 2009 recognises hate crimes based on disability (Sin et al, 2009). The *No Secrets* protection guidelines give social care agencies in England and Wales the lead in responding to crimes against vulnerable people (Department of Health and Home Office, 2000). The Home Office has also produced Good Practice Guidance on tackling hate crime (Home Office Violent Crime Unit, 2008). The Disability Equality Duty, introduced in 2006, places a legal duty on public sector bodies to promote disability equality and eliminate harassment (Sin et al, 2009). However, GPs, as independent practitioners, are exempt from this, and other public bodies are largely ignorant about it (Joint Committee on Human Rights, 2008). Prosecutors are described as being 'still in the foothills' when it comes to prosecuting disability hate crime (Crown Prosecution Service, 2011: 1).

And as inequality increases, so does economic and social deprivation, and this is fertile ground for scapegoating and stigmatisation. Location 'in the community' in areas where rents are relatively low can render people more visible and vulnerable (Sin et al, 2009).

## The Thompson family

The large Thompson family live on an estate comprised mainly of social housing. At least two family members are learning disabled, though neither is recognised as such by Social Services.

Sandy, aged 17, was raped by a 'friend'. She suffers from PTSD and is unable to leave the house alone. The police have decided they are unable to prosecute. The family of the boy who assaulted her have subjected the Thompson family to a sustained campaign of harassment for the past two years. This includes throwing missiles at the house, pushing used condoms through the letterbox and shouting abuse and threats at anyone who leaves the house.

A policewoman has now been appointed to deal with hate crime. She provides an easy point of access for the Thompsons, and as a result of her work ASBOS have been issued to the offenders. She attends a meeting organised by the psychologist at which working relationships are set up between her, the agencies for social housing, carer support and the CTPLD. Mrs Thompson says how relieved she feels to be listened to and to see that her problems are being addressed.

Women may be particularly vulnerable to stigmatisation and abuse (Brown, 2004), and this can be exacerbated by inadequate levels of support.

> A lonely pensioner has been jailed for having sex with an autistic woman who, because of her condition, was unable to refuse. . . . He forced her to strip and took intimate pictures on her mobile phone before carrying out a sex act. . . . He was a complete stranger, more than three times her age, who had met her at a bus stop just minutes earlier. . . . The woman has an IQ of 60, the communication skills of a three-year old. . . .
>
> (*North Devon Journal* 10 May2012)

People's problems are also compounded when they fail to conform to societal norms for reasons other than their learning disability, for example age, ethnic origin, social class, religion or sexuality (Sin et al, 2009).

---

### Trudine

Trudine was born as a boy, but is now seeking gender reassignment. She wears women's clothes and make-up, but her attempts to pass as a woman result in an appearance that is often bizarre. Trudine has no friends, and is estranged from her parents. Recently she tried to re-establish contact with her brother and his two children. Her brother's new partner Tracey started swearing at Trudine, saying she is a freak and pushing her out of the house. Trudine is devastated at losing contact, particularly with her niece and nephew. She says there is no-one in the world who loves her.

---

Stigmatisation, discrimination and hate crime can all have a devastating effect on psychological wellbeing (Emerson et al, 2011). 'My wife and I were completely terrified. At one point I was going to slit my wrists because I couldn't take it any more' (Sin et al, 2009: 44). In the consulting room their feelings may be expressed in depression, anger, denial or grandiose self-belief.

### *The intellectual context: individualisation*

Individualisation has been described as 'the key site of understanding for the aetiology of disablism' (Goodley, 2011: 68). Clinical Psychology has to some extent been complicit in this process, with its emphasis on individualistic models of explanation and intervention. In both Clinical Psychology and government policy, there is a vogue for cognitive therapy, which conveniently disregards the material and social conditions of people's lives. '*Happiness*' is intrapsychic. This has been linked with a diagnostic model, so that specified conditions are seen as needing standard designated therapies to which a price tag can easily be attached. Government policies and funding allocations for both services and research reinforce this emphasis.

With the tendency towards individualisation, earlier debates about the worth of individual lives have resurfaced, and the ugly spectre of eugenics has again reared its head.

> I love my brothers. . . . Despite my love for them, I can think of many ways in which my life has been adversely affected, not by my brothers, but by their disability. I think my life would be more enriched if I could hold a conversation with my brothers; if I could share more in their lives, and they in mine; if I could see them becoming independent; if they could take pride in the achievements of their nieces and nephew . . .
>
> (Carmichael, 2003: 507)

In this heartfelt article, Carmichael makes a strong case for the availability of 'freedom of choice' in pre-natal genetic testing. However, there is also a body of thought that 'choice' should not be considered apart from its broader social and cultural context (Holland and Clare, 2003). This context includes the modern myth of the individual as the embodiment of beauty and perfection, and the scientific means that hold the promise of the myth being achieved (Fitzgerald, 1998). One might add to this the awareness that adequate resources will not be made available to meet the needs of an unborn child with an impairment. In this context, rather than choosing to 'embrace and care' for their unborn child, potential parents can now choose not to give birth to them. 'Freedom of choice . . . masks deeper cultural influences which actually shape our choice' (Fitzgerald, 1998: 6).

## The implementation of *Valuing People*

*Valuing People* and *Valuing People Now* both emphasised the fact that structural, top-down change would be necessary to achieve the aspirations of Rights, Independence, Choice and Inclusion. But implementation has become increasingly individualistic. This is reflected in policies that tend to emphasise making good individual deficits and ignore the quality of people's relationships. It seems that 'Independence' is valued partly because it fits in with the model of the economically self-sufficient employee and consumer.

### *The scope of 'Inclusion'*

Emerson et al (2009) suggest that social exclusion encompasses restriction on participation in four areas: consumption; production; political and civic engagement and social interaction. They point out that people with disabilities are at significantly higher risk of exclusion in all these areas. However, the interpretation of social inclusion has increasingly narrowed, influenced by the concept of citizenship, which is seen as a status to be earnt through being in paid employment and living independently; 'standards and expectations [that] are very difficult, if not impossible, for many people with intellectual disabilities to reach' (Hall, 2010: 51). The aim of *Valuing Employment Now* (2009b) was to reduce the gap in employment rates between people with learning disabilities and people with disabilities in general, but in 2009/10 only 6.1 per cent of adults were in paid employment, and most of these people were working part-time (Emerson et al, 2010).

Since employment is the main route out of poverty and social deprivation, it is understandable that this is seen as a priority for people with learning disability. However, the emphasis on employment needs to be accompanied by appropriate support. Instead, 'significant impairments . . . [are] glossed over, making the real difficulties in providing supports to enable inclusion, autonomy, good health, meaningful activity and acceptance appear insignificant . . . and thereby not requiring substantial additional investment' (Burton and Kagan, 2006: 305). Where people are pressurised into the open employment market, without adequate support, the effects can be catastrophic.

---

### Hugh

Hugh is aged 20 and has been diagnosed as having autistic spectrum disorder. In order to claim benefits he has been told that he has to sign on at the Job Centre, and complete a certain number of job applications each week.

At home, Hugh's mother completes his forms. He is optimistic about his chances of success and is offered an interview every now and again. The interview is usually disastrous, but eventually Hugh is offered a job as a waiter. He is thrilled. But in the café Hugh is unable to follow the rules he is given, and sees no reason why he should. In less than a week he is fired for shouting at a customer.

Hugh is devastated at losing his job and becomes depressed. He spends the next month sitting on the settee watching TV, not washing, and using his computer to make contact with an obscure religious sect.

Hugh's mother contacts the psychologist. She is distraught. Hugh has become aggressive towards her, and has started attending meetings of the sect. She is concerned for his safety.

---

## The quality of relationships

Hall suggests that Inclusion has been implemented in such a way as to ignore the importance of supportive relationships, or 'Belonging' (Hall, 2005). This goes beyond physical integration, employment or independent living 'in the community'. Some people are locked into invasive social situations in which the absence of control and privacy co-exists paradoxically with an absence of close and meaningful relationships. Others struggle to survive semi-independently and suffer from excruciating loneliness.

In service delivery, 'independence' may be valued above the person's need for closeness and emotional security. This can be expressed in the institutional culture and management systems, 'failing to reward the positive contribution that sensitive, affectively attuned caregiving makes to the wellbeing of persons with disabilities' (Schuengel et al, 2010: 38). This can be a concern for parents. Clegg et al carried out a narrative analysis on interviews with 28 young people leaving specialist schools and their parents. They concluded that parents/carers were 'invoking a different moral horizon which makes social relationships and promoting a sense of belonging primary rather than secondary' (2008: 92).

Finding employment does not guarantee an experience of belonging. 'People with intellectual disabilities are more likely to be in low-paid, low status jobs, and often experience neglect and abuse from their employers and fellow employees' (Hall, 2010: 50). People may prefer to eschew the world of employment in favour of 'new spaces of inclusion' or 'oases . . . where some of those who cannot achieve standard norms of inclusion can gather, share experiences, gain support, be "safe" and crucially be able to be "normal" within an accepting environment' (Hall, 2010: 51). Hall gives the example of arts projects in Edinburgh. 'To achieve belonging is much more than being socially included. . . . To belong is to feel attached, to feel valued, and to have a sense of insiderness and proximity to "majority" people, activities, networks and spaces' (Hall, 2010: 56). This may be especially important for people with learning disability, who are likely to have a precarious sense of identity (Reinders, 1997).

## Assessing the Ecological Domain

Political, social and economic issues may seem well beyond our normal range of interest as psychologists. Nevertheless, they all have an impact on our clients' lives, and we need include them during our assessments (see Burton and Kagan, 2008). Questions we may want to ask include those given below.

- What are the national policies that affect this person's wellbeing? How are they translated into local policies? And how are these local policies implemented?
- What is the philosophy of the service that supports the person? What is the agency's management style? How are support plans developed?
- How are decisions made by, with or for the person? Who holds the power or authority in their social world?
- Has the person been subject to bullying the past, and is this a problem now? How do they get on with their neighbours? How do the person's feelings about themselves reflect stigmatising experiences?

- How does the person spend their time? To what extent do they use mainstream services? How much of their days and evenings do they spend alone at home?
- What are the person's sources of income? Is their income adequate to meet their needs? If they are working, what is the quality of their work relationships? How are they supported to fulfil their work role?
- What impact do the services the person receives have on their need for Belonging?

It is in the minutiae of social interactions that relationships are facilitated or otherwise and the person is thereby empowered. This also needs to be a focus of our assessment.

Rapley used Conversation Analysis to identify three patterns of staff behaviour, two of which excluded people in decision making and reinforced inequality in relationships (Rapley, 2004). Williams (2011) provides an introduction to the tools of Conversation Analysis, which include terms such as 'interactional right'; 'turn allocation points'; 'interpretative repertoire' and 'joint accomplishment'. These are used to analyse issues of empowerment, friendship, self-advocacy and identity.

But what matters is not just how people present themselves in conversation, but what the outcome is in terms of decision-making. Pilnick et al (2010) carried out a Conversation Analysis of formal meetings held at the time of people's transition from child to adult services. Despite their concern during these meetings to empower these young adults, there was a consistent failure to achieve this, due to what might be seen as a failure of scaffolding. This involved, for example, lack of preparation for the meeting, lack of clarity in the questioner and discounting of the person's response.

## Conclusion: beyond Inclusion and Independence?

Inclusion and Independence have been the dominant cultural imperative of the last 50 years for people with learning disability. This has come in different guises: '*de-institutionalisation*'; '*community care*'; '*normalisation*' and, a current favourite, '*user involvement*'. But since 2001 the discourse of humanism and human rights has been pitted against the counter-discourse of individualisation and the market.

It seems we have moved into a less benign and less ethically-driven era. The *Valuing People* project has now been shut down. Financial constraints, fear and marketable value are starting to define relationships, and this is reflected in learning disability services. Despite decades of progressive discourse, people are still more likely to suffer deprivation, unemployment, poor health, abuse, neglect and exclusion from mainstream social spaces.

The ideal of Independence has never been either realistic or desirable. We are all *interdependent* (Carnaby, 1998). And the recognition of people's need for Belonging requires action at a social as well as an individual level. Without this, people will continue to suffer from social devaluation, existing in 'asylums as without walls', with 'continuing unassuaged need' (Dear and Wolch, 1987; Heard, 1982).

## Recommended reading

DH (2009a) *Valuing People Now: The Delivery Plan* London: Department of Health
Kagan C, Burton M, Ducket P, Lawthom R and Siddiquee A (2011) *Critical Community Psychology* Chichester: BPS Blackwell
Williams V (2011) *Disability and Discourse* Chichester: Wiley-Blackwell

# 14　The Inner World

This book is based on the premise that, when people with learning disability fail to meet their needs, through a failure of either Agency or Access (or both), then psychological distress will ensue. In order to begin to understand this distress, and its roots, we need to find ways of exploring the Inner World of the person.

> I want to live as ordinary people do, having my own flat and my own postbox with my name, Janka Provazniková on the door as well as on the ring. If it is possible to manage it, even if I am not married, it would make me very happy. . . . Every day Brano and I would meet in our little flat and enjoy love and joy. We still love each other and if we were not disabled we would marry and live as other people do.
>
> (Janka Hanková, 2000: 60)

A psychologist assessing Janka might translate her experience into clinical language. Maybe she is 'depressed', or 'frustrated'; maybe she wants more 'independence' or a 'relationship'. Such descriptions fail to convey the quality and depth of her feelings, or the complexity of her history and personality. In trying to understand another person we set ourselves a task that is humbling in its enormity. And this is much more the case when the other person has difficulty in expressing their thoughts and feelings. In this chapter I will discuss the various aspects of the Inner World that we need to bear in mind and some of the methods we might want to use to help our understanding.

## Sense of self

> Next to the road, in the field, on a little hill, there is a nice flower. It stands there in the rain, the sweltering heat and in the hot sun, all night and all day. It's got nice light-blue flowers. It looks like a blue-eyed woman, holding a toddler in her arms and waiting for her husband. They call this flower, 'chicory'. I'm chicory too. . . . Healthy people are busy and not full of trouble. And they are free. But I've been waiting and waiting. I'm chicory forever.
>
> (Taimara Kainova, 2000: 29–30)

In the case of both Taimara and Janka there is a sense of yearning, an ongoing and painful lack of fulfilment. This might lead us to wonder how they came to see themselves in this way, to have certain dreams or aspirations, and to have the conviction that these dreams will remain unfulfilled.

A child's sense of self develops in and through their relationship with the primary caregivers. This is the 'looking glass self' of Cooley (1902); the self as seen through the other's eyes. Thus, the self becomes both 'I' and 'me', subject and object. This is the foundation of the self-reflective adult. In addition, through the actions, feelings and words of 'significant others' the child assimilates the views of the wider society, the 'generalised other' (Mead, 1934).

According to Berne, the child also assimilates their life script as someone lovable or not, OK or not OK; as someone who can function as an Adult, or who is condemned to be forever locked in the historical straitjacket of Parent or Child (see Stewart and Joines, 1987). This terminology has particular resonance in the field of learning disability, where people often struggle to achieve adult status.

When a person's experiences with the primary caregivers fail to engender a coherent sense of identity, their adult self may be fractured; a metaphorical 'community of selves' (Mair, 1977). These selves act inconsistently and sometimes in conflict with each other (Brown and Marchant, 2011). Such people are often labelled as having Borderline Personality Disorder. Their erratic connection with services makes them difficult to help, and can result in their exclusion, even where they are at risk of serious harm.

Erickson identified adolescence as the time when a young person develops 'an accrued confidence [in] the inner sameness and continuity of [their] meaning for others' (Erickson, 1984: 235). At this time the peer group becomes central to the person's identity, with membership being a defence against role confusion. Their experiences help them to construct the unique nature and meaning of attributes such as age, gender, family relationships, sexuality, health and abilities (MacIntyre, 2007: 217). But even such fundamental attributes may be beyond the understanding of people with learning disability, and the struggle to establish a sense of identity may extend well into adulthood. Carers may be ignorant of their history and of the importance of helping to reinforce their sense of identity.

## Rhys

The psychologist is carrying out a baseline dementia assessment

| Psychologist: | Can you tell me your name? |
|---|---|
| Rhys: | Rhys |
| Psychologist: | That's an unusual name |
| Rhys: | It's Welsh |
| Psychologist (surprised): | Are you Welsh? |
| Rhys (emphatically): | **Through and through!** |

This aspect of Rhys's identity, which was so important to him, was unknown to the carers who had lived with him for several years.

The person's sense of self refers not only to the question '*Who am I?*' but to the question '*How good am I?*' In other words, it has an evaluative aspect. The person's feelings of self-worth, self-confidence and self-efficacy all reflect both their personal history and their perceptions of the judgements made by others. Feelings of low self-worth are likely to be expressed in the person's perceptions of events, their feelings, behaviour and relationships.

## Personal narrative

The person's biography or history is the material out of which the person's Inner World is constructed. Some of the problems people face can be traced to their cognitive limitations, leading to cumulative negative experience that constantly reinforce their low self-esteem. A learning disabled baby may be relatively uncommunicative, and this can adversely affect the growth of secure attachment. As children they may witness being overtaken, cognitively, physically and socially, by younger siblings. At school they may be bullied and experience repeated academic failure. As adolescents they may see their siblings developing social lives beyond the family, and be unable to do this themselves. As adults, they may struggle to form friendships (Arthur, 2003). They may see others of their age move away from home, pursue careers, marry and have children, and be unable to do any of these things themselves. Throughout their lives, they may be aware of their parents' sadness on their behalf. They are also likely to experience a series of losses: loss of grand-parents, parents and support staff; possible loss of a series of homes and maybe loss of health. There is little compensation for these losses in terms of current relationships and activities. And all this is in the context of cognitive impair-ment that makes finding solutions or ways of accommodating to these difficulties very much more difficult than it would be for other people.

As people mature, they are likely to become increasingly aware of pressure to look a certain way, to achieve financial success, to have relationships, to travel independently and so on. Failure to achieve cultural imperatives may result in exclusion, stigmatisation and a 'spoiled identity' (Goffman, 1963). On the other hand, many people with learning disabilities lead happy and fulfilled lives. Focus on their experience in terms of learning disability may unwittingly serve to reinforce their 'deviancy career', according to which the person's perceived identity becomes synonymous with the way they are perceived as being different (O'Brien and Tyne, 1981).

It has been found that people have various strategies for dealing with stigmatisation. These include '*passing*', or attempting to survive as 'normal'; placing value on non-stigmatising personal characteristics and distancing themselves from others seen as more disabled and from stigmatising services ('downward social comparison') (see Jahoda and Markova, 2004). The strategy used by other stigmatised groups, of asserting their difference in a positive way, is also now being adopted by some people with the label of autistic spectrum disorder, based on research that emphasises difference rather than deficit (e.g. Baron-Cohen, 2000; Happé, 1999; Rudy, 2010).

## Needs

When people's needs are met, they are able to lead happy and fulfilled lives, whereas unmet needs result in psychological distress and disordered behaviour. People with learning disability have particular difficulty in meeting their basic needs for safety, autonomy and belonging. Services privilege 'independence', often without putting the structures in place to allow this to be achieved. This can result in repeated experience of failure, which is likely to engender low self-esteem and a sense of learned helplessness (Reed, 1997). Both the fear that arises from physical threat and the loneliness that arises from isolation can have a devastating impact.

## Feelings and thoughts

Troubled biographies and unmet needs are reflected in psychological problems that include depression, anxiety, psychosis and eating disorders (Dagnan and Wearing, 2004; Jahoda et al, 2006). But it may be hard for the person to express their feelings verbally. Their emotional vocabulary is likely to be impoverished. They may use one word to describe all positive or negative emotions, e.g. 'happy' or 'awful'. Or they may misunderstand the meaning of some emotional labels. Sadness can be submerged in the wish to please carers, and pain may be diverted into anger. Carers may, with the best of intentions, have inadvertently taught the person that sadness is unacceptable (Robbins and Hall, 2003). However, after even a short period of therapy, they may take on board the message that their feelings are legitimate.

### Alex

Alex was referred for his aggressive behaviour and it transpired that he was suffering from multiple bereavements.

| | |
|---|---|
| Psychologist: | What do you remember about your Auntie Emily? |
| Alex: | Having tea in the garden |
| Psychologist: | Can you tell me any more about that? |
| Alex: | Jam doughnuts . . . mmm . . . lovely |
| Psychologist (later): | When you think about tea in the garden with Auntie Emily, how do you feel? |
| Alex: | Unhappy |
| Support Worker: | But you still have tea in the garden with the guys |
| Alex: | (turning to him, indignant voice)<br>We're talking about my family now! |

The person's awareness of their feelings is linked with their capacity for emotional regulation, and their subjective experience of this, which may involve feeling out of control, helpless, depressed and ashamed.

Thoughts are likely to be even more inaccessible than feelings. Studies of Cognitive Therapy have found that people struggle to identify their thoughts and also find it difficult to see the connections between events, beliefs, feelings and behaviour (Bruce et al, 2010). The problems are multiplied where people have little or no means of verbal expression.

## Sense of meaning

In 1959 Frankl described the way in which a profound sense of meaning helped him to survive the horrors of a concentration camp. The issue of meaning has now entered (or rather re-entered) clinical psychology through positive psychology.

Seligman (2003: 127) identifies three desirable lives: the *pleasant life*, which is about the pursuit of positive emotions; the *good life*, which is about being engaged in gratifying activities and the *meaningful life*, which is about 'the use of your strengths and virtues in the service of something much larger than you are'.

> We talk about God sometimes. I used to want to see God. I worried I couldn't find him. He is difficult to see. He doesn't answer questions like other people do. Hard to understand. Lots of questions inside me. I think about God. It is important to talk about God, and also Jesus.
>
> (Jenny and Kristjana Kristiansen, 2000a: 114)

Reinders (2000) has explored the issue of meaning in relation to people with learning disability. He suggests an interpretation of meaning that is relational, contextual and involves a sense of what is given rather than what is found. Simon (2004), working with a child with Asperger Syndrome, used their special interest as a meaningful system that could be used metaphorically with the family.

Our approach towards helping people with learning disabilities can be superficial. We often try to find out what things they enjoy doing, but how often do we attempt to find out what they find important and meaningful in their lives? And how often do we help them to articulate this sense? Meaning-making, whether through religion or otherwise, is an important determinant of psychological wellbeing (Peden, 2012).

> Aslaug works at a restaurant in a hotel in a small city. When asked what she likes best about her job, Aslaug says loud and clear, 'I love being in this beautiful room. Most pretty place I have seen. So many beautiful things. It's why I love my job. Being in this room'. Aslaug has spent most of her life in a rather barren institution and told me, 'I never saw

nice things. . . . Now I am here, in this room . . . I like the candles and the glasses best'.

(Kristiansen, 2000b: 189)

What gives meaning to the person's life? Is it, as with Aslaug, a sense of beauty and wonder? Is it their close relationships? Or their relationship with God? Or music? Or their need to be constantly setting themselves a challenge? Or their love of their pets? Or their creativity? Or does all their energy go into the struggle for survival?

## Resilience

The factors that contribute to psychological wellbeing are encapsulated in the concept of resilience. This word 'has come to describe the human being's ability to survive, recover and persevere against various obstacles and threats' (Furman, 1998: 19). Dagnan (2008) links resilience with self-determination, which has itself been seen in terms of optimism and hope. It involves the person's belief that a desired outcome is attainable and that they have the capacity to achieve that outcome. Contributory factors may be the development of alternative narratives, the presence of a source of love and affirmation somewhere in the child's network, and the 'survival methods' of people who have suffered trauma (Furman, 1998).

Awareness of the issues of psychological wellbeing and resilience can inform our assessments, making them less problem-focused and highlighting the person's resources. For example, at my first meeting with carers I routinely ask a question such as: '*What are the qualities that help him cope with his problems?*' This is sometimes first met with bafflement by carers, but they then go on to give answers that open up a deeper and more positive understanding of the person.

## Routes to understanding the Inner World

### *Questionnaire*

Questionnaires are a blunt tool. They can indicate broad areas of concern, and provide quantitative information, which is useful as a baseline and for monitoring change. However, they provide relatively little in the way of the sort of qualitative information we need in order to begin to understand the person's inner world.

### *Observation*

Our sensitivity to the other person begins with observation. Does the person stand upright or are they stooped? Is their handshake firm or tentative? Do they look at us or avoid our gaze? Do they respond to the offer of tea in an offhand manner, or with a sense of desperation? Have they dressed casually or with care? Is their hair recently washed? The list could go on and on. These are all possible clues as to the person's mood, feelings about their self and self-awareness.

In people with pervasive support needs, the need for sensitive observation of behaviour is especially important. In this case, we are likely to be looking for behaviour that reflects the person's feelings. Hogg et al define *affective communication* as:

> behaviour construed as indicative of positive or negative emotion . . . on the basis of both conventional, cultural knowledge of the ways in which emotion is communicated, and of the construer's experience of the individual's means of conveying emotion, both conventional and idiosyncratic.
>
> (Hogg et al, 2001: 19)

We need to take account of both conventional ways of communicating feelings (e.g. smiling), and the person's idiosyncratic means of expression.

### *Interview with carers*

With people who are more severely disabled, we rely on carers for their everyday experience of the person. This experience may have spread over several years and be very detailed. On the other hand, it may be relatively recent, and the person concerned may have arrived at a placement with next to no historical information. Also, institutional procedures may militate against the staff getting to know the residents. Mansell (2007) reports that clients generally only receive about nine minutes of support and 1.4 minutes of facilitative assistance per hour. In this case the person is likely to be as much a mystery to the care staff as they are to us, and it is particularly important to try to track down people who know them from the past, and past reports. It is also important to interview more than one carer, since they may well have very different ideas about the person (Hogg et al, 2001).

One way to capture current carers' knowledge of the person is through interviewing someone who knows the person well as if they were that person. Haydon-Laurelut and Wilson (2011) describe this 'Internalised Other' procedure, moving through Orienting, Relational, Episodic and Appreciative Questions, to input from the Reflecting Team.

## Therapeutic interventions as an assessment tool

The most helpful way we have of understanding the person's Inner World comes through our therapeutic relationship with them. Different types of therapy will result in us getting to know the person in different ways. All therapies benefit from the scaffolding provided by visual aids.

Elaine has been referred because of her attacks on Sylvia, another resident in her home. Behavioural approaches have been ineffective with her. So far she has never been able to explain to carers the reason for these attacks. This is taken from a report written by a trainee following four counselling sessions.

---

### Elaine

We then spent two sessions discussing emotions. Elaine could understand 'happy' and 'sad' but struggled to understand 'angry'. When I tried to discuss what makes her angry, Elaine would change the subject quickly. Pictures of happy, sad and angry faces seemed to help her discuss her feelings. She identified:

**What made her happy**
Laughing, talking, watching TV, helping Sam in the kitchen, helping Tracy vacuum the floor

**What made her sad**
Crying

**What made her angry**
When Sylvia touches her: 'I tell her "no". I don't want you to touch me. Sometimes she stops touching me, sometimes she keeps touching me'.

---

Shortly after this intervention, Elaine disclosed sexual abuse by her stepfather. Investigations were conducted that were inconclusive. However, the disclosure began to make Elaine's extreme reactions to touch make sense to staff and they began to discuss environmental changes to address the problem with Sylvia.

The person-centred qualities of empathy, warmth and genuineness can foster trust and confidence. This allows the other person to explore their feelings, thoughts, sense of identity, self and meaning, so that understanding of the person, and their self-understanding, can develop in tandem (Rogers, 1951). Reflection, whether of content, meaning or feeling, will often prompt people to elaborate on their first response, without them feeling they are being interrogated or bombarded with questions.

People with learning disability are also likely to benefit from a structured approach, which provides the scaffolding they need to move forward. In this case person-centred counselling skills provide a foundation for more specialised therapeutic approaches. The Skilled Helper Model (Egan, 2002) is a staged counselling approach, which moves through exploration and self-understanding to problem-solving.

A range of clinical problems have been found responsive to *cognitive behaviour therapy* (CBT), which suggests that both cognitive deficits and cognitive distortions play a part in the genesis and maintenance of these problems. According to this model, the beliefs people hold about themselves and others influence their feelings and their interpretation of events in ways that are unhelpful to them (Jahoda et al, 2009). Cognitive negativity may reflect negative life experiences, suggesting the interpersonal nature of self (see Jahoda et al, 2006, 2009; Kroese et al, 1997). The process of cognitive therapy may also reveal other issues, leading both therapist and client to a better understanding of the problems, and suggesting fresh interventions.

---

### Ben

Ben is aged 20 and has a diagnosis of autism. He has been referred because of his aggressive behaviour towards other members of his family. The psychologist finds that these incidents take place when Ben is anxious about something. This often happens when there has been some unexpected change. She works with him to consider how he is feeling and thinking, and the way in which this influences his behaviour. Together they work out coping strategies and they engage the support of his parents in using these ways of coping.

As they come towards the end of their time working together, Ben starts to talk more about the difficulty he has in coping with change. The psychologist mentions that this may be to do with his diagnosis of autism. Ben says that he has never understood that word, and would like to know more about autism. They agree that when their first lot of work is finished, Ben will receive some further psycho-educational sessions to help him better understand his condition.

---

Most people we see are not able to express a coherent personal narrative, and, whatever our therapeutic approach, a central part of our work involves helping them construct this story. 'Unity and uniqueness of the self is achieved through the coherence of a person's life story – narrative coherence . . . stories are formed, or constructed, from an interaction of lived experience through time and meaning . . . stories are at the core of our identities' (Engel et al, 2008: 41, 45 and 46). *Life Story Work* (Meininger, 2006) is a tool we can use in this (see Ahmed's vignette, p. 169).

Within the narrative therapy approach, White (2007) provides an accessible way for us to explore meaning with people, through his concepts of *landscape of action* and a *landscape of meaning*. It can be drawn out as two parallel timelines, both covering the same time period. The first, the landscape of action refers to what the person did and events they experienced. The second, the landscape of meaning or value refers to the meaning of these events for their self concept and values. Whereas actions (and thoughts) can be evaluated negatively, values invariably reflect well on the person, so working on this

## Ahmed

Ahmed is aged 19, and is due to leave college. He was adopted as a young child, and has a close relationship with his adoptive parents, who are both now elderly and in poor health. Ahmed has become anxious about meeting Asian people, either in the college or the street. His mother thinks that he is afraid that they will abduct him.

The trainee sees Ahmed for six sessions of Life Story Work. Ahmed makes a lovely treasure box in which he collects many things that are important to him, including a little teddy that he had as a child. He and the psychologist also prepare a photo album, which includes photos of both his adoptive family and his birth family. As he puts the album together, Ahmed talks about his memories of Asian families coming to visit him when he was a child, and how afraid he was that he would be taken away from his adoptive family.

In the course of the work, Ahmed comes to be able to separate the past from the present, and to begin to accept his dual identity. He gains the confidence to cope with his transition from college, and to express his distress at his parents' health problems.

with the person can help them to reconsider their lives and see themselves in a more positive light.

*Mindfulness training* involves cultivating awareness of the present moment and doing so in an accepting, non-judgemental way. These are both features that suggest it could be beneficial for people with learning disabilities, who are likely to suffer from limited self-awareness, combined with a poor self-concept. Singh has shown mindfulness training to be effective in helping people with learning disabilities (Singh et al, 2007). It has been incorporated into other integrative therapies such as *Dialectical Behaviour Therapy*, which has been developed in learning disability service (Baillie et al, 2010).

As people's capacity for reflection develops, the nature of their early attachment relationships is likely to unfold (Corbett, 2009). In the case of *psychodynamic psychotherapy*, early working models of attachment are played out through the therapist–client relationship and brought into consciousness (Schore, 1994). Psychodynamic psychotherapy has been developed and evaluated in relation to people with learning disability (Baxter, 2011; Beail et al, 2005).

## Communicating with people with pervasive support needs

People without verbal communication can only let us know how they feel through their behaviour. If the person is distressed their behaviour can become stereotyped and hard to penetrate. Moreover, they may not have reached the stage of intentional communication (see Chapters 10 and 11). *Intensive interaction* is a structured, developmental, one-to-one approach that provides a route into communicating with people who are hard to reach (Nind and Hewett, 2001). Information can be found on http://www.intensiveinteraction. co.uk/ and from http://www.phoebecaldwell.co.uk/. Goldbart and Caton (2011) give a general introduction to communication. Communication is often a first step to decision making, and the *Involve Me* guide gives helpful information on how this can be achieved (Mencap et al, 2011).

## A responsive environment

An alternative to individual therapeutic work is to institute systemic changes to facilitate communication. Ware's work provides a structure for working with staff so as to enhance the sensitivity and reliability of their understanding and so encourage the person to communicate their feelings (Ware, 2003). This begins with detailed observations, if possible including video recording, which are used with the staff team to discuss the person's early attempts at intentional behaviour. Staff then use techniques such as 'catching an alert moment' and 'turnabouts' to start and to develop conversations. This is an extract from a teacher's conversation with a nonverbal pupil.

| | |
|---|---|
| **Teacher** | Are you ready? Here we go! |
| **Suzannah** | looks at teacher |
| **Teacher** | Round and round the garden like a teddy bear. |
| **Suzannah** | Vocalises & continues to look at teacher |
| **Teacher** | One step, two step, and tickle S there (tickles) |
| | PAUSE |
| **Teacher** | What do you think, shall we do it again? |

(Ware, 2003: 83–84)

As this dialogue progresses, Suzannah stops vocalising and her head drops down her chest. The teacher responds with: '*No, you don't want any more, shall we chat instead?*' She then goes on to talk about a coming school outing, Suzannah begins to vocalise and smile, and they discuss her participation. This moving extract shows the way in which, as carers learn to apply the philosophy and techniques suggested by Ware, this allows the person to express their feelings and make choices.

## Conclusions

Understanding another person's inner world is a long, slow and often chastening process. It is inextricably linked with an understanding of all the circumstances and conditions that have given birth to that world. It is a privilege for us to accompany the person on the journey of self-understanding, and to be able to share our own understanding with them. This is a first step in helping them to meet their needs.

## Recommended reading

Nind M and Hewett D (2001) *A Practical Guide to Intensive Interaction* Kidderminster: British Institute of Learning Disabilities

Traustadòttir R and Johnson K (eds) (2000) *Women with Intellectual Disabilities: Finding a Place in the World* London: Jessica Kingsley

Ware J (2003) *Creating a Responsive Environment for People with Profound and Multiple Learning Difficulties* (2nd edition) London: David Fulton

# Part III

# Making sense

## Three Stories

# 15 Formulating a coherent narrative

The BPS has produced very helpful Good Practice Guidelines on the use of formulation, and the first part of this chapter should be considered alongside these guidelines (BPS, 2011). Formulation has been described succinctly as 'a hypothesis about a person's difficulties, which draws from psychological theory' (Johnstone and Dallos, 2006: 4). I think of it as a coherent story that helps to make sense of the person's problems and provides a foundation for working with them to develop an effective intervention plan. We consider formulation to be a distinctively psychological competence, and it is seen by the Division of Clinical Psychology as a core skill (Division of Clinical Psychology, 2001). Without it we might be inclined to jump from assessment to intervention without an explicit theoretical rationale, or even ignore the assessment phase completely (*'have you thought of . . .?'*; *' I always find . . . very helpful'*).

## Formulating within alternative paradigms

When we arrive at the point of developing our formulation, the tension between the positivist, phenomenological and narrative paradigms comes to the fore. In Chapter 1 I described these three paradigms as varying along the dimensions of ontology, explanation, methodology, values and concept of human nature. I feel that each of the three paradigms is valuable, whilst also either being incomplete or imposing conditions in one or other of the five dimensions that are impossible to meet in the clinical context.

Although I have previously stressed the importance of giving credence to the different stories people tell, and to the meaning they give to those stories, when it comes to trying to put together my own formulation, I do see myself as trying to approach the truth of the situation:

> Let us assume also that there is indeed a real world out there, one that is largely independent of our assumptions. . . . While we do hold that perceptions are anchored in constructs, we hold also that some constructions serve us better than others in our efforts to anticipate comprehensively what is actually going on.
>
> (Kelly, 1977: 5–6)

Moreover, the narrative form arises at least in part from the nature of our lives.

Action has a basically historical character. It is because we live out narratives in our lives and because we understand our own lives in terms of narratives that we live out that the form of narrative is appropriate for understanding the action of others. Stories are lived before they are told.

(MacIntyre, 2007: 212)

According to Kuhn, different paradigms are inherently incompatible. Nevertheless, it seems to me that our formulations should be constructed in a spirit of openness and respect for all three of the clinical paradigms I have identified.

Valentine suggests that 'causal explanations explain a given event by reference to a past event' (1982: 100). She identifies the essential ingredients of causality as *conditionality*, *relevance* and *temporal contiguity*. Paxton (1976) suggests that to qualify as scientific, our explanation should meet the following criteria:

- be backed by supporting evidence
- be amenable to empirical refutation
- find reasons for the event in the antecedent situation
- imply the relevance of these antecedent events
- (other things being equal) Be simple/economical rather than complicated
- be fruitful in the sense of being predictive and also leading to new generalisations.

In the clinical context we are often concerned with establishing a relationship involving the influence of one set of variables over another that does not meet these strict criteria. Nevertheless, they do draw our attention to important factors, particularly the need for evidence. 'Empirical refutation' refers to Popper's (1963) criterion of falsifiability, which is hard to achieve, but may in the clinical context involve the weaker criterion of testability through conversation or through intervention. We also need to be aware of the danger of circular explanations. For example, if a person is referred because they are self-injuring, this cannot be explained by reference to the idea that they 'have' challenging behaviour.

The phenomenological paradigm emphasises issues of meaning and subjective interpretation. Crellin suggests that formulation is incompatible with humanistic and phenomenological approaches to psychotherapy that are concerned not with problem solving or removing symptoms but with 'helping the client to arrive at a meaningful narrative, and to make sense of things over time' (1998: 19). According to Crellin, the only person who can arrive at a formulation is the client, and that only after an extended period of therapy.

Though issues of experience and meaning-making are as significant for people with learning disability as for anyone else, they will rarely (if ever) enter the consulting room and tell us that they want to be able to make sense of their lives. Instead, they will present as confused, worried, depressed, angry or in any number of other ways. Our role is to provide the secure structure, the scaffolding that will help the person begin to make sense of their lives. And this includes gathering information from diverse sources, offering tentative suggestions, making initial inferences and helping the person fashion this information and make sense of it. In this way, we hope to arrive with the person at a shared understanding of their problems.

This necessitates simplification of language and concepts, as well as a willingness to listen and take on board the views of the client. Where our initial formulation is complex, it is unlikely that we would share it all with the client in a single session. Simplification may mean just sharing with the client that part of the initial formulation that explains our proposed intervention. Over time, other elements of the formulation will be clarified, developed and shared.

I suggested earlier that there has been a welcome tendency towards rapprochement between the three approaches, and I believe that we should work explicitly, reflectively and reflexively with this rapprochement in our clinical work. But how do we reconcile our quest for understanding (grounded in an ideal of objectivity and truth) with our belief in the value and worth of each individual and the socially constructed nature of their reality? Thankfully, while in philosophy and principle the paradigms may be irreconcilable, in real life clinical practice the situation is less clear cut, even murky. We work with our clients to construct explanations that are meaningful for them and that will work in the sense of guiding our interventions and helping us intervene effectively.

## The place of formulation within the care pathway

In the linear care pathway, as traditionally conceived, assessment, formulation and intervention proceed in neat progression. In some circumstances this can happen, but as mentioned in Chapter 6, the reality is usually more complex. First, our choice of factors for assessment will depend on our theoretical perspective. So formulation is intrinsic to the process from the very beginning, guiding the form that our assessment takes. Second, our relationship with the person we are trying to help is at the core of all three processes, but is ignored in care pathways as usually described. And as the therapeutic relationship progresses (whether this is with our client or their carers), different knowledges emerge and are woven into an increasingly complex narrative.

Formulation is thus usually not a one-off conceptualisation, but an ongoing process, arrived at collaboratively. The BPS suggests that it should be seen as a working model or map that can be changed as new evidence emerges and as the intervention proceeds (BPS, 2004). Dallos et al suggest that it should be termed 'formulating' rather than 'formulation'. They describe 'formulating' as

> an interactive, vibrant and live activity during which we start to get to know and engage with our clients. . . . What we learn about our clients unfolds

over time and is based on the development of trust and openness, so that any early formulation must by definition be tentative and open to revision.

(Dallos et al, 2006: 167–68).

## Integrative formulation

Formulation is not just a question of filling boxes with arrows between them, but of creating a dynamic narrative that makes sense of those links and outcomes. It is relatively uncomplicated when we are working within a single theoretical perspective. However in the field of learning disability, the complexity of the problems we face, and the wide range of potential contributory factors, will often require us to refer simultaneously to different theories. In order to fashion these theories and the assessment information into a coherent whole we generally need to adopt an integrative approach. This means considering what theories might enter into the formulation, and how these theories will be related to each other and to the presenting problems.

Dallos (2006) distinguishes between this sort of 'conceptual synthesis' and eclectic approaches, which simply bring together different theories within an organising framework. An example of this is the 'Four Ps' model, in which the organising categories are predisposing, precipitating, protective and perpetuating factors (Weerasekara, 1996). This is an a-theoretical model, which allows a wide variety of factors to be included. It can be helpful in a situation where we need to make an idiosyncratic synthesis in the case of a particular client. However, it can also result in a repetitive and piecemeal listing of factors, which fails to amount to a coherent story.

Where a conceptual synthesis is attempted, theories aim to extract core features from different models 'in order to create a fresh and vibrant new perspective' (Dallos et al, 2006: 157). Three such integrative theories are: Attachment Narrative Therapy (Dallos, 2006); Cognitive Analytic Therapy (Ryle, 1990) and Positive Behaviour Support. Any one of these approaches could be helpful, and indeed adequate to explain our clients' problems. However, they each tend to neglect one or other of the Eight Domains.

What follows is a fresh approach to formulation, which builds on the holistic understanding provided by the Eight Domains model to provide a simple and flexible structure for integrative formulation. I will illustrate this model by reference to three people.

## An integrative model: Three Stories and needs

Notwithstanding the range of factors that we consider when carrying out a holistic assessment, it is also usually the case that one of these sets of factors appears to be particularly salient for the person. I call this the ***Core Story.*** This may come from any one of the Eight Domains.

Stories from other Domains will often serve to reinforce the Core Story. For example, the Core Story may relate to Anxiety (Inner World domain); but this is reinforced by cognitive deficits that mean that the person is unable to make use of anxiety management strategies suggested by generic services. These additional stories, which serve to increase the impact of the Core Stories, are termed *Supporting Stories*.

Most people have sources of resilience, which have helped them survive often horrendous circumstances. These may involve, for example, a relationship with a kindly relative or neighbour; a particular skill in drawing; or a feisty personality that refuses to succumb to adversity. Borrowing a term from Michael White, I call these *Sparkling Stories*.

## Needs

In Chapter 2 I discussed my belief that a humanistic approach should be grounded in an idea of what constitutes a human being. The concept of need provides an anchor for this idea. Failure to meet a person's needs results in the development of problems, either internal to the person, in their relationships, in their management of their lives or in all these areas. In my clinical work and in the literature, three needs appear to be particularly salient. These are the needs for Safety, Belonging and Self-Determination. In addition, I believe there is a human thirst for Meaning, which remains largely unrecognised and unexplored in the field of learning disability, though we may spot it tangentially. For example, where a person lacks daytime activities, they may lack opportunities to engage in the creative activities through which they find meaning in their lives.

When we plan our intervention we do so with the aim of helping the person meet their needs. This may mean prioritising needs, partly because it is not possible to do everything at once, and partly because needs may conflict. In particular the person's need and wish for Self-determination may conflict with their need for Safety. In this case intervention should be negotiated with the person and their carers in the context of a risk assessment, a risk management plan and possibly a capacity assessment.

## Intervention: Agency and Access

In order to be effective, intervention is likely to be needed at the level of both the individual and the system. This dual-level approach is expressed in the concepts of Agency and Access, as described in Chapter 2. In the examples that follow you will see the way in which the intervention plan links with the formulation and the person's perceived needs.

## Empathy and the process of formulating

Empathic understanding is central to the process of selecting the Core, Supporting and Sparkling Stories. Empathy is often described in terms of metaphor. It involves 'seeing things from another person's point of view' or 'standing in the shoes of another'. Since we can never fully know another person, it requires an imaginative leap and also curiosity and attentiveness (Lederach, 2004). Werhane (2002) suggests that the practice of empathy involves starting with self-reflection, moving on to a reflection on a wider situation, and from there to imagining 'new possibilities', which include imagining the other person's way of thinking. But empathy is not just about thinking, but also about seeking 'to understand the patient's lived experience, and come to operate in the narrative of that lived experience' (Engel et al, 2008: 109). Lovett (1985: 14) suggests that we begin our work by asking ourselves simply: *'How would I feel in that position?'*

We can only achieve empathic understanding by committing ourselves emotionally as well as intellectually:

> Except as I involve myself deeply with a person whose life is at the turning point, unless I seek to anticipate the outcomes of his decisions at this point, unless I myself make some commitment to joining him in a common understanding . . . I shall accomplish little more than to accumulate a bibliography to attach to my next application for a job.
>
> (Kelly, 1977: 11–13)

Thus we find ourselves both seeking objectively for the truth of the situation and also seeking to immerse ourselves empathically in the person's lived experience. This also involves seeking an empathic understanding of the social group that surrounds the person we are trying to help. Out of this process emerges our formulation.

## Example one: Brian's story

Brian is aged 35. He was referred after he stopped eating and drinking and was admitted to hospital. Over a period of several months, he resumed a more normal pattern of eating and drinking, though with a tendency to binge and put on weight. He was also verbally and physically aggressive towards his support workers.

Brian hated himself. He hated the fact that he was learning disabled, that he swore at other people and was fat. He felt ashamed, guilty, worthless. He repeatedly told others that they would all be better off if he threw himself under a train. No amount of reassurance served to percolate his self-loathing.

Brian's father had a diagnosis of schizophrenia and belonged to a Christian fundamentalist sect that placed strong emphasis on sin and punishment. He was physically violent to his wife and his three children and also sexually abused at least two of his children. Brian incurred extra punishment and castigation on account of his inability to do well in school. When he was nine years old, Brian was sent away to boarding school, where he was deeply unhappy. Visits home for holidays involved a renewal of the longstanding physical and sexual abuse. He was repeatedly told that this was his own fault, because he was so stupid.

Brian's living situation exacerbated his problems. He spent many hours of the day alone. Loneliness and boredom resulted in binge eating. A fluctuating staff group did not respond consistently to Brian's temper, and he took each outburst as further evidence of his worthlessness. In addition, Brian was in poor physical health.

As I got to know Brian, I began to appreciate the central importance of Safety for him. His whole life was suffused with a sense of threat, first from his parents, later from children at school and more recently from his physical health problems. Indeed, he explained his aggression towards staff in terms of his fear and belief that they were going to hit him, though this had never happened.

But the situation was not all bleak. One day, we decided to go out into town and spend our session time in a local café. I found to my surprise that in this social situation, Brian was quite skilled. He knew where to go to get the cheapest cup of tea in town. He knew the first name of the lady in the café and they chatted about their local church. I discovered that Brian came here every Saturday morning for a cup of tea. Later, when we returned to his flat, I saw him teasing and being teased by his support worker, and I realised how much Brian was helped to cope by his sense of humour.

Brian's formulation is summarised in Figure 15.1.

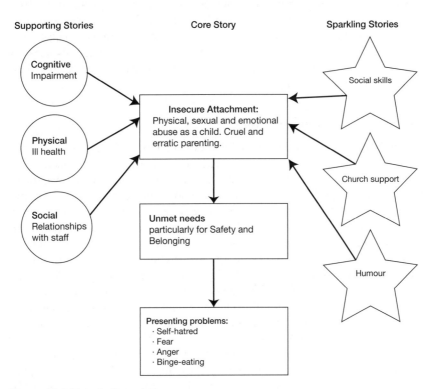

*Figure 15.1* Brian's formulation.

Brian's formulation suggested a number of 'entry points' for intervention. For example, at the level of Agency, Brian's sense of threat could be reduced by narrative therapy to help him externalise his fear, understand its historical roots and learn to deal with it in a more helpful way. His temper could be helped by working with him to develop in assertiveness skills. At the level of Access, his sense of threat could be reduced by working with staff to provide a more consistent, stable and boundaried environment. His sense of belonging could be enhanced by setting up a Circle of Support, building on his existing community links. These possible interventions are summarised in Table 15.1.

*Table 15.1* Helping Brian

|  | *Agency* | *Access* |
| --- | --- | --- |
| **Need for Safety** | Narrative therapy | Work with staff to create 'safe' environment |
| **Need for Belonging** | Assertiveness training; anger management | Circle of Support |

Brian's intellectual limitations and his physical illness meant that it was difficult to achieve continuity between his individual sessions. Nevertheless, I was able to continue contact with him, working on simple anger management strategies. I also continued to work with staff to help enhance his sense of safety. His relationship with staff improved and his eating ceased to present a serious threat to his health.

## Example two: Maurice's story

Maurice was referred for help with his obsessional behaviours. My initial formulation was in terms of anxiety, and we embarked on a cognitive-behavioural programme to manage this. However, as time went on I noticed Maurice's inability to remember things from one session to the next. Moreover, despite some initial conversations with staff, they were not giving him the level of support he needed to help him implement the programme. This was partly due to lack of time and partly to staff lack of understanding of Maurice's problems.

Maurice also expressed worries about his parents. I therefore decided to re-visit my assessment, in three ways: first with an interview with Maurice's parents; second with a cognitive assessment and third in a meeting with the staff manager. When I met with Maurice's parents, they were baffled at the worries that Maurice was expressing. I was convinced by their genuineness, and the likelihood that Maurice's worries were ground in his own lack of understanding rather than any real threat to his parents or their relationship.

When I carried out a cognitive assessment with Maurice, the results confirmed that he had severe memory problems, previously unrecognised by those supporting him. Moreover, his superficial facility with language masked severe communication problems. I referred Maurice to the Speech and Language Therapist for assessment. Following this, we worked together on a revised programme to help Maurice manage his anxiety, which I now saw as being secondary to his cognitive deficits. This programme included visual aids and prompts, which were put in place each day by the support staff. Maurice also learnt to write a list of his worries each day, so that these could be discussed with staff when they visited and answers could be written down (e.g. letting him know who would be coming to help him that evening). Maurice's formulation is summarised in Figure 15.2.

The interventions for Maurice are summarised in Table 15.2.

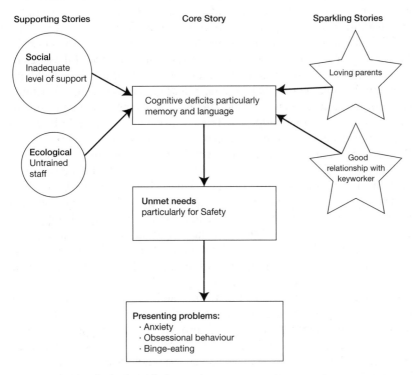

*Figure 15.2* Maurice's formulation.

*Table 15.2* Helping Maurice.

|  | *Agency* | *Access* |
|---|---|---|
| **Need for Safety** | Training in use of communication aids, based on Speech and Language Therapy assessment | Work with staff to help them understand Maurice's problems |
|  | Use of memory aids Behavioural programme for obsessions | Training in use of communication and memory aids |

This approach proved to be effective for Maurice in helping reduce his anxiety and the associated obsessional behaviours. Changes were maintained at three-month follow-up.

## Example three: Trudine's story

Trudine, who was mentioned in Chapter 14, is just at the start of her therapeutic journey. She was born as a male, but has a strong conviction that her gender identity is female. Trudine was first referred for counselling, but despite attempts to support her, her attendance was extremely erratic. I suspected that this apparent non-compliance may have been due to Trudine's anxiety about leaving her flat. Later, the Community Nurse referred her for a cognitive assessment, in order to help staff support her more effectively.

A Clinical Psychology trainee carried out the cognitive assessment, which did reveal significant impairments. However, the significance of these results was overshadowed by the calamitous nature of the rest of her life: abandoned by her family, shunned by neighbours, refused a gender change operation because of her failure to attend appointments and facing a change in support workers. As these stories unfolded, Trudine became increasingly bizarre in her appearance, and her flat became increasingly dirty and chaotic.

While I might have seen Attachment issues as constituting Trudine's Core Story, the trainee was clear that the Core Story was about Trudine's Inner World and her fragile sense of identity. This was exacerbated by negative attitudes towards trans-gender people, expressed by both her neighbours and her family. Her assessment also suggested a daunting array of Supporting Stories. Trudine's Sparkling Story was largely about her personal qualities: her cognitive strengths, her sense of humour and her determined belief in her female identity, in the face of massive difficulties and negative consequences for herself. Her formulation is shown in Figure 15.3.

This formulation was discussed in a simplified form with Trudine, and the beginning of an intervention plan agreed with her. We believed she would benefit from some input being targeted through her new support agency, to help them understand her problems, help her gain a feeling of security and develop new relationships. We also believed she would benefit from cognitive behavioural therapy, to begin to address her problems in a structured and contained way. For example, work on her anxiety could help her to overcome the difficulties she has in engaging with services. These interventions are summarised in Table 15.3. This was a predictably long process, which is ongoing as I write.

## Formulating and its links with assessment

If we find that we need to explore only one of the Eight Domains in our initial assessment, then it is likely that we will be able to construct an adequate formulation using a single theory. If we find that we need to explore more than

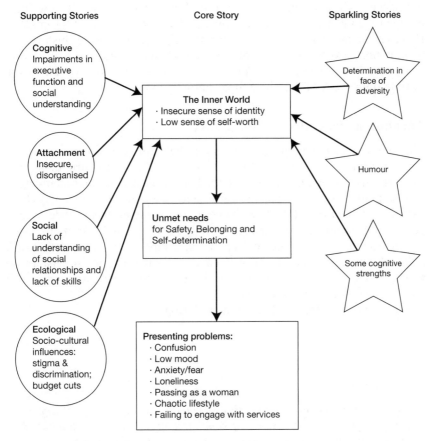

*Figure 15.3* Trudine's formulation.

*Table 15.3* Helping Trudine.

|  | *Agency* | *Access* |
| --- | --- | --- |
| **Need for Safety** |  |  |
| **Need for Belonging** | Long term psychotherapy, using cognitive-behavioural model | Work with staff, beginning with '*Getting to Know You*' (see Chapter 8). |
| **Need for Self-determination** |  |  |

one of the Eight Domains to make sense of the person's story, then we may be able to draw on an 'off the shelf' integrative theory such as ANT or CAT. However, if the person we are trying to help has a complex history and presentation, involving several of the Eight Domains, then we will need to construct an idiosyncratic integrative formulation. In this case, we can use the flexible framework of the Three Story Formulation.

## Turning the formulation into a story

The summary formulations given so far in the form of boxes and arrows do not constitute coherent narratives. Our next step is to turn them into explanations that can make sense to the person themselves and their carers, and help them on their path towards understanding and change. These narratives make explicit the links between presenting problems, theories and possible interventions. For clients, they may be written in the form of a letter, in user-friendly language and with appropriate illustrations. It is helpful to ask a Speech and Language Therapist to check the letter and advise on ways in which it may be made more accessible. For carers, the formulation will constitute part of a formal report.

Below is a letter that could be written to Brian.

*Dear Brian*

*Since we met I have seen how bravely you cope with all the problems in your life: your health problems; your difficult mother; your loneliness when you are too ill to leave your flat; your worries about how to cope with everyday life.*

*Even with all these problems, you carry on coping. You tease your carers, go to church and go on outings into town when you feel well enough. Last year you even managed to go on holiday on your own! That was a big achievement.*

*Sometimes it all gets too much for you. You are in pain, and that makes you irritable. You can't remember what you have been told. You think people are getting at you. You feel very anxious. Then you get angry with other people. Afterwards you blame yourself. You think you are a terrible person. Then you get more upset and angry. It is vicious circle.*

*In our work together we have talked about the reasons that you think you are a terrible person.*

• *One reason could be that you really are terrible.*
• *The other reason could be that your father kept telling you that you are terrible.*

*We invited your older brother to come to some of our meetings. He told us about the cruel way your father treated you both.*

*I think you started to see that maybe your problems are not all your fault. Your parents never gave you love and affection. Your mother was too afraid to help you. Your father hit you and told you that you were useless. You grew up believing that. You struggled with your work at school. When you were sent away to boarding school other children bullied you. You could not cope with your hurt feelings. You became angry and sometimes hit other people.*

*Now, you have a nice flat and kind carers. They never hit you. Still, sometimes you think that they will. You feel afraid and get angry with them.*

*We will carry on working together to feel better about yourself. You are not a bad person. You are the way you are because of the way your parents treated you. Now you are an adult. You can start to put the past behind you and enjoy your life.*

*Thank you for sharing the story of your life with me.*
*I have enjoyed getting to know you.*
*My good wishes for the future*

*Jenny*

This letter and report could have been written in other ways. For example, Brian's problems could have been given a cognitive-behavioural formulation in terms of schemas and negative automatic thoughts. I have presented them in terms of attachment theory because that is what seemed most meaningful to me and what I thought could make sense to Brian. The letter does not necessarily cover every element of the formulation. Some aspects may be mentioned only in a few words, and some omitted altogether, whilst the main points may be repeated. The aim is to convey a simple message in an accessible way, and to provide a basis for future work together.

I see this letter as a gift to the person I am trying to help, but this is not a one-way process. It gives back to them the information they have given to me and the trust that went with that. It also gives them back part of myself: my commitment to helping them and the investment in time and emotion that I have made. It is something tangible that they can keep, share if they want to, and maybe treasure.

## Conclusions

Formulating goes beyond an attempt at scientific explanation. It is an ongoing and developing process rooted in our relationship with the person and our empathic understanding of their situation.

There is no one 'correct' formulation. The problems of the three people described could have been constructed in different ways, drawing on alternative theoretical perspectives. The formulation is a working model. Its value lies partly in the meaning it has for the person concerned, in helping them to understand themselves and make sense of their lives. Its value also lies in its usefulness as a therapeutic tool, indicating where we might target our interventions. However, our first intervention is not the end of the story. Through this we will learn to better understand the person, test our hypotheses and maybe lay the ground for helping the person in other ways, as well as enabling them to help themselves.

## Recommended reading

British Psychological Society (2011) *Good Practice Guidelines on the Use of Psychological Formulation* Leicester: BPS.

Johnstone L and Dallos R (2006) *Formulation in Psychology and Psychotherapy* Hove: Routledge

# 16 Conclusions

I see Clinical Psychology as being built on the foundations of science, humanism and reflection. Science is based on the conviction that truth exists and can be discovered through objective methods. Humanism involves a belief in the shared humanity of all, which can be appreciated through empathic feeling and understanding. Reflection requires that we take a broad view, in which we ourselves form part of the subject of study.

It is in the nature of the human condition that we view our situation from an egocentric perspective – as if we are walking along a path guided by the single beam of a torch. But if we are to function scientifically and humanistically then we need to attempt to question our own taken-for-granted view. This involves seeing ourselves both personally and professionally in a broad context, at the confluence of multiple currents, intellectual and social, historical and personal. Mace, in discussing mindfulness, uses the analogy of starlight: a view that is 'literally infinite, yet unique to the spot from which it is seen' (1996: viii).

In writing this guide I have attempted to begin to construct this broad view, starting with the various contexts of our work, and going on to discuss the framework of the Eight Domains and the Three Stories. In this picture we also see ourselves, with our own needs for safety, self-determination and belonging, and our faltering attempts to make sense of our lives. In our professional role we may feel impotent, the product of a historical and political process over which we have little influence. But Giddens (1991) reminds us that we are also agents, helping to shape the world of which we form a part. Clinical Psychology provides us with a body of expertise to help us in our enterprise. Working in the field of Learning Disability is particularly challenging and interesting, not only because of the people we meet, but also because of the potential relevance of the whole range of psychological theories from all the clinical specialties.

In choosing our direction, we need to be aware of the ways in which the idealistic approaches of the past have been hijacked and warped in the service of lesser motives. Changes of nomenclature have resulted in stigma attaching itself to new labels: normalisation developed into a denial of individual needs and neglect of the need for social change; personalisation turned into individualisation; inclusion has been used as a reason to deny difference; a human rights-based approach has been accused of perpetuating otherness (Clapton and Fitzgerald, 2010). And the needs-based approach advocated in this book could be criticised on the grounds that it ignores values and goals that need to be articulated at a societal level (Kagan et al, 2011). We therefore need to stay on our toes, constantly questioning and in a spirit of humility. But also we need to feel confident about our unique role as clinical psychologists contributing to the wellbeing of people with learning disabilities.

As I reach the end of this book I also come close to reaching the end of my career in the NHS. The story of this book coincides with the story of my own professional history and its roots in my personal life.

## Robert

It is 1976. The scene is a Mental Handicap Hospital in Essex. Boys and men of all ages are lined up on seats in a cavernous hall in front of a distant TV. They have been sitting there a long time. One side of the hall is all windows. A door on the second side leads off into the toilets. The efforts of staff are focused on keeping the boys away from the fragile glass and whatever could happen in the toilets.

Robert is nine years old. He takes no interest in the TV. His legs jitter constantly and every now and then he jumps up and makes a dash for one of the forbidden areas. The staff nurse is fed up with him. She yells at Robert to sit still, but to no avail. Finally, she picks up a strip of plastic. She rushes up to Robert and hits him hard on his bare calves several times.

The new nursing assistant is watching, with a sense of horror and helplessness. She runs across to the staff nurse and wrenches the plastic strip out of her hand. The nurse turns to her, initially dumbstruck. Finally, she explains herself. 'You don't understand', she says. 'These boys aren't like us. They don't feel pain. They're animals!'

We have come far since 1976. And, as I observed earlier, therapeutically these are hopeful times. I conclude with a vignette that describes what for me was a magical moment.

## Heena

Heena has a diagnosis of autism. She spends most of her time sitting in front of the TV, but not watching it or communicating with the other three women in her house. She shows an interest only in food, which she eats at great speed. Her parents say she enjoys classical music. She has a CD player in her room, but it is out of her reach, and rarely seems to be used. She is also said to enjoy walking round the garden and looking at the light on the leaves of the trees, but this also seems to happen rarely. The psychologist has never seen Heena make eye contact or initiate an activity.

The psychologist works with the staff to experiment with activities and find things that Heena enjoys. They gather together a box of things that offer her sensory stimulation and start to use them regularly. A short daily session of Intensive Interaction between Heena's keyworker and the Speech and Language Therapist is introduced.

Heena is also referred to a day centre, and a few weeks later, the psychologist goes to find out how she is getting on. The psychologist is astonished to see Heena turn to the person sitting next to her, look at her, smile and reach out to hold hands.

# Appendix 1

## Initial assessment – prompt sheet

**PART ONE: BACKGROUND INFORMATION**

| **THE PERSON'S DETAILS** | **THE REFERRER'S DETAILS** |
|---|---|
| Name | Name |
| Date of birth | Relationship/organisation |
| Phone numbers | Address |
| Diagnoses | Phone numbers |
| Significant others | |
| Assessment dates | |
| Present at interviews | |
| Address | |

**INTRODUCTORY DISCUSSION AND OUTCOME**
Introductory leaflet sent and discussed
Capacity to give consent to the assessment
Confidentiality; its limitations, recording and sharing of information

**PRESENTING PROBLEMS**
*(Difficulties or concerns/when problem began/why help is being sought now/impact on daily life and inclusion/expectations of service)*

Person's views
Carer's views
What has been tried so far?
What are the qualities, values or strengths that the person has shown in their attempts to tackle the problem? How do others see these qualities?

**CURRENT SITUATION**
Home environment: location/safety/adaptations/transport
Other residents
Support
Occupation
Weekly routine
Lifestyle
Income/benefits/control of money/debt/funding for services

## PART TWO: THE EIGHT DOMAINS

### 1. THE BEHAVIOURAL DOMAIN
Verbal aggression
Physical aggression to people
Physical aggression to environment
Self injury
Sexually inappropriate behaviour
Frequency/severity/duration
Setting conditions
Triggers
Consequences
Forensic history

### 2. THE SOCIAL DOMAIN
Family relationships
Friendships
Intimate/sexual relationships
Community relationships
Relationships with staff

### 3. THE PHYSICAL DOMAIN
Medical history
Health screening
Health action plan
Sight and hearing tests
Sensory impairment
Pain
Epilepsy
Swallowing
Continence
Mobility
Medication/need for review
Other medical conditions

### 4. THE NEUROLOGICAL DOMAIN
Psychiatric diagnoses
History of brain injury
History of illnesses affecting brain function

### 5. THE COGNITIVE DOMAIN
Previous cognitive assessments
Educational history and qualifications
Employment history
General intellectual ability

Orientation/attention
Language
Memory
Motor function
Visual Perception
Executive Function and Reasoning
Social Understanding
Self care skills
Domestic skills
Community living skills
Evidence of loss of skills

## 6. THE ATTACHMENT DOMAIN
Birth and early development
Family history and relationships
Genogram
History of relationships and loss
History of abuse/trauma

## 7. THE INNER WORLD
Anxiety
Obsessionality
Depression
Hallucinations
Energy/interest/motivation
Appetite/sleep
Likes/dislikes
Interests/strengths
Sense of identity
Expressed needs or wishes
Resilience

## 8. THE ECOLOGICAL DOMAIN
Spiritual/racial/cultural aspects
Community involvement
Financial situation

## PART THREE: RISK & SUPPORT

### RISK ASSESSMENT

Physical harm
Sexual harm
Emotional harm
Neglect
Self-injury
Exploitation (sexual, financial)
Harm to others

Ability to maintain physical health
Ability to maintain psychological
    wellbeing
Ability to maintain safety
Risk of placement breakdown
Failure to maintain contact with
    services
Need for crisis intervention
Need for multi-professional risk
    assessment and risk management
    plan

### FAMILY AND INFORMAL CARERS

Physical health
Psychological wellbeing
Request for help/support
Need for carer's assessment
Address
Phone numbers

### PROFESSIONAL SUPPORT RECEIVED/CONTACT DETAILS

Support at home
Advocacy
Speech and Language
    Therapy
Clinical Psychology
Other Consultants

Day care
Community Nursing
Physiotherapy
Social work
Other agencies

Respite care
Occupational Therapy
Dietetics
Psychiatry

## PART FOUR: PLANNING

## INITIAL FORMULATION

**PERSON'S VIEWS:** hopes and wishes/expectations of service/response to initial formulation

**CARER'S VIEWS:** beliefs about client/response to initial formulation

## OUTCOME OF INITIAL ASSESSMENT
**Advice given**                **Signposted**
**Referred on**                 **Discharged**
**Further assessment agreed**
**Intervention agreed**
**Signed with date and time**

# Appendix 2

## My Life – initial assessment sheet for client*

**What I want to talk about**

- My family and friends
- My health
- How I spend my time
- My control over my life

- My support
- My abilities
- My safety
- My feelings

**What I want**

**What we decided**

**What will happen next**

---

\* Visual aids should be added.

# Appendix 3
## Cognitive assessment

**GENERAL INTELLECTUAL ABILITY**
Previous assessments?

**ORIENTATION/ATTENTION**
Orientation (time/place/person)
Attention (focused/sustained/divided)

**LANGUAGE/COMMUNICATION**
Previous Speech and Language Reports?

Nonverbal communication:
- Intentional/pre-intentional
- Use of gestures/Makaton signs/symbols/other visual aids
- Body language

Receptive language
Understanding/use of abstract concepts
Understanding/use of idioms
Expressive language/examples
Emotional expression/vocabulary
Pragmatic use of language

**MEMORY**
Immediate memory
Working memory
Delayed verbal
Delayed visual
Autobiographical
Procedural
Prospective
Everyday memory problems

**VISUAL PERCEPTION**
Object recognition
Space/depth perception

**EXECUTIVE FUNCTION**
Planning
Initiation/motivation
Organisation
Inhibition/impulsivity
Perseveration
Rigidity/flexibility
Impulsivity
Abstract thinking
Reasoning
Processing speed
Self-monitoring/self-awareness
General behaviour

**SOCIAL UNDERSTANDING**
Emotion recognition
Theory of mind
Understanding of social rules

**ACADEMIC ABILITY**
Educational attainment/exams
Reading
Writing
Arithmetic
Telling the time
Using money

**DEMENTIA**
Previous assessments?
Evidence of loss of skills
Direct assessments
Carer report
Everyday living skills

# Bibliography

Abbeduto L, Seltzer M M, Shattuck P, Krauss M W, Osmond G, Murphy M M (2004) Psychological well-being and coping in mothers of youths with autism, Down Syndrome or Fragile X-Syndrome *American Journal on Mental Retardation, 109,* 466–74

Abbeduto L, Pavetto M, Kesin E, Weissman M, Karadottir S, O'Brien A and Cawthon S (2001) *The Linguistic and Cognitive Profile of Down Syndrome: Evidence From a Comparison with Fragile X Syndrome.* Available from http://www.down-syndrome.org/reports/109/ (accessed 22.5.2011)

Abbey J, Piller N, De Bellis A, Esterman A, Parker D, Giles L and Lowcay B (2004) The Abbey pain scale: a 1-minute numerical indicator for people with end-stage dementia *International Journal of Palliative Nursing, 10,* 6–13

Abbott P and Sapsford R (1988) *Community Care for Mentally Handicapped Children* Milton Keynes: Open UniversIty Press

Aitken S and Buultjens M (1992) *Vision for Doing: Assessing Functional Vision of Learners who are Multiply Disabled* Edinburgh: Moray House

Ajzen I (1991) The theory of planned behaviour, in *Organisational Behaviour and Human Decision Processes*; cited in E Martin, K McKenzie, E Newman, K Bowden and P Morris (2011) Care staff intentions to support adults with intellectual disability to engage in physical activity: an application of the Theory of Planned Behaviour *Research in Developmental Disabilities, 12,* 2535–41

Alborz A (2003) Transitions: placing a son or daughter with intellectual disability and challenging behaviour in alternative residential provision *Journal of Applied Research in Intellectual Disabilities, 16,* 75–88

Allderidge P (1979) Hospital, madhouses and asylums: cycles in the care of the insane *British Journal of Psychiatry, 134,* 321–34

Allen D, James W, Evans J, Hawkins S and Jenkins R (2005) Positive Behavioural Support: definition, current status and future directions *Tizard Learning Disability Review, 10*(2), 4–11

American Association of Intellectual and Development Disability (2009) *Public Comments Regarding Draft Definition of Intellectual Disability.* Available from http://www.aaidd.org/ (accessed 6.10.2011)

American Association on Mental Retardation (1992) *Mental Retardation: Definitions, Classification and Systems of Support* (10th edition) Washington, DC: American Association on Mental Retardation.

American Psychiatric Association (2000) *Diagnostic and Statistical Manual of Mental Disorders, 4th Edition* Washington, DC: American Psychiatric Association

Anastasi A and Urbina S (1997) *Psychological Testing* (7th edition) London: Prentice-Hall

Andersen T (2006) Significant new voices, Foreword to S Baum and H Lynggaard (eds) *Intellectual Disabilities: A Systemic Approach* London: Karnac Books

Andrews G, Goldberg D P, Krueger R F, Carpenter Jr W T, Hyman S E, Sachdev P and Pine D S (2009a) Exploring the feasibility of a meta-structure for DSM-V and ICD-11: could it improve utility and validity? *Psychological Medicine, 39,* 1993–2000

Andrews G, Pine D S, Hobbs M J, Anderson T M and Sunderland M (2009b) Neurodevelopmental disorders: Cluster 2 of the proposed meta-structure for DSM-V and ICD-11 *Psychological Medicine, 39,* 2013–23

Arscott K, Dagnan D and Stenfert Kroese B (1999) Assessing the ability of people with a learning disability to give informed consent to treatment *Psychological Medicine, 29,* 1367–75

Arthur A R (2003) The emotional lives of people with learning disability *British Journal of Learning Disabilities, 31,* 25–30

Atkinson D, Jackson M and Walmsley J (1997) *Forgotten Lives: Exploring the History of Learning Disability* Kidderminster: British Institute of Learning Disabilities

Atkinson L, Chisholm V C, Scott B, Goldberg S, Vaughn B, Blackwell J, Dickens S and Tam F (1999) Maternal sensitivity, child functional level and attachment in Down Syndrome *Monographs for the Society of Research in Child Development, 64*(3), 45–66

Aylward E H, Burt D B, Thorpe L U, Lai F and Dalton A(1997) Diagnosis of dementia in individuals with intellectual disability *Journal of Intellectual Disability Research, 41*(2), 152–64

Backer C, Chapman M and Mitchell D (2009) Access to secondary healthcare for people with intellectual disabilities: a review of the literature *Journal of Applied Research in Intellectual Disabilities, 22,* 514–25

Baillie A, Slater S, Millington R, Webb H, Keating G, Akroyd S, Ford C, Brady C, Swash J and Twist E (2010) What it takes to set up a DBT service for adults with a learning disability: the lessons so far *Clinical Psychology & People with Learning Disabilities, 8*(1&2), 12–20

Baker S, Hooper S, Skinner M, Hatton D, Schaaf J, Ornstein P and Bailey D (2011) Working memory subsystems and task complexity in young boys with Fragile X syndrome *Journal of Intellectual Disability Research, 55*(1), 19–29

Ball S L, Holland A J, Treppner P, Watson P C and Huppert F A (2008) Executive dysfunction and its association with personality and behaviour changes in the development of Alzheimer's disease in adults with Down Syndrome and mild to moderate learning disabilities *British Journal of Clinical Psychology, 47,* 1–29

Bandura A (2001) Social Cognitive Theory: an agentic perspective *Annual Review of Psychology, 52,* 1–26

Bannister D and Fransella F (1980) *Inquiring Man* Harmondsworth: Penguin

Baron-Cohen S (2000) Asperger's Syndrome/High-Functioning Autism necessarily a disability? *Special Millenium Issue of Developmental and Psychopathology.* Available from http://trehinp.dyndns.org/prehistautistic/a_different_view_of_autism.htm (accessed 21.5.2012)

—— (2001) Theory of mind in normal development and autism *Prisme, 34,* 174–83

—— (2011) *Zero Degrees of Empathy: A New Theory of Human Cruelty* London: Allen Lane

Baron-Cohen S, Ring H A, Bullmore E T, Wheelwright S, Ashwin C and Williams S C R (2000) The amygdala theory of autism *Neuroscience and Biobehavioural Reviews*, *24*, 355–64

Barr M and Shields N (2011) Physical activity in Down Syndrome *Journal of Intellectual Disability Research*, *55*, 1020–33

Barrett M and Eames K (1996) Sequential developments in children's human figure drawing *British Journal of Developmental Psychology*, *14*, 219–36

Baum S and Lynggaard H (2006) *Intellectual Disabilities: A Systemic Approach* London: Karnac Books

Baum S and Webb J (2002) 'Valuing People': what will it mean for clinical psychology services for people with learning disabilities? *Clinical Psychology*, *14*, 20–24

Baxter L (2011) Working psychodynamically with a young woman with a learning disability *Clinical Psychology & People with Learning Disabilities*, *9*(2&3), 67–72

Beacroft M and Dodd K (2011) 'I feel pain' – audit of communication skills and understanding of pain and health needs with people with learning disabilities *British Journal of Learning Disabilities*, *39*, 139–47

Beail N, Warden S, Morsley K and Newman D (2005) Naturalistic evaluation of the effectiveness of psychodynamic psychotherapy with adults with intellectual disabilities *Journal of Applied Research in Intellectual Disabilities*, *18*, 245–51

Beery K E, Buktenica N A and Beery N A (2010) *Developmental Test of Visual Motor Integration* (6th edition) San Antonia, TX: Pearson

Bender M (1993) The unoffered chair: the history of therapeutic disdain towards people with a learning difficulty *Clinical Psychology Forum*, *54*, 7–12

Berne E (1961, 1973) *Transactional Analysis in Psychotherapy: A Systematic Individual and Social Psychiatry* New York: Grove Press

Binet A and Simon T H (1905) Methodes nouvelles pour le diagnostic du niveau intellectual des anormaux *Année Psychologique*, *11*, 191–244; cited in A Anastasi and S Urbina (1997) *Psychological Testing* (7th edition) London: Prentice-Hall

Blackman N (2008) The development of an assessment tool for the bereavement needs of people with learning disabilities *British Journal of Learning Disabilities*, *36*, 165–70

Blakemore S (2007) The social brain of a teenager *The Psychologist*, *20*, 600–602

Blatt B (1969) Purgatory, in R Kugel and W Wolfensberger (eds) *Changing Patterns in Residential Services for the Mentally Retarded* Washington, DC: President's Committee on Mental Retardation

Blatt B and Kaplan F (1967) *Christmas in Purgatory* Boston, MA: Allyn & Bacon. Available from http://www.disabilitymuseur.org/lib/docs/1728card.htm

Bloomberg K, West D, Johnson H and Iacono T (2009) *The Revised Triple C: Checklist of Communication Competencies* Victoria, Australia: Severe Communication Impairment Outreach Projects

BMA and Law Society (2004) *Assessment of Mental Capacity: Guidance for Doctors and Lawyers* (2nd edition) London: BMJ Books

Boake C (2002) From the Binet-Simon to the Wechsler-Bellevue: tracing the history of intelligence testing *Journal of Clinical and Experimental Neuropsychology*, *24*, 383–405

Board of Education (1924) *The Hadow Report. Psychological Tests of Educable Capacity and Their Possible Use in the Public System of Education* London: HMSO

Bogdashina O (2003) *Sensory Perceptual Issues in Autism and Asperger Syndrome* London: Jessica Kingsley

Booth T and Booth W (1998) Risk, resilience and competence: parents with learning difficulties and their children, in R Jenkins (ed.) *Questions of Competence: Culture, Classification and Intellectual Disability* Cambridge: Cambridge University Press

Boring E (1923) Intelligence as the tests test it *New Republic*, June 6, p. 35; cited in S Murdoch (2007) *IQ: The Brilliant Idea That Failed* London: Duckworth Overlook

Bowlby J (1953) *Child Care and the Growth of Love* Harmondsworth: Penguin

—— (1969, 1971) *Attachment and Loss, Volume 1* Harmondsworth: Penguin

Boyle M (2002) *Schizophrenia: A Scientific Delusion?* (2nd edition) London: Routledge

BPS (2001) *Learning Disability: Definitions and Contexts* Leicester: BPS

—— (2004) *Psychological Interventions for Severely Challenging Behaviours Shown by People with Learning Disabilities: Clinical Practice Guidelines* Leicester: BPS

—— (2006) *Assessment of Capacity in Adults: Interim Guidance for Psychologists* Leicester: BPS

—— (2007) *Best Interests: Guidance on Determining the Best Interests of Adults who Lack the Capacity to Make a Decision (or decisions for themselves) (England and Wales)* Leicester: BPS

—— (2008) *Generic Professional Practice Guidelines* (2nd edition) Leicester: BPS

—— (2009a) *Code of Ethics and Conduct* Leicester: BPS

—— (2009b) *Dementia and People with Learning Disabilities* Leicester: BPS

—— (2011) *Good Practice Guidelines on the Use of Psychological Formulation* Leicester: BPS

Braveman P and Gruskin S (2003) Poverty, equity, human rights and health *Bulletin of the World Health Organisation, 81*(7), 539–45

Brazier C (2003) *Buddhist Psychology: Liberate Your Mind, Embrace Life* London: Constable & Robinson

Breckon S and Simpson J (2011) The case for a role for cognitive analytic therapy in learning disability services *Clinical Psychology & People with Learning Disabilities, 9*(1), 2–7

Brown H (2004) A rights-based approach to abuse of women with learning disabilities *Learning Disability Review, 9*(4), 41–44

—— (2011) The role of emotion in decision-making *Journal of Adult Protection, 13*(4), 194–202

Brown H and Marchant E (2011) *Best Interests Decision-Making in Complex Cases* London: Office of the Public Guardian

Brown H and Smith H (eds) (1992) *Normalisation: A Reader* London: Routledge

Brown I, Brown R I, Baum N T, Isaacs B J, Myerscough T, Neikrug S, Roth D, Shearer J and Wang M (2006) *Family Quality of Life Survey: Main Caregivers of People with Intellectual or Developmental Disabilities* Toronto, ON, Canada: Surrey Place Centre

Bruce M, Collins S, Langdon P, Powlitch S and Reynolds S (2010) Does training improve understanding of core concepts in cognitive behaviour therapy by people with intellectual disabilities? A randomized experiment *British Journal of Clinical Psychology, 49*, 1–13

Bruner J S (1983) *Child's Talk: Learning to Use Language* New York: Norton

Brylewski J and Duggan L (2004) Antipsychotic medication for challenging behaviour in people with learning disability (Cochrane Review), in *The Cochrane Library, Issue 4* Chichester: Wiley

Bubenzer D L, West J D and Boughner S R (Interviewers) (1995) The narrative perspective in therapy, in M White *Reauthoring Lives: Interviews and Essays* Adelaide, Australia: Dulwich Centre Publications

Bunning K (2009) Making sense of communication, in J Palwyn and S Carnaby (eds) *Profound Intellectual and Multiple Disabilities: Nursing Complex Needs* Chichester: Wiley-Blackwell

Burleigh M (2000) *The Third Reich: A New History* London: Pan Macmillan

Burnham J, Alvis Palma D and Whitehouse L (2008) Learning as a context for differences and differences as a context for learning *Journal of Family Therapy*, *30*, 529–42

Burns J (1992) Normalisation through the looking glass *Clinical Psychology Forum*, *January*, 22–24

Burton M (with additions by C Kagan) (2008) Societal case formulation. Available from http://www.compsy.org.uk/listb.htm (accessed 30.4.2012)

Burton M and Kagan C (2006) Decoding Valuing People *Disability & Society*, *21*, 299–313

Cambridge P and Carnaby S (2005) *Person Centred Planning and Care Management with People with Learning Disabilities* London: Jessica Kingsley

Cardone D and Hilton A (2006) Engaging people with intellectual disabilities in systemic therapy, in S Baum and H Lynggaard (eds) *Intellectual Disabilities: A Systemic Approach* London: Karnac Books

Carmichael B (2003) The Human Genome Project – threat or promise? *Journal of Intellectual Disability Research*, *47*(7), 505–508

Carnaby S (1998) Reflections on social integration for people with learning disabilities: does interdependence have a role? *Journal of Intellectual and Developmental Disability Research*, *23*, 219–28

Carr A, O'Reilly C, Noonan Walsh P and McEvoy J (2007) *The Handbook of Intellectual Disability and Clinical Psychology Practice* London: Routledge

Carr E G (1996) The transfiguration of behavior analysis: strategies for survival *Journal of Behavioral Education*, *6*(3), 263–70

Carr E G, Horner R H, Turnbull A P, Marquis J G, McLaughlin D M, McAtee M L, Smith C E, Ryan K A, Ruef M B and Doolabh A (1999) *Positive Behavior Support for People with Developmental Disabilities* Washington, DC: American Association on Mental Retardation

Carr E G, Dunlap G, Horner R H, Koegel R L, Turnbull A P, Sailor W, Anderson J L, Albin R W, Koegel L K and Fox L (2002) Positive behavior support; evolution of an applied science *Journal of Positive Behavior Interventions*, *4*(1), 4–16

Carr E H (1961) *What is History?* Harmondsworth: Pelican

Chamberlain P, Woolston A and Thompson S (2005) Person Centred Planning – will psychologists strangle it at birth? *Clinical Psychology & People with Learning Disabilities*, *3*(1), 2–7

Chaney R H and Eyman R K (2000) Patterns in mortality over 60 years among people with mental retardation in a residential facility *Mental Retardation*, *38*, 289–93

Changeux J-B and Dehaene S (1993) Neuronal models of cognitive functions, in M H Johnson (ed.) *Brain Development and Cognition: A Reader* Oxford: Blackwell

Chaytor N and Schmitter-Edgecombe M (2003) The ecological validity of neuropsychological tests: a review of the literature on everyday cognitive skills *Neuropsychological Review*, *14*(4), 181–97

Clapton J and Fitzgerald J (2010) The history of disability: a history of 'otherness' *Renaissance Universal*. Available from http://www.ru.org/human-rights/the-history-of-disability-a-history-of-otherness.html (accessed 30.3.2012)

Clare I (2005) *Consent to Treatment* presentation 12 September 2005

Clare I C H and Gudjonsson G H (1993) Interrogative suggestibility, confabulation, and acquiescence in people with mild learning disabilities (mental handicap): implications for reliability during police interrogations *British Journal of Clinical Psychology*, *32*(3), 295–302

Clarkson P (1989) *Gestalt Counselling in Action* London: Sage

Clegg J A and Lansdall-Welfare R (1995) Attachment and learning disability: a theoretical review informing three clinical interventions *Journal of Intellectual Disability Research*, *39*(4), 295–305

Clegg J and Sheard C (2002) Challenging behaviour and insecure attachment *Journal of Intellectual Disability Research*, *46*(6), 503–506

Clegg J, Murphy E, Almack K and Harvey A (2008) Tensions around inclusion: reframing the moral horizon *Journal of Applied Research in Intellectual Disabilities*, *21*, 81–94

Clements J (2002) *Assessing Behaviors Regarded as Problematic for People with Developmental Disabilities* London: Jessica Kingsley

Coles S (2010) Clinical psychology's interest in the conceptualisation and use of power *Clinical Psychology Forum*, 212, 22–26

Conboy-Hill S (2001) The cognitive interview: a multipurpose approach to interviewing people with learning disabilities *Clinical Psychology*, *2*(June), 17–20

Cooley C H (1902) *Human Nature and the Social Order* New York: Scribner's; cited in A N Schore (1994) *Affect Regulation and the Origin of the Self: The Neurobiology of Emotional Development* Hillsdale, NJ: Lawrence Erlbaum Associates

Corbett A (2009*)* Words as a second language: the therapeutic challenge of severe intellectual disability, Chapter 3 in T Cottis (ed.) *Intellectual Disability, Trauma and Psychotherapy* London: Routledge

Corker M and Shakespeare T (eds) (2002) *Disability/Postmodernity: Embodying Disability Theory* New York: Consortium

Cottis T (ed.) (2009) *Intellectual Disability, Trauma and Psychotherapy* London: Routledge

Coupe O'Kane J and Goldbart J (1998) *Communication Before Speech: Development and Assessment* London: David Fulton

Coupe O'Kane J, Barton L, Barber M, Collins L, Levy D and Murphy D (1985) *Affective Communication Assessment* Manchester: Manchester Education Committee

Cozolino L (2006) *The Neuroscience of Human Relationships* London: Norton

CPS (2011) *DPP Says Prosecuting Disability Hate Crime is "the Next Frontier" for the Criminal Justice System.* Available from http://www.cps.gov.uk/news/press_releases/110_11/ (accessed 5.5.2012)

CQC (2011) *CQC Report on Winterbourne View Confirms its Owners Failed to Protect People from Abuse.* Available from www.cqc.org.uk/media (accessed 13.5.2012)

Crellin C (1998) Origins and social contexts of the term 'formulation' in psychological case-reports *Clinical Psychology Forum*, *112*(February), 18–27

Criminal Justice Act (2003) London: HMSO. Available from http://www.legislation.gov.uk/ukpga/2003/44/contents

Crocker T M (1990) Assessing client participation in mental handicap services: a pilot study *The British Journal of Mental Subnormality*, *36*(2), 98–107

Cronbach L J and Meehl P E (1955) Construct validity in psychological tests *Psychological Bulletin*, *52*(4), 281–302

Cummins R A (2005a) Moving from the quality of life concept to a theory *Journal of Intellectual Disability Research*, *49*(10), 699–706

—— (2005b) Issues in the systematic assessment of quality of life, in J Hogg and A Langa (eds) *Assessing Adults with Intellectual Disabilities* Oxford: Blackwell/BPS

—— (2005c) Instruments assessing quality of life, in J Hogg and A Langa (eds) *Assessing Adults with Intellectual Disabilities* Oxford: Blackwell/BPS, pp. 119–37

Dagnan D (2008) Psychological and emotional health and well-being of people with intellectual disabilities *Learning Disability Review*, *13*(1), 3–9

Dagnan D and Wearing M (2004) Linking stigma to psychological distress: testing a social-cognitive model of the experience of people with intellectual disabilities *Clinical Psychology & Psychotherapy*, *11*, 247–54

Dallos R (2006) *Attachment Narrative Therapy* Maidenhead: Open University Press

Dallos R and Draper R (2000) *An Introduction to Family Therapy* Buckingham: Open University Press

Dallos R and Vetere A (2009) *Systemic Theory and Attachment Narra*tives Hove: Routledge

Dallos R, Wright J, Stedmon J and Johnstone L (2006) Integrative formulation, in L Johnstone and R Dallos (eds) *Formulation in Psychology and Psychotherapy* Hove: Routledge

Darwin C (1859) *On the Origin of Species* London: John Murray

Daynes S, Doswell, S, Gregory N, Haydon-Laurelut M and Millett E (2011) Emergent cake: a plurality of systemic practices *Context*, *April*, 21–25

Dear M and Wolch J (1987) *Landscapes of Despair: From Deinstitutionalisation to Homelessness* Cambridge: Polity; cited in E Hall (2010) Spaces of social inclusion and belonging for people with intellectual disabilities *Journal of Intellectual Disability Research*, *54*, 48–57

Deb S, Clarke D and Unwin G (2006) *Using Medication to Manage Behaviour Problems Among Adults with a Learning Disability* Birmingham: University of Birmingham, Royal College of Psychiatrists and Mencap

Decety J and Jackson P L (2004) The functional architecture of human empathy *Behavioural & Cognitive Neuroscience Reviews*, *3*(2), 71–100

Deci E L and Ryan R M (1985) *Intrinsic Motivation and Self-Determination in Human Behavior* New York: Plenum

—— (2000) The what and the why of goal pursuits: human needs and the self-determination of behaviour *Psychological Inquiry*, *11*, 227–68

Department for Constitutional Affairs (2007) *Mental Capacity Act: Code of Practice* London: HMSO

Department of Health (1997) *Signposts for Success in Commissioning and Providing Health Services for People with Learning Disabilities* London: NHS Executive

—— (1999) *Once a Day* London: HMSO

—— (2001a) *Valuing People: A New Strategy for Learning Disability for the 21st Century* London: HMSO

—— (2001b) *Reference Guide to Consent for Examination or Treatment* London: Department of Health

—— (2001c) *Good Practice in Consent Implementation Guide* London: Department of Health

—— (2001d) *Seeking Consent: Working with People with Learning Disabilities* London: Department of Health

—— (2001e) *Planning with People: Towards Person Centred Approaches* London: Department of Health

——— (2002a) *Action for Health – Health Action Plans and Health Facilitation: Detailed Good Practice Guidance on Implementation for Learning Disability Partnership Boards* London: Department of Health

——— (2002b) *Planning with People: Towards Person-Centred Approaches* London: Department of Health

——— (2007) *Putting People First: A Shared Vision and Commitment to the Transformation of Adult Social Care* London: Department of Health

——— (2008) *Transforming Social Care* London: Department of Health

——— (2009a) *Valuing People Now: the Delivery Plan* London: Department of Health

——— (2009b) *Valuing Employment Now: Real Jobs for People with Learning Disabilties* London: Department of Health

Department of Health and Home Office (2000) *No Secrets: Guidance on Developing and Implementing Multi-Agency Policies and Procedures to Protect Vulnerable Adults from Abuse* London: Department of Health

Department of Health and Social Security (1980) *Mental Handicap: Progress, Problems and Priorities. A Review of Mental Handicap Services in England since the 1971 White Paper – 'Better services for the mentally handicapped'* London: HMSO

Department of Health and Social Security and Welsh Office (1971) *Better Services for the Mentally Handicapped* Cmnd 4683. London: HMSO

De Schipper J C and Schuengel C (2010) Attachment behaviour towards support staff in young people with intellectual disabilities: associations with challenging behaviour *Journal of Intellectual Disability Research, 54*, 584–96

Devereux J, Hastings R and Noone S (2011) Staff stress and burnout in intellectual disability services: work stress theory and its application *Journal of Applied Research in Intellectual Disabilities, 22*, 561–73

Didden R, Sigafoos J, Korzilius H, Baas A, Lancioni G E, O'Reilly M and Curfs L M G (2009) Form and function of communicative behaviours in individuals with Angelman Syndrome *Journal of Applied Research in Intellectual Disabilities, 22*, 526–37

Digby A (1996) Contexts and perspectives, in D Wright and A Digby (eds) *From Idiocy to Mental Deficiency* London: Routledge, pp. 1–12

Disability Discrimination Act (1995) London: HMSO. Available from http://www.legislation.gov.uk/ukpga/1995/50/contents

Disability Rights Commission (2004) *Equal Treatment: Closing the Gap. Background Evidence for the DRC's Formal Investigation into Health Inequalities Experienced by People with Learning Disabilities or Mental Health Problems* London: DRC

Diversi M (2003) Glimpses of street children through short stories, in M Gergen and K J Gergen (eds) *Social Construction: A Reader* London: Sage

Division of Clinical Psychology (1995) *Professional Practice Guidelines* Leicester: BPS

——— (2001) *Core Purpose and Philosophy of the Profession* Leicester: BPS

Dobson S and Upadhyaya S (2002) Concepts of autism in Asian communities in Bradford, UK *Good Autism Practice, 3*(2), 43–51

Driver J, Haggard P and Shallice T (eds) (2007) *Mental Processes in the Human Brain* Oxford: Oxford University Press

Duffy S (2010) The Citizenship Theory of social justice: exploring the meaning of personalisation for social workers *Journal of Social Work Practice, 24*(3), 253–67

Dunn M C, Cloare I C H and Holland A J (2008) To empower or protect? Constructing the 'vulnerable adult' in English law and public policy *Legal Studies*, *28*(2), 234–53

Durand V M and Crimmins D B (1992) *The Motivation Assessment Scale (MAS)* Topeica, KS: Monaco & Associates

Edgin J O, Kumar A, Spanò G and Nadel L (2011) Neuropsychological effects of second language exposure in Down Syndrome *Journal of Intellectual Disability Research*, *55*(3), 351–56

Edmunds G and Bliss V (2006) Solution focused Asperger Syndrome *Solution News*, *2*(2), 8–9

Education Act (1944) London: HMSO. Repealed 1.11.1996. Available from http://www.legislation.gov.uk/ukpga/Geo6/7-8/31/contents

Edwardraj S, Mumtaj K, Prasad J H, Kuruvilla A, and Jacob K S (2010) Perceptions about intellectual disability: a qualitative study from Vellore, South India *Journal of Intellectual Disability Research*, *54*(8), 736–48

Egan G (2002) *The Skilled Helper* Pacific Grove, CA: Brooks/Cole

Emerson E (1992) What is normalisation?, in H Brown and H Smith (eds) *Normalisation: A Reader* London: Routledge

——— (2001, 1995) *Challenging Behaviour: Analysis and Intervention in People with Severe Intellectual Disabilities* (2nd edition) Cambridge: Cambridge University Press

Emerson E and Baines S (2010) *Health Inequalities and People with Learning Disabilities in the UK: 2010* Manchester: Learning Disabilities Observatory, supported by the Department of Health

Emerson E, McGill P and Mansell J (eds) (2001) *Severe Learning Disabilities and Challenging Behaviours* London: Chapman & Hall

Emerson E, Hatton C and MacLean W E (2007) Contribution of socioeconomic position to health inequalities of British children and adolescents with intellectual disabilities *American Journal on Mental Retardation*, *112*(2), 140–50

Emerson E, Baines S, Allerton L and Welch V (2011) *Health Inequalities and People with Learning Disabilities in the UK: 2011* Manchester: Learning Disabilities Observatory

Emerson E, Madden R, Robertson J, Graham H, Hatton C and Llewellyn G (2009) *Intellectual and Physical Disability, Social Mobility, Social Inclusion and Health* Lancaster: Centre for Disability Research

Emerson E, Hatton C, Robertson J, Roberts H, Baines S and Glover G (2010) *People with Learning Disabilities in England 2010: Services and Supports* Manchester: Learning Disabilities Observatory

Emerson E, Hatton C, Dickson K, Gone R, Caine A and Bromley J (2012) *Clinical Psychology and People with Intellectual Disabilities* (2nd edition) Chichester, UK: Wiley-Blackwell

Engel J D, Zarconi J, Pethtel L L and Missimi S A (2008) *Narratives in Health Care* Oxford: Radcliffe

Ephraim G (1998) Exotic communication, conversations and scripts – or tales of the pained, the unheard and the unloved, in D Hewett (ed.) *Challenging Behaviour: Principles and Practices* London: David Fulton

Erickson E (1984) *Childhood & Society* London: Granada

Espie C A, Watkins J, Curtice L, Espie A, Duncan R, Ryan J A, Brodie M J, Mantala K and Sterrick K (2003) Psychopathology in people with epilepsy and intellectual disability; an investigation of potential explanatory variables *Journal of Neurology, Neurosurgery & Psychiatry*, *74*, 1485–92

Eysenck H J (1972) Behavior therapy is behavioristic *Behavior Therapy*, *3*, 609–13

Felce D (1997) Defining and applying the concept of quality of life *Journal of Intellectual Disability Research*, *41*(2), 126–35

Fitzgerald J (1998) Geneticizing disability: the Human Genome Project and the commodification of the self *Issues in Law & Medicine*, *10.1.1998*. Available from http://www.metafuture.org/articlesbycolleagues/JenniferFitzgerald (accessed 30.4.2012)

Fletcher H (2008) Attachment theory and learning disabilities: connections between early beginnings and later challenges *Advancing Practice Conference* 8 May 2008

Flynn J R (1987) Massive IQ gains in 14 nations: what IQ tests really measure *Psychological Bulletin*, *101*(2), 171–91

—— (2000) The hidden history of IQ and special education *Psychology, Public Policy and Law*, *6*(1), 191–98

Fogel A (2009) What is a transaction?, in A Sameroff (ed.) *The Transactional Model of Development* Washington, DC: American Psychological Association

Fonagy P, Steele H, Moran G S, Steele M and Higgit A (1991) The capacity for understanding mental states: the reflective self in parent and child and its significance for security of attachment *Infant Mental Health Journal*, *13*, 200–17

Foucault M (1967, 1989) *Madness and Civilisation* London: Routledge

Fox H (2009) A good citizen: using narrative in contexts of trauma *Context, October*, 46–49

Fox P (2008) Positive behavioural support: quality of life and social validity *Clinical Psychology & People with Learning Disabilities*, *6*(4), 6–12

Frankl V (1959, 2004) *Man's Search for Meaning* London: Random House

Fromm E (1957, 1985) *The Art of Loving* Hammersmith: Thorsons

Fromm E and Xirau R (1968) *The Nature of Man* New York: Macmillan

Furman B (1998) *It's Never Too Late to Have a Happy Childhood* London: BT Press

Gallagher S (2007) The natural philosophy of agency *Philosophy Compass*, *2*, 1–9

Galton F (1883) *Inquiries into Human Faculty and its Development*; cited in A Anastasi and S Urbina (1997) *Psychological Testing* (7th edition) London: Prentice-Hall

Garner C, Callias M and Turk J (1999) Executive function and theory of mind performance of boys with Fragile-X Syndrome *Journal of Intellectual Disability Research*, *43*, 466–74

Gelsthorpe S (1995) Consent, compliance and coercion *Clinical Psychology Forum*, *October*, 36–38

George C, Kaplan N and Main M (1985) *The Berkeley Adult Attachment Interview* unpublished document, Department of Psychology, University of California, Berkeley, CA; cited in R Dallos (2006) *Attachment Narrative Therapy* Maidenhead: Open University Press

Gergen K J (2003) Knowledge as socially constructed, in M Gergen and K Gergen (eds) *Social Construction: A Reader* London: Sage

Gergen M and Gergen K J (2003) *Social Construction: A Reader* London: Sage

Gerhardt S (2004) *Why Love Matters* Hove: Brunner-Routledge

—— (2010) *The Selfish Society* London: Simon & Schuster

Giddens A (1991) *Modernity and Self-Identity* Cambridge: Polity Press

Gilbert P (ed.) (2005) *Compassion: Conceptualisations, Research and Use in Psychotherapy* Hove: Routledge

—— (2010) *The Compassionate Mind* London: Constable

Gillath O, Shaver P R and Mikulinger M (2005) An attachment-theoretical approach to compassion and altruism, Chapter 4 in P Gilbert (ed.) *Compassion: Conceptualisations, Research and Use in Psychotherapy* Hove: Routledge

Gladstone D (1996) The changing dynamic of institutional care, in D Wright and A Digby (eds) *From Idiocy to Mental Deficiency* London: Routledge

Glover G and Ayub M (2010) *How People with Learning Disabilities Die* Manchester: Learning Disabilities Observatory

Goddard H (1912) *The Kallikak Family: A Study in the Heredity of Feeble-Mindedness* New York: Macmillan; cited in J W Trent (1994) *Inventing the Feeble Mind: A History of Mental Retardation in the United States* Berkeley, CA: University of California Press

Goffman E (1961) *Asylums: Essays on the Social Situation of Mental Patients and Other Inmates* Harmondsworth: Penguin

—— (1963) *Stigma: Notes on the Management of Spoiled Identity* Harmondsworth: Penguin

Goldbart J and Caton S (2011) *Communication and People with the Most Complex Needs: What Works and Why This is Essential* London: Mencap

Goodey C F (1996) The psychopolitics of learning and disability in seventeenth century thought, in D Wright and A Digby (eds) *From Idiocy to Mental Deficiency* London: Routledge

—— (2001) What is developmental disability? The origin and nature of our conceptual models *Journal on Developmental Disabilities, 8*(2), 1–18

—— (2011) *A History of Intelligence and Intellectual Disability: The Shaping of Psychology in Early Modern Europe* Farnham, Surrey: Ashgate

Goodley D (2011) *Disability Studies: An Interdisciplinary Introduction* London: Sage

Graham H (2005) Intellectual disabilities and socioeconomic inequalities in health: an overview of research *Journal of Applied Research in Intellectual Disabilities, 18*, 101–11

Greenough W T, Black J E and Wallace C S (1993) Experience and brain development, in M Johnson (ed.) *Brain Development and Cognition: A Reader* Oxford: Blackwell, pp. 290–318

Greenspan S (1994) Review of 'Mental Retardation: Definition, Classification and Systems of Supports, 9th ed.' *American Journal of Mental Retardation, 98*(3), 544–49

Greenspan S, Switzky H N and Woods G W (2011) Intelligence involves risk-awareness and intellectual disability involves risk-unawareness: implications of a theory of common sense *Journal of Intellectual and Developmental Disability, 36*, 246–57

Grove N, Bunning K, Porter J and Morgan M (2000) *See What I Mean: Guidelines to Aid Understanding of Communication by People with Severe and Profound Learning Disabilities* Kidderminster: BILD and Mencap

Guralnick M J (1996). Future directions in early intervention for children with Down Syndrome, Chapter 8 in J A Rondal, J Perera, L Nadel and A Comblain (eds) *Down Syndrome: Psychological, Psychobiological and Socio-educational Perspectives* London: Whurr

Hall E (2005) The entangled geographies of social exclusion/inclusion for people with learning disabilities *Health and Place, 11*, 107–15

—— (2010) Spaces of social inclusion and belonging for people with intellectual disabilities *Journal of Intellectual Disability Research, 54*, 48–57

Hanková J and Hanková J, with Holukbová (2000) Coming home, Chapter 3 in R Traustadòttir and K Johnson (2000) *Women with Intellectual Disabilities: Finding a Place in the World* London: Jessica Kingsley

Hanna L M, Taggart L and Cousins W (2010) Cancer prevention and health promotion for people with intellectual disabilities: an exploratory study of staff knowledge *Journal of Intellectual Disability Research*, *55*(3), 281–91

Happé F (1999) Autism: cognitive deficit or cognitive style? *Trends in Cognitive Sciences*, *3*(6), 216–22

Happé F and Frith U (1996) The neuropsychology of autism *Brain*, *119*, 1377–1400

Harrison J A, Mullen P D and Green L W (1992) A meta-analysis of studies of the Health Belief Model with adults *Health Education Research*, *7*, 107–16; cited in M Barr and N Shields (2011) Physical activity in Down Syndrome *Journal of Intellectual Disability Research*, *55*(11), 1020–33

Harvey D (2005) *A Brief History of Neoliberalism* Oxford: Oxford University Press; cited in W Bivens-Tatum *Libraries and the Commodification of Culture.* Available from http://blogs.princeton.edu/librarian/2012/002 (accessed 30.4.2012)

Haydon-Laurelut M (2011) Disablement, systemic therapy and people with learning disabilities *Context, April*, 7–11

Haydon-Laurelut M and Nunkoosing K (2010) 'I want to be listened to': systemic psychotherapy with a man with intellectual disabilities and his paid supporters *Journal of Family Therapy*, *32*, 73–86

Haydon-Laurelut M and Wilson J C (2011) Interviewing the internalised Other: attending to voices of the 'Other' *Journal of Systemic Therapies*, *30*(1), 24–37

Heard D (1982) Family systems and the attachment dynamic *Journal of Family Therapy*, *4*, 99–116

Hensel E, Rose J, Stenfert Kroese B and Banks-Smith J (2002) Subjective judgements of quality of life: a comparison study between people with intellectual disability and those without disability *Journal of Intellectual Disability Research*, *46*(2), 95–107

Heslop P (2011) Supporting people with learning disabilities who self-injure *Tizard Learning Disability Review*, *16*(1), 5–15

Hewett D (ed.) (1998) *Challenging Behaviour: Principles and Practices* London: David Fulton

Hill J (1982) Reasons and causes: the nature of explanations in psychology and psychiatry *Psychological Medicine*, *12*, 501–14

Hillery J, Tomkin D, McAuley A, Keane V and Staines M (1998) Consent to treatment and people with learning disabilities *Irish Journal of Psychological Medicine*, *15*(4), 117–18

Hobson R P, Lee A and Brown R (1999) Autism and congenital blindness *Journal of Autism and Developmental Disorders*, *29*(1), 45–56

Hogg J and Sebba J (1986) *Profound Mental Retardation and Multiple Impairment, Volume 1: Development and Learning* London: Croom Helm

Hogg J and Langa A (2005) *Assessing Adults with Intellectual Disabilities: A Service Provider's Guide* Oxford: BPS Blackwell

Hogg J, Reeves D, Roberts J and Mudford O C (2001) Consistency, context and confidence in judgements of affective communication in adults with profound intellectual and multiple disabilities *Journal of Intellectual Disability Research*, *45*(1), 18–29

Holland A and Clare I (2003) The Human Genome Project: considerations for people with intellectual disabilities *Journal of Intellectual Disability Research*, *47*(7), 515–25

Home Office Violent Crime Unit (2008) *Learning Disability Hate Crime: Good Practice Guidance for Crime and Disorder Reduction Partnerships and Learning Disability Partnership Boards* London: Home Office

Hughes D (2009) The communication of emotions and the growth of autonomy and intimacy within family therapy, in D Fosha, D S Siegel and M F Solomon (eds) *The Healing Power of Emotion: Affective Neuroscience, Development and Clinical Practice* New York: Norton

Human Rights Act (1998) London: HMSO. Available from http://www.legislation. gov.uk/ukpga/1998/42/contents

Iarocci C and Burack G (1998) Understanding the development of attention in persons with mental retardation: challenging the myths, in J A Burack, R M Hodapp and E Zigler (eds) *Handbook of Mental Retardation and Development* Cambridge: Cambridge University Press

Iwata B A and DeLeon I G (1996) *The Functional Analysis Screening Tool* Gainesville, FL: University of Florida

Jackson M (1996) Institutional provision for the feeble-minded in Edwardian England: Sandlebridge and the scientific morality of permanent care, in D Wright and A Digby (eds) *From Idiocy to Mental Deficiency* London: Routledge

Jahoda A and Markova I (2004) Coping with social stigma: people with intellectual disabilities moving from institutions and family home *Journal of Intellectual Disability Research*, 48(8), 719–29

Jahoda A, Dagnan D, Jarvie P and Kerr W (2006) Depression, social context and cognitive behavioural therapy for people who have intellectual disabilities *Journal of Applied Research in Intellectual Disabilities*, 19, 81–89

Jahoda A, Dagnan D, Stenfert Kroese B, Pert C and Trower P (2009) Cognitive behaviour therapy: from face to face interaction to a broader contextual understanding *Journal of Intellectual Disability Research*, 53(9), 759–71

Janssen C G C, Schuengel C and Stolk J (2002) Understanding challenging behaviour in people with severe and profound intellectual disability: a stress-attachment model *Journal of Intellectual Disability Research*, 46, 445–53

Jefferies L (2009) Introducing Intensive Interaction *The Psychologist*, 22(9), 756–59

Jeffery L (2011) *Understanding Agency* Bristol: The Policy Press

Jenkins R (2006) Working with the support network: applying systemic practice in learning disabilities services *British Journal of Learning Disabilities*, 34, 77–81

—— (ed.) (1998) *Questions of Competence: Culture, Classification and Intellectual Disability* Cambridge: Cambridge University Press

Johnson M H (2005) *Developmental Cognitive Neuroscience* (2nd edition) Oxford: Blackwell

Johnstone E (2010) Systemic perspectives about therapeutic change working in a social services team context *Clinical Psychology Forum*, 214, 41–45

Johnstone L (1997) 'I hear what you're saying' – how to avoid jargon in therapy *Psychotherapy Section Newsletter 22, December*, 3–11

Johnstone L and Dallos R (2006) *Formulation in Psychology and Psychotherapy* Hove: Routledge

Joint Committee on Human Rights (2008) *A Life Like Any Other? Human Rights of Adults with Learning Disabilities* House of Lords, House of Commons

Jones K (1972) *A History of the Mental Health Services* Routledge: London

Kagan C and Burton M (2001) *Critical Community Psychology Praxis for the 21st Century* paper presented to BPS Conference Glasgow, March 2001

Kagan C, Burton M, Ducket P, Lawthom R and Siddiquee A (2011) *Critical Community Psychology* Chichester: BPS Blackwell

Kainova T, with Cerna M (2000) What is life like, Chapter 1 in R Traustadòttir and K Johnson (eds) *Women with Intellectual Disabilities: Finding a Place in the World* London: Jessica Kingsley

Karmiloff-Smith A (1995) Annotation: the extraordinary cognitive journey from foetus through infancy *Journal of Child Psychology and Psychiatry, 38*(8), 1293–1313

—— (2009) Nativism versus neuroconstructivism: rethinking the study of developmental disorders *Developmental Psychology, 45*(1), 56–63

Kaufman A S and Lichtenberger E O (2006) *Assessing Adolescent and Adult Intelligence* (3rd edition) Hoboken, NJ: Wiley

Keegan S (2007) Science, but not as we know it *Qualitative Methods in Psychology Newsletter, 4*, 32–33

Kelly G (1969) Man's construction of his alternatives, in B Maher (ed.) *Clinical Psychology and Personality: Selected Papers of George Kelly* Chichester: Wiley

—— (1977) The psychology of the unknown, in D Bannister (ed.) *New Perspectives in Personal Construct Theory* London: Academic Press

Kent L, Evans J, Paul M and Sharp M (1999) Comorbidity of autistic spectrum disorders in children with Down Syndrome *Developmental Medicine & Child Neurology, 41*, 153–58

Keywood K and Flynn M (2006) Healthcare decision-making by adults with learning disabilities: ongoing agendas, future challenges *Psychiatry, 5*(10), 360–62

Keywood K, Fovargue S and Flynn M (1999) *Best Practice? Health Care Decision Making By, With and for Adults with Learning Disabilities* Manchester: National Development Team

King R D, Raynes N V and Tizard J (1970) *Patterns of Residential Care: Sociological Studies in Institutions for Handicapped Children* London: Routledge & Kegan Paul

Klotz J (2004) Sociocultural study of intellectual disability: moving beyond labelling and social constructionist perspectives *British Journal of Learning Disabilities, 32*, 93–104

Kreuger L, van Exel J and Nieboer A (2008) Needs of persons with severe intellectual disabilities: a Q-methodological study of clients with severe behavioural disorders and severe intellectual disabilities *Journal of Applied Research in Intellectual Disabilities, 21*, 466–76

Kristiansen K (2000a) Learning from and with women: the story of Jenny, Chapter 7 in R Traustadòttir and K Johnson (eds) *Women with Intellectual Disabilities: Finding a Place in the World* London: Jessica Kingsley

—— (2000b) The social meaning of work, Chapter 13 in R Traustadòttir and K Johnson (eds) *Women with Intellectual Disabilities: Finding a Place in the World* London: Jessica Kingsley

Kroese B S, Dagnan D and Loumidis K (1997) *Cognitive-Behaviour Therapy for People with Learning Disabilities* Hove: Brunner-Routledge

Kuhn S (1996) *The Structure of Scientific Revolutions* (3rd edition) London: University of Chicago Press

Lacey P and Ouvry C (eds) (1998) *People with Profound and Multiple Learning Disabilities: A Collaborative Approach to Meeting Complex Needs* London: Fulton

Lacey T (2012) Developing a conversational assessment tool for the detection of Asperger's Syndrome in adults *Clinical Psychology Forum, 236*, 41–45

Laing R D (1960) *The Divided Self* Harmondsworth: Penguin

Lanfranchi S, Jerman O, Dal Pont E, Alberti A and Vianello R (2010) Executive function in adolescents with Down Syndrome *Journal of Intellectual Disability Research*, *54*(4), 308–19

Larkin M (2002) Using scaffolded instruction to optimize learning. Available from http://ww.cec.sped.org/AM/Template.cfm (accessed 1.6.2002)

LaVigna G W and Willis T J (2005) A Positive Behavior Support Model for breaking the barriers to social and community inclusion *Learning Disability Review*, *10*(2), 16–23

LaVigna G, Willis T J, Shaull J F, Abedi M and Sweltzer M (1994) *Periodic Service Review: A Total Quality Assurance System for Human Services and Education* London: Paul H Brookes

Leahy R L (2005) A social-cognitive model of validation, Chapter 7 in P Gilbert (ed.) *Compassion: Conceptualisations, Research and Use in Psychotherapy* Hove, E Sussex: Routledge

Leaning B (2007) The use of Narrative Therapy in the treatment of a 19-year-old man with learning disabilities whose life was invaded by anger *Clinical Psychology & People with Learning Disabilities*, *5*(3), 2–7

Lederach J P (2004) *The Moral Imagination* Oxford: Oxford University Press

Lee D (2005) The perfect nurturer: a model to develop a compassionate mind within the context of cognitive therapy, Chapter 11 in P Gilbert (ed.) *Compassion: Conceptualisations, Research and Use in Psychotherapy* Hove: Routledge

Leeder S R and Dominello A (2005) Health, equity and intellectual disability *Journal of Applied Research in Intellectual Disabilities*, *18*, 97–100

Ley P (1988) *Communicating with Patients* London: Stanley Thornes

Ley P and Florio T (1996) The use of readability formulas in health care *Psychology, Health & Medicine*, *1*(1), 7–28

Lezak M, Howieson D B and Loring D W (2004) *Neuropsychological Assessment* (4th edition) Oxford: Oxford University Press

Lichtenberger E O and Kaufman A S (2009) *Essentials of WAIS-IV Assessment* Hoboken: Wiley

Lindsay W, Steptoe L and Haut F (2011) The sexual and physical abuse histories of offenders with intellectual disability *Journal of Intellectual Disability Research*, *56*, 326–31

Lloyd E (2009) Speaking through the skin: the significance of shame, Chapter 4 in T Cottis (ed.) *Intellectual Disability, Trauma and Psychotherapy* London: Routledge

Lloyd J (2011) Consulting with staff teams *Clinical Psychology & People with Learning Disabilities*, *9*(1), 22–31

Lombard D (2009) Valuing People Now 'unrealistic' due to lack of new funding *Community Care*, 19 January

Lovett H (1985) *Cognitive Counselling and Persons with Special Needs* Westport, CT: Praeger

—— (1996) *Learning to Listen: Positive Approaches and People with Difficult Behaviour* Baltimore, MD: P H Brookes Publishing

Lowe K and Felce D (1996) Challenging behaviour services: how effective are they? *Clinical Psychology Forum*, *93*, 20–23

Luria A R (1970) The functional organization of the brain *Scientific American*, *222*(3), 66–78

—— (1976) *Cognitive Development: Its Cultural and Social Foundations* Cambridge, MA: Harvard University Press

McCarthy M (2000) Consent, abuse and choices: women with intellectual disabilities and sexuality, Chapter 9 in R Traustadòttir and K Johnson (eds) *Women with Intellectual Disabilities: Finding a Place in the World* London: Jessica Kingsley

MacCorquodale K and Meehl P E (1948) On a distinction between hypothetical constructs and intervening variables *Psychological Review*, *55*, 95–107

McDonagh P (2000) Diminished men and dangerous women: representations of gender and learning disability in early- and mid-nineteenth-century Britain *British Journal of Learning Disabilities*, *28*, 49–53

—— (2008) *Idiocy: A Cultural History* Liverpool: Liverpool University Press

Mace C (1996) *Mindfulness and Mental Health* Hove: Routledge

McGill P (2003) Challenging behaviour, challenging environments and challenging needs *Clinical Psychology Forum*, *June*, 14–18

MacIntyre A (2007) *After Virtue* (3rd edition) Notre Dame, IN: University of Notre Dame Press

Mackay E and Dodd K (2010) Evaluation and effectiveness of pain recognition and management training for staff working in learning disability services *British Journal of Learning Disabilities*, *39*, 243–51

Mair J M M (1977) The community of self, in D Bannister (ed.) *New Perspectives in Personal Construct Theory* London: Academic Press

Mansell J (2007, 1993) *Services for People with Learning Disabilities and Challenging Behaviour or Mental Health Needs* (Revised edition) London: Department of Health

Mansell J and Beadle-Brown J (2005) Person Centred Planning and Person-Centred Action: A Critical Perspective, Chapter 2 in P Cambridge and S Carnaby *Person Centred Planning and Care Management with People with Learning Disabilities* London: Jessica Kingsley

Marvin R S and Planta R C (1996) Mothers' reactions to their child's diagnosis: relations with security of attachment *Journal of Clinical Child Psychology*, *25*(4), 436–45

Martin D M, Roy A and Wells M B (1997) Health gain through health checks: improving access to primary health care for people with intellectual disability *Journal of Intellectual Disability Research*, *45*, 401–408

Marwick A (1970) *The Nature of History* London: Macmillan

Maslow A H (1971, 1976) *The Farther Reaches of Human Nature* London: Penguin

Mead G H (1934, 1962) *Mind, Self and Society* Chicago, IL: University of Chicago Press

Meininger H P (2006) Narrating, writing, reading: life story work as an aid to (self) advocacy *British Journal of Learning Disabilities*, *34*, 181–88

Mencap (1997) *Prescription for Change* London: Mencap

—— (1999) *Living in Fear* London: Mencap

—— (2001) *No Ordinary Life* London: Mencap

—— (2004) *Treat Me Right* London: Mencap

—— (2007) *Death by Indifference* London: Mencap

Mencap, BILD and The Renton Foundation (2011) *Involve Me: Practical Guide* London: Mencap

Michael J (2008) *Healthcare for All: Independent Inquiry into Access to Healthcare for People with Learning Disabilities* London: Department of Health

Mental Capacity Act (2005) London: HMSO. Available from http://www.legislation.gov.uk/ukpga/2005/9/contents

Mental Deficiency Act (1913) London: HMSO

Mental Health Act (1959) London: HMSO. Available from http://www.legislation. gov.uk/ukpga/Eliz2/7-8/72/contents

—— (1983) London: HMSO. Available from http://www.legislation.gov.uk/ukpga/ 1983/20/contents

Midgeley C (2007) A life, stolen *The Times* 7 November. Available from http://www. thetimes.co.uk/tto/health/article178788.ece

Midlands Psychology Group (2010) Post qualification training in selective ignorance: a report from two recent national conferences for therapeutic psychologists *Clinical Psychology Forum 212*, 46–51

Miller W and Rollnick S (1991) *Motivational Interviewing: Preparing People to Change Addictive Behaviour* New York: Guilford Press

Mirandola (undated) *Oration on the Dignity of Man*; cited in E Fromm and R Xirau (1968) *The Nature of Man* New York: Macmillan

Mitchell G and Hastings R P (1998) Learning disability care staff's emotional reactions to aggressive challenging behaviours: development of a measurement tool *British Journal of Clinical Psychology, 37*, 441–49

Money D (2002) *Speech and Language Therapy Management Models*; cited in S Abudarham and A Hurd (2002) *Management of Communication Needs in People with Learning Disability* London: Whurr

Morgan A (2000) *What is Narrative Therapy?* Adelaide: Dulwich Centre Publications

Morris C D, Niederbuhl J M and Mahr J M (1993) Determining the capability of individuals with mental retardation to give informed consent *American Journal on Mental Retardation, 98*(2), 263–72

Morris J, Bush A and Joyce T (2012) *Outcome Measures for Challenging Behaviour Interventions* London: British Psychological Society

Morton J (2004) *Understanding Developmental Disorders: A Causal Modelling Approach* Oxford: Blackwell

Morton J and Frith U (1994) Causal modelling: a structural approach to developmental psychopathology, cited in Happé *Autism: An Introduction to Psychological Theory* London: UCL Press

Mowbray, D (1989) *Review of Clinical Psychology Services* Cheltenham: Management Advisory Service to the NHS

Murdoch S (2007) *IQ: The Brilliant Idea That Failed* London: Duckworth Overlook

Murphy G and Clare I (2009) Intellectual disability, in S Young, M Kopelman and G Gudjonsson (eds) *Forensic Neuropsychology in Practice* Oxford: Oxford University Press

National Assistance Act (1948) London: HMSO. Available from http://www. legislation.gov.uk/ukpga/Geo6/11-12/29/contents

NCCL (1951) *50,000 Outside the Law* London: National Council for Civil Liberties

Neugebauer R (1996) Mental handicap in medieval and early modern England, in D Wright and A Digby (eds) *From Idiocy to Mental Deficiency* London: Routledge

New Possibilities NHS Trust (2001) *Turner Village, 1935–2001* Colchester: New Possibilities NHS Trust

Newman D W and Beail N (1994) The assessment of need: a psychological perspective on people with learning disabilities *Clinical Psychology forum, September*, 21–25

NHS and Community Care Act (1990) London: HMSO. Available from http://www.legislation.gov.uk/ukpga/1990/19/contents

Nieboer A, Lindenberg S, Boomsma A and van Bruggen A C (2005) Dimensions of well-being and their measurement: the SPF-IL Scale *Social Indicator Research, 73*, 313–53

Nind M and Hewett D (2001) *A Practical Guide to Intensive Interaction* Kidderminster: British Institute of Learning Disabilities

Numminen H, Service E, Ahonen T, Korhonen T, Tolvanen A, Patja K and Ruoppila I (2000) Working memory structure and intellectual disability *Journal of Intellectual Disability Research*, *44*(5), 579–90

Nuttall M (1998) States and categories: indigenous models of personhood in northwest Greenland, in R Jenkins (ed.) *Questions of Competence: Culture, Classification and Intellectual Disability* Cambridge: Cambridge University Press

O'Brien J (2004) If person-centred planning did not exist, *Valuing People* would require its invention *Journal of Applied Research in Intellectual Disabilities*, *17*, 11–15

O'Brien C L and O'Brien J (2000) *The Origins of Person-Centred Planning: A Community of Practice Perspective* Responsive Systems Associates Inc.

O'Brien J and Tyne A (1981) *The Principle of Normalisation: A Foundation for Effective Services* London: The Campaign for Mentally Handicapped People

Offences (Aggravation by Prejudice) Bill (2009) Edinburgh: Scottish Government. Available from http://www.scotland.gov.uk/Topics/People/Equality/18507/EQIASearch/offencesaggravation

Oliver C, McClintock K, Hall S, Smith M, Dagnan D and Stenfert-Kroese B (2003) Assessing the severity of challenging behaviour: psychometric properties of the Challenging Behaviour Interview *Journal of Applied Research in Intellectual Disabilities*, *16*, 53–61

Oliver M (2004) If I had a hammer: the social model in action, in J Swain, V Finkelstein, S French and M Oliver (eds) (2004) *Disabling Barriers – Enabling Environments* London: Sage

Osgood T (2005) Managing tensions: organisations and service users, in P Cambridge and S Carnaby *Person Centred Planning and Care Management with People with Learning Disabilities* London: Jessica Kingsley

Oswin M (1991) *Am I Allowed to Cry?* London: Souvenir Press

Owens R G and Ashcroft J B (1982) Functional analysis in applied psychology *British Journal of Clinical Psychology*, *21*, 181–89

Pawlyn J and Carnaby S (eds) (2009) *Profound Intellectual and Multiple Disabilities: Nursing Complex Needs* Chichester: Wiley-Blackwell

Paxton R (1976) Note: some criteria for choosing between explanations in psychology *Bulletin of the British Psychological Society*, *29*, 396–99

Peckham G (2007) The vulnerability and sexual abuse of people with learning disabilities *British Journal of Learning Disabilities*, *35*, 131–37

Peden A (2012) The potential benefits of religious beliefs and practices for psychological well-being *Clinical Psychology Forum*, *233*, 33–35

Penketh V and Hare D (2011) Manchester Attachment Scale (MAST) 3rd part observation measure of secure attachment behaviours *Unpublished Doctoral Thesis*, cited in H Fletcher (2008) Attachment theory and learning disabilities: connections between early beginnings and later challenges *Advancing Practice Conference*, 8 May 2008

Pennington B F (2009) How neuropsychology informs our understanding of developmental disorders *Journal of Child Psychology and Psychiatry*, *50*(1–2), 72–78

Perry J and Felce D (2003) Quality of Life outcomes for people with intellectual disabilities living in staffed community housing services: a stratified random sample of statutory, voluntary and private agency provision *Journal of Applied Research in Intellectual Disabilities*, *16*, 11–28

Petrie S (2011) The experience of the reflecting team for people with learning disabilities in family therapy *Context*, *April*, 34–37

Pilgrim D (2011) Some limitations of the Biopsychosocial Model *History and Philosophy of Psychology*, *13*(2), 23

Pilling D and Midgley G (1992) Does PASS measure up? Evaluating a measure of service quality *Clinical Psychology Forum*, *January*, 25–28

Pilnick A, Clegg J, Murphy E and Almack K (2010) Questioning the answer: questioning style, choice and self-determination in interactions with young people with intellectual disabilities *Sociology of Health & Illness*, *32*, 415–36

Pitt V (2010) Progress report on Valuing People Now *Community Care*, 15 January

Pockney R (2006) Friendship or facilitation: people with learning disabilities and their paid carers *Sociological Research Online*, *11*(3). Available from http://www.socresonline.org.uk/11/3/pockney.html (accessed 23.7.2010)

Potts M and Fido R (1993) A fit person to be removed: personal accounts of life in a Mental Deficiency Institution *Clinical Psychology Forum*, *51*(January), 4

Prochaska J and DiClemente C C (1982) Transtheoretical therapy: toward a more integrative model of change *Psychotherapy: Theory, Research and Practice*, *19*(3), 276–89

Race D G (ed.) (2002) *Learning Disability – A Social Approach* London: Routledge

Raczka R, Williams J and Theodore K (2013) *Pilot Evaluation of Routine Outcome Measures for Use with Adults with Learning Disabilities* London: Central London Community Healthcare NHS Trust

Rapley M (1990) Is normalisation a scientific theory? *Clinical Psychology Forum*, *October*, 16–20

—— (2004) *The Social Construction of Intellectual Disabilities* Cambridge: Cambridge University Press

RCP, BPS and Royal College of Speech & Language Therapists (2007) *Challenging Behaviour: A Unified Approach*. Available from http://www.rcpsych.ac.uk/files/pdfversion/cr144.pdf

RCPsyche (1996–1999) *Health of the Nation Outcome Scales (HoNOS)* London: Royal College of Psychiatrists

Reed J (1997) Understanding and assessing depression in people with learning disabilities, in B S Kroese, D Dagnan and K Loumidis (1997) *Cognitive-Behaviour Therapy for People with Learning Disabilities* Hove: Brunner-Routledge

Regnard C, Reynolds J, Watson B, Matthews D, Gibson L and Clarke, C. (2007) Understanding distress in people with severe communication difficulties: developing and assessing the Disability Distress Assessment Tool (DisDAT) *Journal of Intellectual Disability Research*, *51*(4), 277–92

Reinders H S (1997) The ethics of normalisation *Cambridge Quarterly of Healthcare Ethics*, *6*, 481–89; cited in J Clegg, E Murphy, K Almack and A Harvey (2008) Tensions around inclusion: reframing the moral horizon *Journal of Applied Research in Intellectual Disabilities*, *21*, 81–94

—— (2000) Mental retardation and the quest for meaning, Chapter 5 in J Stolk, T A Boer and R Seldenrijk (eds) *Meaningful Care* London: Kluwer Academic Publishers

Reynolds Whyte S (1998) Slow cookers and madmen: competence of heart and head in rural Uganda, in R. Jenkins (ed.) *Questions of Competence: Culture, Classification and Intellectual Disability* Cambridge: Cambridge University Press

Rhodes P (2003) Behavioural and family systems interventions in developmental disability: towards a contemporary and integrative approach *Journal of Intellectual and Developmental Disability*, *28*(1), 51–64

Richardson K (2002) What IQ tests test *Theory & Psychology, 12*(2), 283–314

Robbins L and Hall P (2003) Experiences of an emotional awareness group for adults with learning disabilities *Clinical Psychology, 25*, 31–34

Rogers C R (1951) *Client-Centered Therapy* London: Constable

Rojahn J, Matson J L, Lott D, Esbensen A J and Smalls Y (2001) The Behavior Problem Inventory: an instrument for the assessment of self-injury, stereotyped behavior, and aggression/destruction in individuals with developmental disabilities *Journal of Autism and Developmental Disorders, 31*, 577–88

Rondal J A and Perera J (2006) *Down's Syndrome: Neurobehavioral Specificity* London: Whurr

Rondal J A, Perera J, Nadel L and Comblain A (1996) *Down's Syndrome: Psychological, Psychobiological and Socio-Educational Perspectives* London: Whurr

Rose N (1991) *Power and Subjectivity: Critical History and Psychology.* Available from http://www.academyanalyticarts.org/rose1.htm (accessed 29.8.2012)

Rudy L J (2010) *Top 10 Terrific Traits of Autistic People.* Available from http://autism.about.com/od/inspirationideas/tp/besttraits.htm (accessed 21.5.2012)

Rushton, P (1988) Lunatics and idiots: mental disability, the community, and the Poor Law in North-East England, 1600–1800 *Medical History, 32*, 34–50

Ryan J and Thomas F (1980) *The Politics of Mental Handicap* Harmondsworth: Penguin

Ryle A (1990) *Cognitive-Analytic Therapy: Active Participation in Change* Chichester: Wiley

Sabbadini M, Bonanni R, Carlesimo G A and Caltagirone C (2001) Neuropsychological assessment of patients with severe neuromotor and verbal disabilities *Journal of Intellectual Disability Research, 45*(2), 169–79

Sacks H (1992) *Lectures on Conversation, Volumes 1 & 2* Oxford: Basil Blackwell; cited in M Rapley (2004) *The Social Construction of Intellectual Disabilities* Cambridge: Cambridge University Press

Samuel P S, Rillotta F and Brown I (2012a) The development of family quality of life concepts and measures *Journal of Intellectual Disability Research, 56*(1), 1–16

Samuel P S, Hobden K L, LeRoy B W and Lacey K K (2012b) Analysing family service needs of typically underserved families in the USA *Journal of Intellectual Disability Research, 56*(1), 111–28

Saxe R, Carey S and Kanwisher N (2004) Understanding other minds: linking developmental psychology and functional neuroimaging *Annual Review of Psychology, 55*, 87–124

Schalock R L (2004) Quality of life: what we know and do not know *Journal of Intellectual Disability Research, 48*, 203–16

Schore A N (1994) *Affect Regulation and the Origin of the Self: the Neurobiology of Emotional Development* Hillsdale, NJ: Lawrence Erlbaum Associates

Schuengel C (2011) Stress, Attachment and Mental Health *MHID Congress, 2 September 2011.* Available from http://tinyurl.com/MHIDAttachment (accessed 10.1.2012)

Schuengel C and Janssen C G C (2006) People with mental retardation and psychopathology: stress, affect regulation and attachment: a review *International Review of Research in Mental Retardation, 32*, 229–60

Schuengel C, Kef S, Damen S and Worm N (2010) 'People who need people': attachment and professional caregiving *Journal of Intellectual Disability Research, 54*(1), 38–47

Schutz A (1962) *Collected Papers, Volume One: The Problem of Social Reality* The Hague: Martinus Nijhoff; cited in M Rapley (2004) *The Social Construction of Intellectual Disabilities* Cambridge: Cambridge University Press

Schwarzer R (2008) Modelling health behavior change: how to predict and modify the adoption and maintenance of health behaviors *Applied Psychology: An International Review, 57,* 1–29

Scior K and Lynggaard H (2006) New stories of intellectual disabilities: a narrative approach, Chapter 6 in S Baum and H Lynggaard (eds) *Intellectual Disabilities: A Systemic Approach* London: Karnac Books

The Scottish Executive (2000) *The Same as You? A Review of Services for People with Learning Difficulties* Edinburgh: The Scottish Executive. Available from http://www.scotland.gov.uk/Resource/Doc/1095/0001661.pdf

Scottish Government (2012) *The Same as You? 2000–2012: Consultation Report* Edinburgh: The Scottish Government

Seale J and Nind N (eds) (2010) *Understanding and Promoting Access for People with Learning Difficulties* London: Routledge

Seligman M (2003) Positive psychology *The Psychologist, 16*(3), 126–27

Sexual Offences Act (2003) London: HMSO. Available from http://www.legislation. gov.uk/ukpga/2003/42/contents

Siegel D J (2007) *The Mindful Brain* New York: W W Norton

Sigelman C, Budd E C, Spaniel C and Schoenrock C (1981) When in doubt say yes: acquiescence in interviews with mentally retarded persons *Mental Retardation, 19,* 53–58

Simon G (2004) Systemic family therapy with families with a child who has a diagnosis of Asperger Syndrome *Human Systems: The Journal of Systemic Consultation and Management, 15*(4), 257–74

Simpson G and Price V (2009) From inclusion to exclusion: some unintended consequences of Valuing People *British Journal of Learning Disabilities, 38,* 180–86

Sin C H, Hedges A, Cook C, Mguni N and Comber N (2009) *Disabled People's Experiences of Targeted Violence and Hostility* Manchester: Equality and Human Rights Commission

Singh N N, Lancioni G E, Wingon A S W, Adkins A D, Singh J and Singh A N (2007) Mindfulness training assists individuals with moderate mental retardation to maintain their community placements *Behaviour Modification, 31,* 800–13

Singleton J and Kalsy S (2008) It hurts! Pain and older adults with learning disabilities and dementia *Clinical Psychology & People with Learning Disabilities, 6*(1)

Skinner B F (1953) *Science and Human Behaviour* New York: Macmillan

Skirrow P and Perry E (2009) *The Maslow Assessment of Needs Scales* Mersey Care NHS Trust

Smith P and McCarthy G (1996) The development of a semi-structured interview to investigate the attachment-related experiences of adults with learning disabilities *British Journal of Learning Disabilities, 24,* 154–60

Spencer H (1864) *The Principles of Biology* London: Williams and Norgate

Spreen O, Risser A H and Edgell D (1995) *Developmental Neuropsychology* Oxford: Oxford University Press

Steele H (2002) Attachment Theory *The Psychologist, 15*(10), 518–22

Sterkenburg P S, Janssen C G C and Schuengel C (2008) The effect of an attachment-based behaviour therapy for children with visual and severe intellectual disabilities *Journal of Applied Research in Intellectual Disabilities, 21,* 126–35

Sternberg R J, Grigorenko E L and Bundy D A (2001) The predictive value of IQ *Merrill-Palmer Quarterly*, *47*(1), 1–41

Stewart I and Joines V (1987) *TA Today: A New Introduction to Transactional Analysis* Nottingham: Lifespan Publishing

Stolk J, Boer T A and Seldenrijk R (2000) *Meaningful Care: A Multidisciplinary Approach to the Meaning of Care for People with Mental Retardation* Dordrecht: Kluwer

Stolk J and Kars H (2000) Parents' experiences of meaning, Chapter 2 in J Stolk, T A Boer and R Seldenrijk *Meaningful Care* London: Kluwer

Swain J, Finkelstein V, French S and Oliver M (eds) (1993) *Disabling Barriers – Enabling Environments* London: Sage

Swain J, French S, Barnes C and Thomas C (eds) (2004) *Disabling Barriers – Enabling Environments* London: Sage

Swaine J, Parish S L, Luken K and Atkins L (2011) Recruitment and consent of women with intellectual disabilities in a randomised control trial of a health promotion intervention *Journal of Intellectual Disability Research*, *55*(5), 474–83

Taggart L, Truesdale-Kennedy M and McIlfatrick S (2011) The role of community nurses and residential staff in supporting women with intellectual disability to access breast screening services *Journal of Intellectual Disability Research*, *55*(1), 41–52

Terman L (1916) *The Measurement of Intelligence: An Explanation of and a Complete Guide for the Use of the Stanford Revision and Extension of the Binet-Simon Intelligence Scale* Boston, MA: Houghton Mifflin, cited in S Murdoch (2007) *IQ: The Brilliant Idea That Failed* London: Duckworth Overlook

Thomas C (1999) *Female Forms: Experiencing and Understanding Disability* Buckingham: Open University Press

—— (2004) Disability and impairment, in J Swain, S French, C Barnes and C Thomas (eds) *Disabling Barriers – Enabling Environments* London: Sage

Tizard J (1953) The effects of different types of supervision on the behaviour of mental defectives in a sheltered workshop *American Journal of Mental Deficiency*, *58*, 43–61; cited in P Williams (2005) The work of Jack Tizard 1: 1950–1964 *Tizard Learning Disability Review*, *10*(1), 7–11

Tizard J and Loos F (1954) The learning of a spatial relations test by adult imbeciles *American Journal of Mental Deficiency*, *59*, 85–90; cited in P Williams (2005) The work of Jack Tizard 1: 1950–1964 *Tizard Learning Disability Review*, *10*(1), 7–11

Tomm K (1999) Co-constructing responsibility; cited in M Haydon-Laurelut and J C Wilson (2011) Interviewing the internalised Other: attending to voices of the 'Other' *Journal of Systemic Therapies*, *30*(1), 24–37

Towell D and Sanderson H (2004) Person-centred planning in its strategic context: reframing the Mansell/Beadle-Brown critique *Journal of Applied Research in Intellectual Disabilities*, *17*, 17–21

Traustadòttir R (2000) Friendship: love or work?, Chapter 8 in R Traustadòttir and K Johnson *Women with Intellectual Disabilities: Finding a Place in the World* London: Jessica Kingsley

Traustadòttir R and Johnson K (eds) (2000) *Women with Intellectual Disabilities: Finding a Place in the World* London: Jessica Kingsley

Tredgold A F (1908, 1952) *Mental Deficiency – Amentia* Baillière, Tindall, and Cox

Trent, J W (1994) *Inventing the Feeble Mind: A History of Mental Retardation in the United States* Berkeley, CA: University of California Press

—— (2011) Review of *A History of Intelligence and 'Intellectual Disability': The Shaping of Psychology in Early Modern Europe* (review no 1140). Available from http://www.history.ac.uk/reviews/review/1140 (accessed 20.4.2012)

Tulsky D S, Saklofske D H, Chelune G J, Heaton R K, Ivink R J, Bornstein R, Prifitera A and Ledbetter M (eds) (2003) *Clinical Interpretation of the WAIS-III AND WMS-III* London: Academic Press

Turk V and Brown H (1993) The sexual abuse of adults with learning disabilities: results of a two year incidence survey *Mental Handicap Research*, 6, 193–216

UN (1948) *Preamble to the Universal Declaration of Human Rights*. Available from http://www.un.org/en/documents/udhr

—— (1971) *United Nations Declaration on the Rights of Mentally Retarded Persons*

—— (1975) *The Declaration on the Rights of Disabled Persons* Available from http://www.ohchr.org/EN/ProfessionalInterest/Pages/RightsOfDisabledPersons.aspx (accessed 14.2.2011)

UPIAS (1976) *Fundamental Principles of Disability* London: UPIAS; cited in J Swain, S French, C Barnes and C Thomas (eds) (2004) *Disabling Barriers – Enabling Environments* London: Sage

Valentine E R (1982) *Conceptual Issues in Psychology* London: Allen & Unwin

Van Nijnatten C (2010) *Children's Agency, Children's Welfare* Bristol: The Policy Press

Vansteenkiste M and Sheldon K M (2006) There's nothing more practical than a good theory: integrating motivational interviewing and self-determination theory *British Journal of Clinical Psychology*, 45, 63–82

Vygotsky L S (1978) *Mind in Society* London: Harvard University Press

Waddell H and Evers C (2000) Psychological services for people with learning disabilities living in the community: focus group view *Clinical Psychology Forum*, 141, 34–38

Wahler R J and Fox J J (1981) Setting events in applied behaviour analysis: toward a conceptual and methodological expansion *Journal of Applied Behaviour Analysis*, 14, 327–38

Waitman A and Conboy-Hill S (1991) *Psychotherapy and Mental Handicap* London: Sage

Walker J (2008) The use of attachment theory in adoption and fostering *Adoption & Fostering*, 32, 49–57

Walmsley J (2000) Women and the Mental Deficiency Act of 1913: citizenship, sexuality and regulation *British Journal of Learning Disabilities*, 28, 65–70

Warburg M (2001) Visual impairment in adult people with intellectual disability: literature review *Journal of Intellectual Disability Research*, 45, 424–38

Ware, J. (2003) *Creating a Responsive Environment for People with Profound and Multiple Learning Difficulties* (2nd edition) London: David Fulton

Wechsler D (1939) *Wechsler–Bellevue Intelligence Scale* New York: The Psychological Corporation

Webb J (2011) Working with systems: a long journey *Context*, April, 26–28

Webb J and Stanton M (2005) Better access to primary healthcare for adults with learning disability: how can clinical psychologists contribute? *Clinical Psychology*, 48, 21–25

—— (2008) Better access to primary healthcare for adults with learning disabilities: evaluation of a group programme to improve knowledge and skills *British Journal of Learning Disabilities*, 37, 116–22

—— (2009) Working with primary care practices to improve service delivery for people with learning disabilities – a pilot study *British Journal of Learning Disabilities*, *37*, 221–27

Webb J and Whitaker S (2012) Defining learning disability *The Psychologist*, *25*(6), 440–43

Webster A and Roe J (1998) *Children with Visual Impairments: Social Interaction, Language and Learning* London: Routledge

Wechsler D, Coalson D L and Raiford S E (2008) *WAIS-IV Technical and Interpretive Manual* San Antonio, TX: Pearson

Weerasekara P (1996) *Multiperspective Case Formulation: A Step Towards Treatment Integration* Malabar, FL: Kriegeer

Wehmeyer M L and Garner N W (2003) The impact of personal characteristics of people with intellectual and developmental disability on self-determination and autonomous functioning *Journal of Applied Research in Intellectual Disabilities*, *16*, 255–65

Weigel L, Langdon P E, Collins S and O'Brien Y (2006) Challenging behaviour and learning disabilities: the relationship between expressed emotion and staff attributions *British Journal of Clinical Psychology*, *45*, 205–16

Weiss L G, Saklofske D H, Coalson D and Engi Raiford S (2010) *WAIS-IV: Clinical Use and Interpretation* London: Elsevier

Werhane P (2002) Moral imagination and systems thinking *Journal of Business Ethics*, *38*, 33–42; cited in J D Engel, J Zarconi, L L Pethtel and S A Missimi (2008) *Narrative in Health Care* Oxford: Radcliffe

Whitaker S (2003) Should we abandon the concept of mild learning disability? *Clinical Psychology*, *29*, 16–19

—— (2008a) Intellectual disability: a concept in need of revision? *British Journal of Developmental Disabilities*, *54*(1), 3–9

—— (2008b) The merits of mental age as an additional measure of intellectual ability in the low ability range *Clinical Psychology Forum*, *191*, 44–47

White C, Holland E, Marsland D and Oakes P (2003) The identification of environments and cultures that promote the abuse of people with intellectual disabilities: a review of the literature *Journal of Applied Research in Intellectual Disabilities*, *16*, 1–9

White M (2005) Children, trauma and subordinate storyline development *The International Journal of Narrative Therapy and Community Work*, *38*(4), 10–21

—— (2007) *Maps of Narrative Practice* London: Norton

Whittington A and Burns J (2005) The dilemmas of residential care staff working with the challenging behaviour of people with learning disabilities *British Journal of Clinical Psychology*, *44*, 59–76

Whittington J and Holland T (2011) Recognition of emotion in facial expression by people with Prader-Willi Syndrome *Journal of Intellectual Disability Research*, *55*, 75–84

Wilcox E, Finlay W M and Edmonds J (2006) 'His brain is totally different': an analysis of care-staff explanations of aggressive challenging behaviour and the impact of gendered discourses *British Journal of Social Psychology*, *45*(1), 197–216

Wilkinson R and Pickett K (2010) *The Spirit Level* Harmondsworth: Penguin

Williams P (2005) The work of Jack Tizard 1: 1950–1964 *Tizard Learning Disability Review*, *10*, *1*, 7–11

Williams V (2011) *Disability and Discourse* Chichester: Wiley-Blackwell

Winch P (1958, 1990) *The Idea of Social Science and its Relation to Philosophy* London: Routledge

Wing L and Gould J (1979) Severe impairments of social interaction and associated abnormalities in children: espidemiology and classification *Journal of Autism and Developmental Disorders*, 9, 11–29

De Winter C F, Jansen A A C and Evenhuis H M (2011) Physical conditions and challenging behaviour in people with intellectual disability: a systematic review *Journal of Intellectual Disability Research*, 55(7), 675–98

Wittchen H-U, Beesdo K and Gloster A T (2009) A new meta-structure of mental disorders: a helpful step into the future or a harmful step back to the past? *Psychological Medicine*, 39, 2083–89

Wolfensberger W (1972) *The Principle of Normalization in Human Services* Toronto: National Institute on Mental Retardation

——— (1980) A brief overview of the principle of normalization, in R Flynn and K Nitsch (eds) *Normalization, Social Integration and Community Services* Baltimore, MD: University Park Press

——— (1983) Social role valorization: a proposed new term for the principal of normalization *Mental Retardation*, 21, 234–39

Wolfensberger W and Glenn L (1975) *PASS 3: Program Analysis of Service Systems Field Manual* (3rd edition) Toronto: National Institute on Mental Retardation

Wong J G, Clare I C H, Gunn M J and Holland A J (1999) Capacity to make health care decisions: its importance in clinical practice *Psychological Medicine*, 29, 437–46.

Wong J G, Clare I C H, Holland A J, Watson P C and Gunn M J (2000) The capacity of people with a 'mental disability' to make a particular healthcare decision *Psychological Medicine*, 30, 295–306

Wood J and Emerson E (2005) *Measuring Deprivation at the Local Neighbourhood Level* Lancaster University: Institute for Health Research

WHO (1980) *International Classification of Impairments, Disabilities and Handicaps: A Manual of Classification Relating to the Consequences of Disease* Geneva: WHO

——— (1993) *The DCR-10 Classification of Mental and Behavioural Disorders: Diagnostic Criteria for Research (ICD-10-DCR)* Geneva: WHO

——— (1994) *The ICD-10 Classification of Mental and Behavioural Disorder* London: Churchill Livingstone

Wright D (1996) Childlike in his innocence, in D Wright and A Digby (eds) *From Idiocy to Mental Deficiency* London: Routledge

Wright D and Digby A (eds) (1996) *From Idiocy to Mental Deficiency* London: Routledge

Young F (2000) A parent's search for meaning in family life, Chapter 2 in J Stolk, T A Boer and R Seldenrijk *Meaningful Care: A Multidisciplinary Approach to the Meaning of Care for People with Mental Retardation* Dordrecht: Kluwer

Zarkowska E and Clements J (1994) *Problem Behaviour and People with Severe Learning Disabilities: The S.T.A.R. Approach* (2nd edition) London: Chapman & Hall

# Index